# STAR WARS®
# DARK TIMES

## VOLUME ONE

## THE PATH TO NOWHERE

# THE RISE OF THE EMPIRE

*From 1,000 to 0 years before the Battle of Yavin*

After the seeming final defeat of the Sith, the Republic enters a state of complacency.
In the waning years of the Republic, the Senate rife with corruption, the ambitious
Senator Palpatine causes himself to be elected Supreme Chancellor.
This is the era of the prequel trilogy.

The events in this story take place approximately nineteen years before
the Battle of Yavin.

# STAR WARS®
# DARK TIMES

## VOLUME ONE

## THE PATH TO NOWHERE

Story
**WELLES HARTLEY**

Script
**MICK HARRISON**
with additional dialogue from the novel
*Dark Lord: The Rise of Darth Vader*,
by James Luceno

Art
**DOUGLAS WHEATLEY**

Colors
**RONDA PATTISON**

Lettering
**MICHAEL DAVID THOMAS**
**MICHAEL HEISLER**

Cover art
**DOUGLAS WHEATLEY**

DARK HORSE BOOKS®

Publisher
**MIKE RICHARDSON**

Collection Designer
**TONY ONG**

Art Director
**LIA RIBACCHI**

Editor
**RANDY STRADLEY**

Assistant Editor
**DAVE MARSHALL**

special thanks to Elaine Mederer, Jann Moorhead, David Anderman, Leland Chee, Sue Rostoni,
and Carol Roeder at Lucas Licensing

STAR WARS DARK TIMES—Volume One: The Path to Nowhere

This volume collects issues one through five of the Dark Horse comic-book series
*Star Wars: Dark Times*.

Published by
Dark Horse Books
A division of Dark Horse Comics, Inc.
10956 SE Main Street
Milwaukie, OR 97222

darkhorse.com
starwars.com

To find a comics shop in your area, call the Comic Shop Locator Service
toll-free at 1-888-266-4226

First printing: January 2008
ISBN: 978-1-59307-792-1

1 3 5 7 9 10 8 6 4 2
Printed in China

**"FOR OVER A THOUSAND GENERATIONS THE JEDI KNIGHTS WERE THE GUARDIANS OF PEACE AND JUSTICE IN THE OLD REPUBLIC. BEFORE THE DARK TIMES, BEFORE THE EMPIRE."**
**—BEN KENOBI**

The dark times are here. Order 66 destroyed the Jedi Order and dispersed its survivors. With their droid armies shut down, the Separatist resistance fighters are no longer a match for Palpatine's clone stormtroopers. The worlds of the former Republic are drawn inexorably into the iron grip of the Empire, while other systems are adrift in a sea of chaos, lawlessness, and despair.

For billions of sentient beings across the galaxy, what they believed was a road to a better future has become an uncertain path . . .

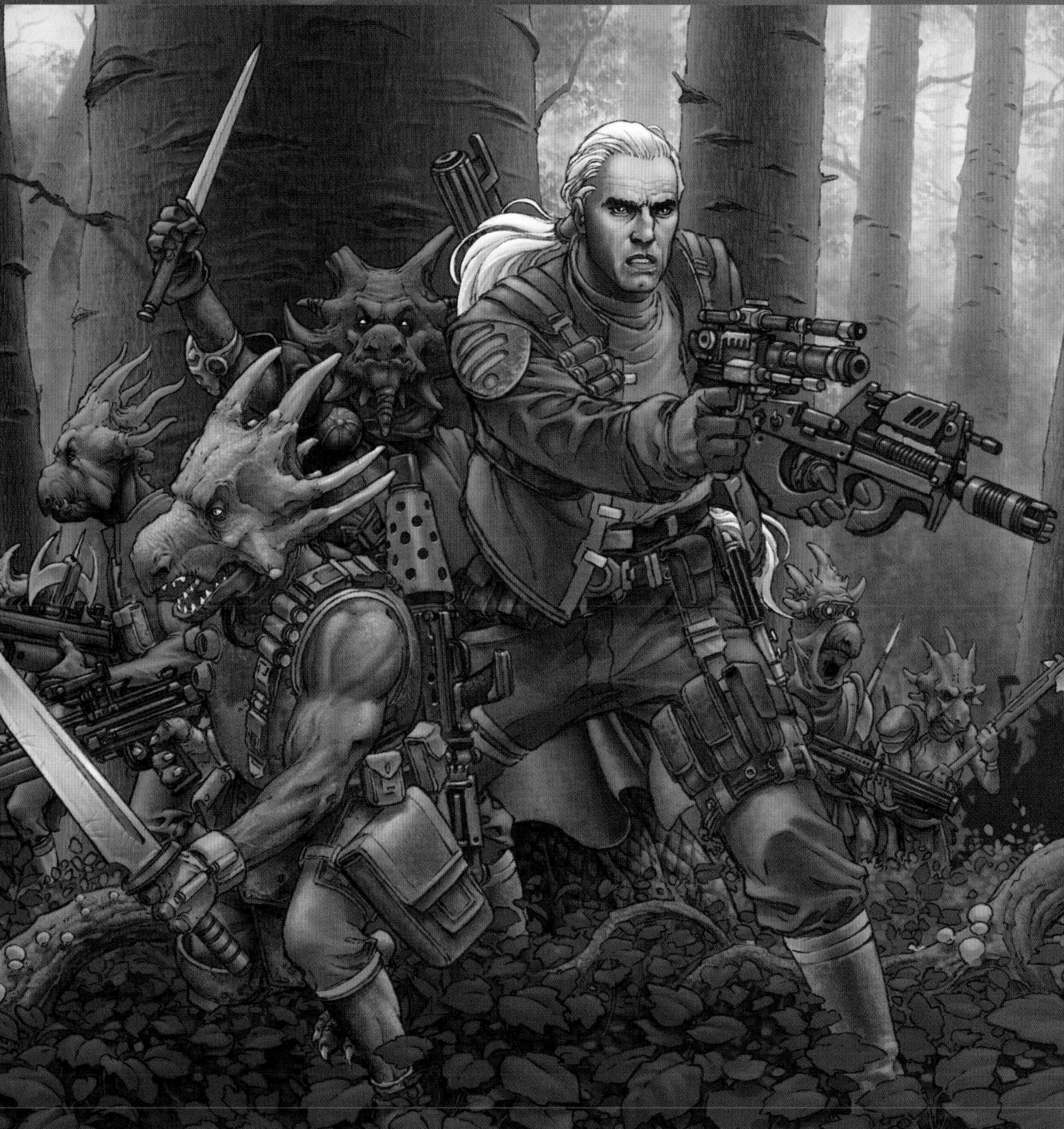

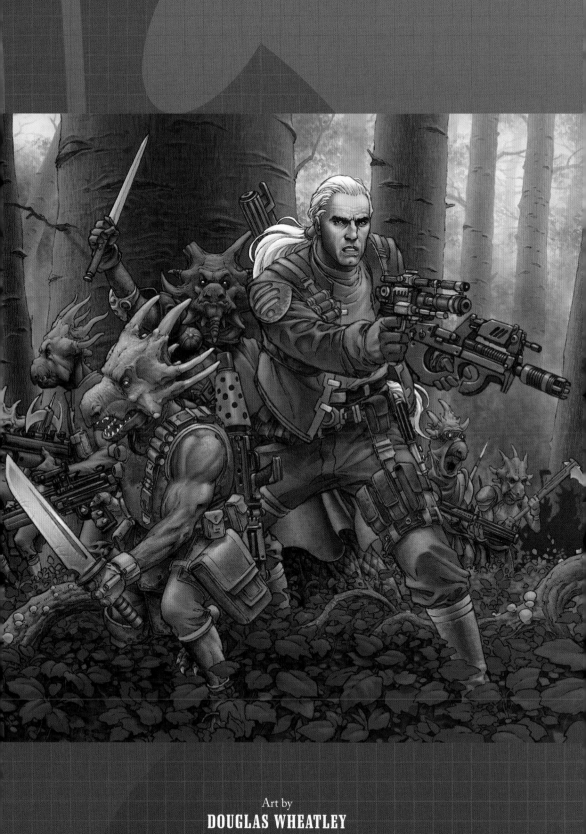

Art by
**DOUGLAS WHEATLEY**

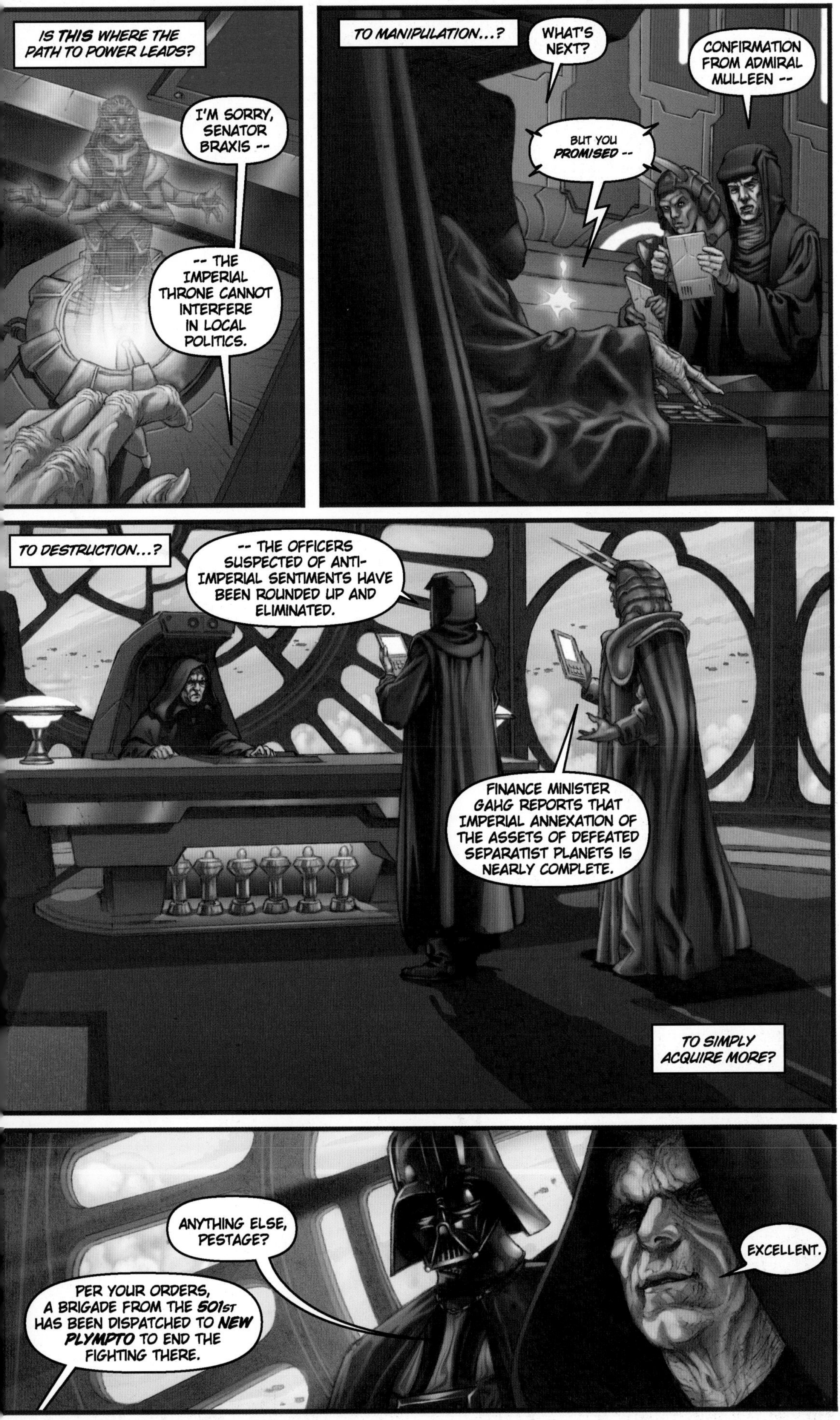
IS THIS WHERE THE PATH TO POWER LEADS?
I'M SORRY, SENATOR BRAXIS --
-- THE IMPERIAL THRONE CANNOT INTERFERE IN LOCAL POLITICS.
TO MANIPULATION...?
WHAT'S NEXT?
BUT YOU PROMISED --
CONFIRMATION FROM ADMIRAL MULLEEN --
TO DESTRUCTION...?
-- THE OFFICERS SUSPECTED OF ANTI-IMPERIAL SENTIMENTS HAVE BEEN ROUNDED UP AND ELIMINATED.
FINANCE MINISTER GAHG REPORTS THAT IMPERIAL ANNEXATION OF THE ASSETS OF DEFEATED SEPARATIST PLANETS IS NEARLY COMPLETE.
TO SIMPLY ACQUIRE MORE?
ANYTHING ELSE, PESTAGE?
PER YOUR ORDERS, A BRIGADE FROM THE 501ST HAS BEEN DISPATCHED TO NEW PLYMPTO TO END THE FIGHTING THERE.
EXCELLENT.

THAT WILL BE ALL FOR NOW.

GUARDS, YOU ARE DISMISSED.

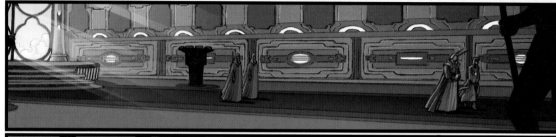

ARE THE LESSONS OF KESSEL SO SOON FORGOTTEN, APPRENTICE? GIVING IN TO YOUR EMOTIONS NEARLY LED TO YOUR DESTRUCTION.

MASTER ... I...

YOU FEEL YOU SHOULD BE DOING *SOMETHING*, DON'T YOU, LORD VADER?

WHAT WOULD YOU DO? LEAD THE 501st? *HUNT* THE JEDI? *TRACK DOWN* ANAKIN SKYWALKER'S FORMER MASTER?

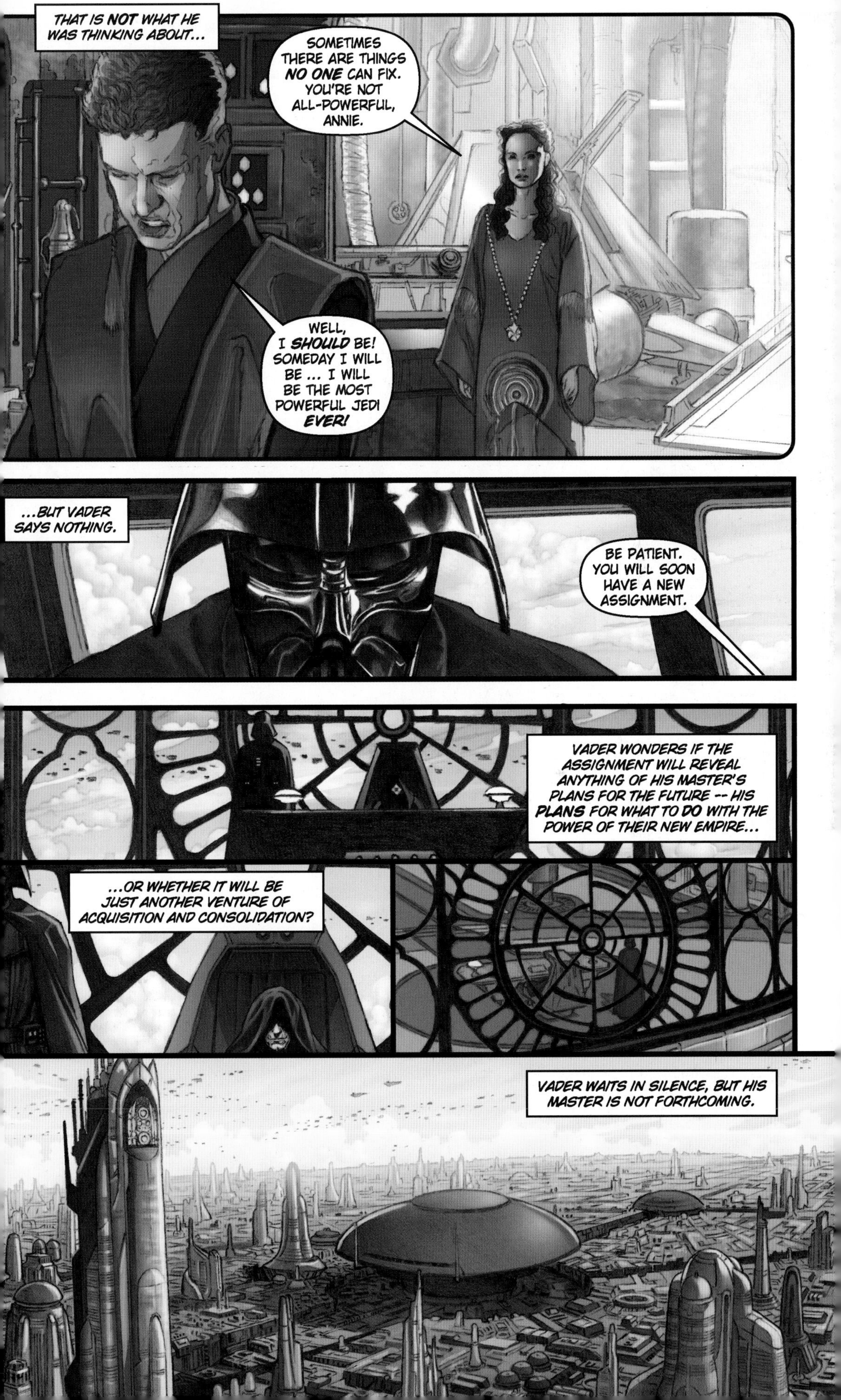
THAT IS NOT WHAT HE WAS THINKING ABOUT...
SOMETIMES THERE ARE THINGS NO ONE CAN FIX. YOU'RE NOT ALL-POWERFUL, ANNIE.
WELL, I SHOULD BE! SOMEDAY I WILL BE ... I WILL BE THE MOST POWERFUL JEDI EVER!
...BUT VADER SAYS NOTHING.
BE PATIENT. YOU WILL SOON HAVE A NEW ASSIGNMENT.
VADER WONDERS IF THE ASSIGNMENT WILL REVEAL ANYTHING OF HIS MASTER'S PLANS FOR THE FUTURE -- HIS PLANS FOR WHAT TO DO WITH THE POWER OF THEIR NEW EMPIRE...
...OR WHETHER IT WILL BE JUST ANOTHER VENTURE OF ACQUISITION AND CONSOLIDATION?
VADER WAITS IN SILENCE, BUT HIS MASTER IS NOT FORTHCOMING.

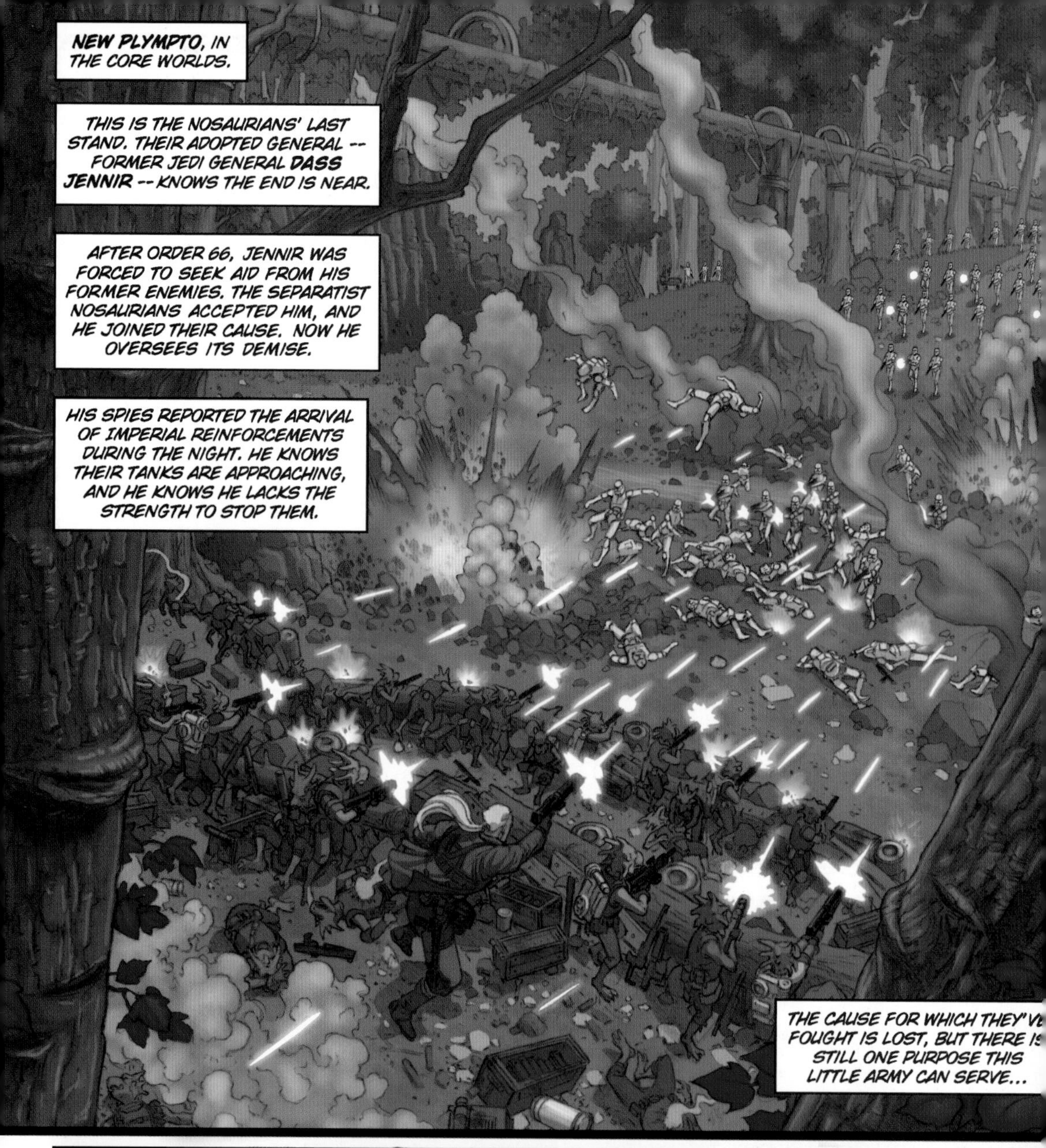
NEW PLYMPTO, IN THE CORE WORLDS.
THIS IS THE NOSAURIANS' LAST STAND. THEIR ADOPTED GENERAL -- FORMER JEDI GENERAL DASS JENNIR -- KNOWS THE END IS NEAR.
AFTER ORDER 66, JENNIR WAS FORCED TO SEEK AID FROM HIS FORMER ENEMIES. THE SEPARATIST NOSAURIANS ACCEPTED HIM, AND HE JOINED THEIR CAUSE. NOW HE OVERSEES ITS DEMISE.
HIS SPIES REPORTED THE ARRIVAL OF IMPERIAL REINFORCEMENTS DURING THE NIGHT. HE KNOWS THEIR TANKS ARE APPROACHING, AND HE KNOWS HE LACKS THE STRENGTH TO STOP THEM.
THE CAUSE FOR WHICH THEY'VE FOUGHT IS LOST, BUT THERE IS STILL ONE PURPOSE THIS LITTLE ARMY CAN SERVE...
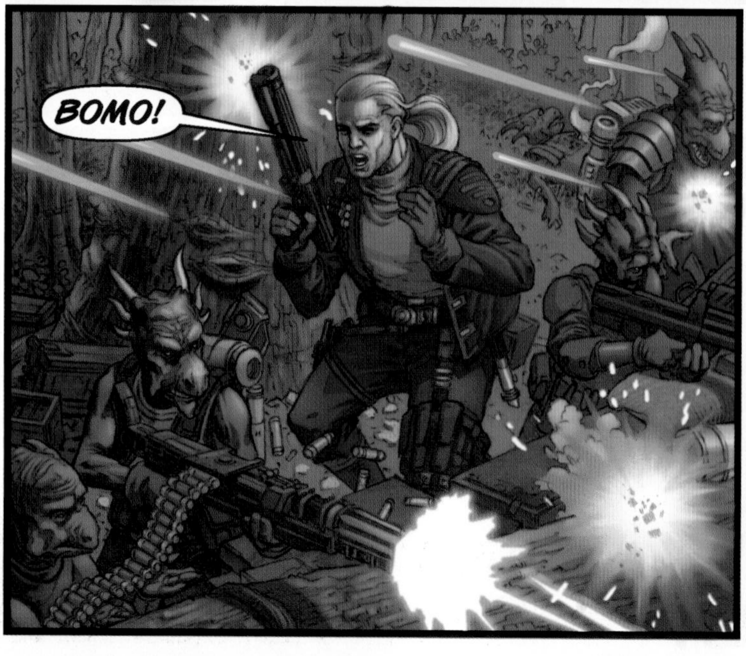
BOMO!
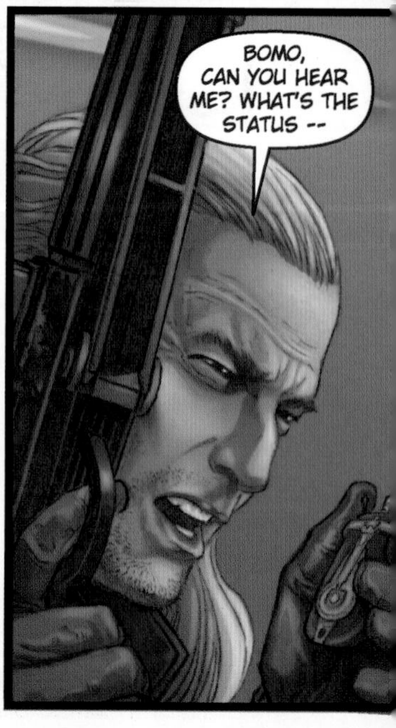
BOMO, CAN YOU HEAR ME? WHAT'S THE STATUS --

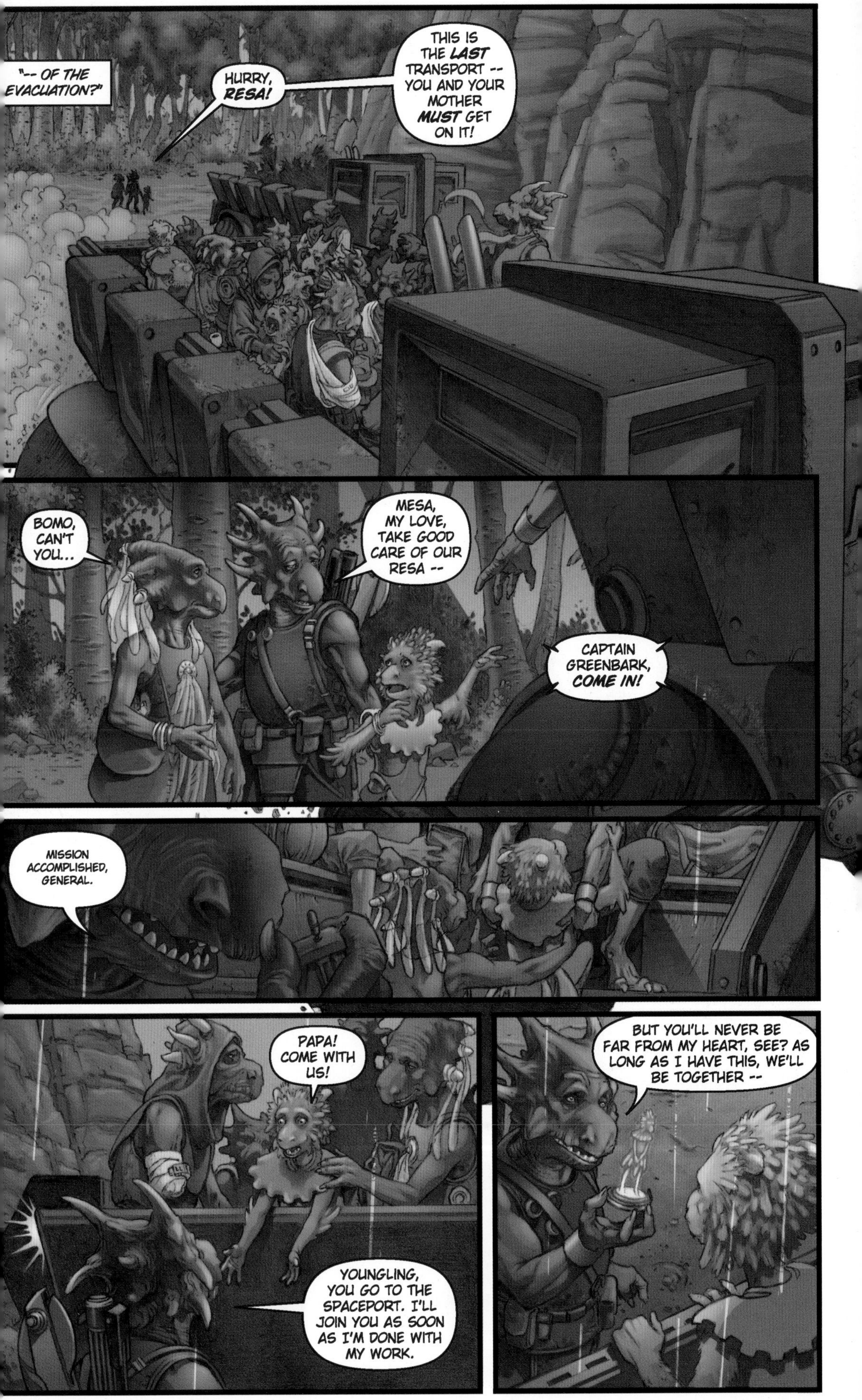
"-- OF THE EVACUATION?"
HURRY, RESA!
THIS IS THE LAST TRANSPORT -- YOU AND YOUR MOTHER MUST GET ON IT!
BOMO, CAN'T YOU...
MESA, MY LOVE, TAKE GOOD CARE OF OUR RESA --
CAPTAIN GREENBARK, COME IN!
MISSION ACCOMPLISHED, GENERAL.
PAPA! COME WITH US!
YOUNGLING, YOU GO TO THE SPACEPORT. I'LL JOIN YOU AS SOON AS I'M DONE WITH MY WORK.
BUT YOU'LL NEVER BE FAR FROM MY HEART, SEE? AS LONG AS I HAVE THIS, WE'LL BE TOGETHER --

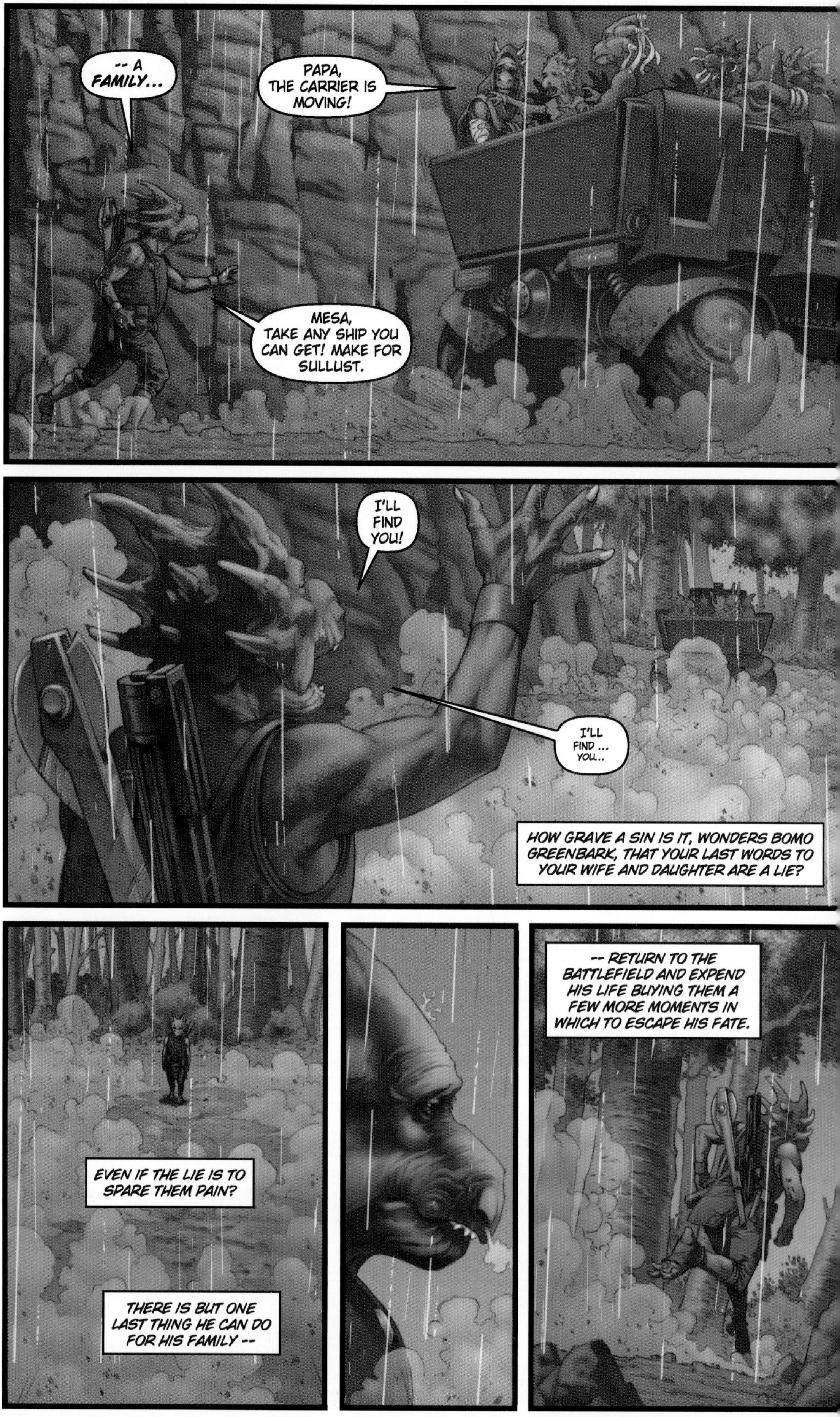
-- A FAMILY...
PAPA, THE CARRIER IS MOVING!
MESA, TAKE ANY SHIP YOU CAN GET! MAKE FOR SULLUST.
I'LL FIND YOU!
I'LL FIND ... YOU...
HOW GRAVE A SIN IS IT, WONDERS BOMO GREENBARK, THAT YOUR LAST WORDS TO YOUR WIFE AND DAUGHTER ARE A LIE?
EVEN IF THE LIE IS TO SPARE THEM PAIN?
THERE IS BUT ONE LAST THING HE CAN DO FOR HIS FAMILY --
-- RETURN TO THE BATTLEFIELD AND EXPEND HIS LIFE BUYING THEM A FEW MORE MOMENTS IN WHICH TO ESCAPE HIS FATE.

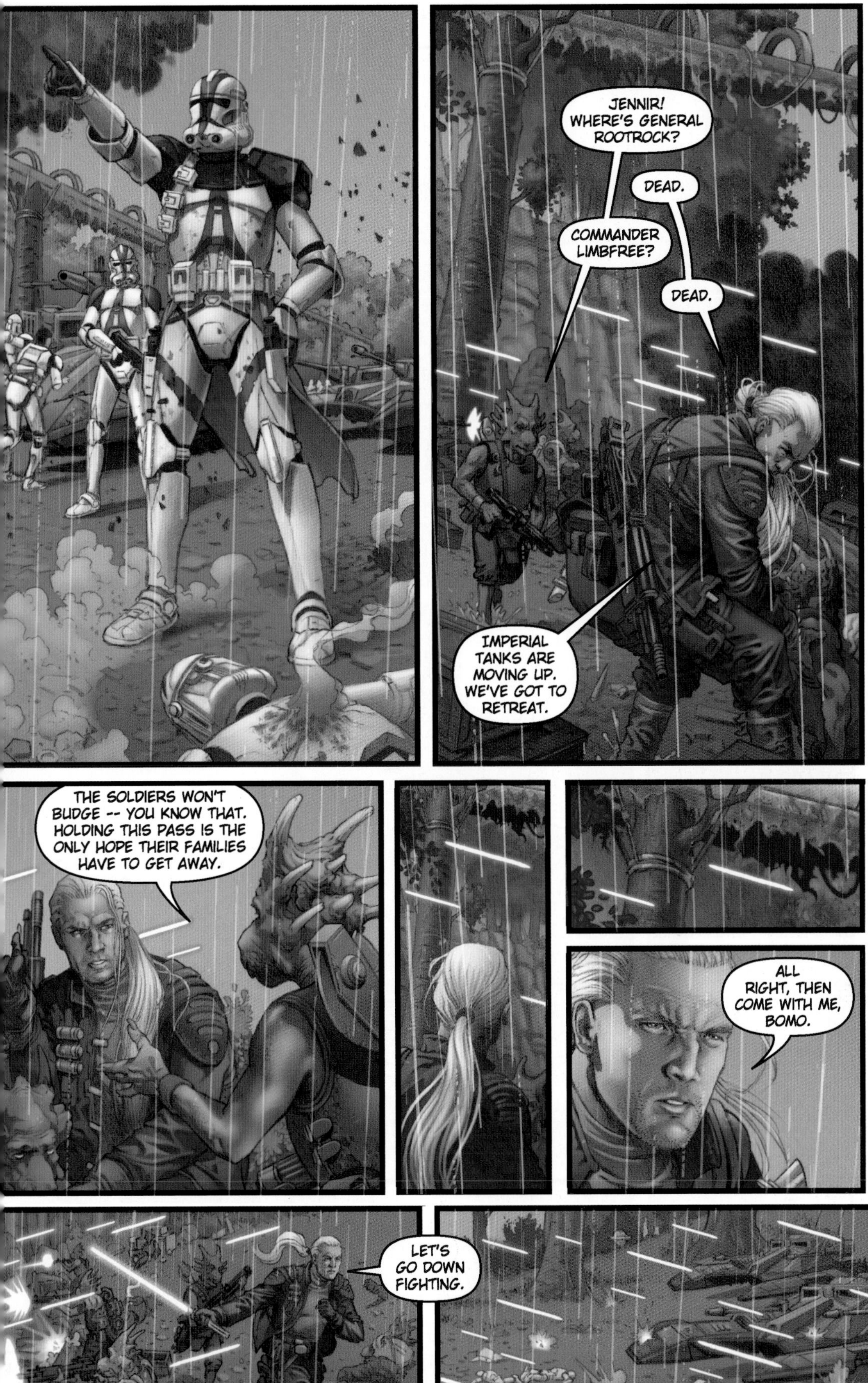
JENNIR! WHERE'S GENERAL ROOTROCK?
DEAD.
COMMANDER LIMBFREE?
DEAD.
IMPERIAL TANKS ARE MOVING UP. WE'VE GOT TO RETREAT.
THE SOLDIERS WON'T BUDGE -- YOU KNOW THAT. HOLDING THIS PASS IS THE ONLY HOPE THEIR FAMILIES HAVE TO GET AWAY.
ALL RIGHT, THEN COME WITH ME, BOMO.
LET'S GO DOWN FIGHTING.

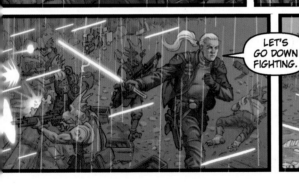

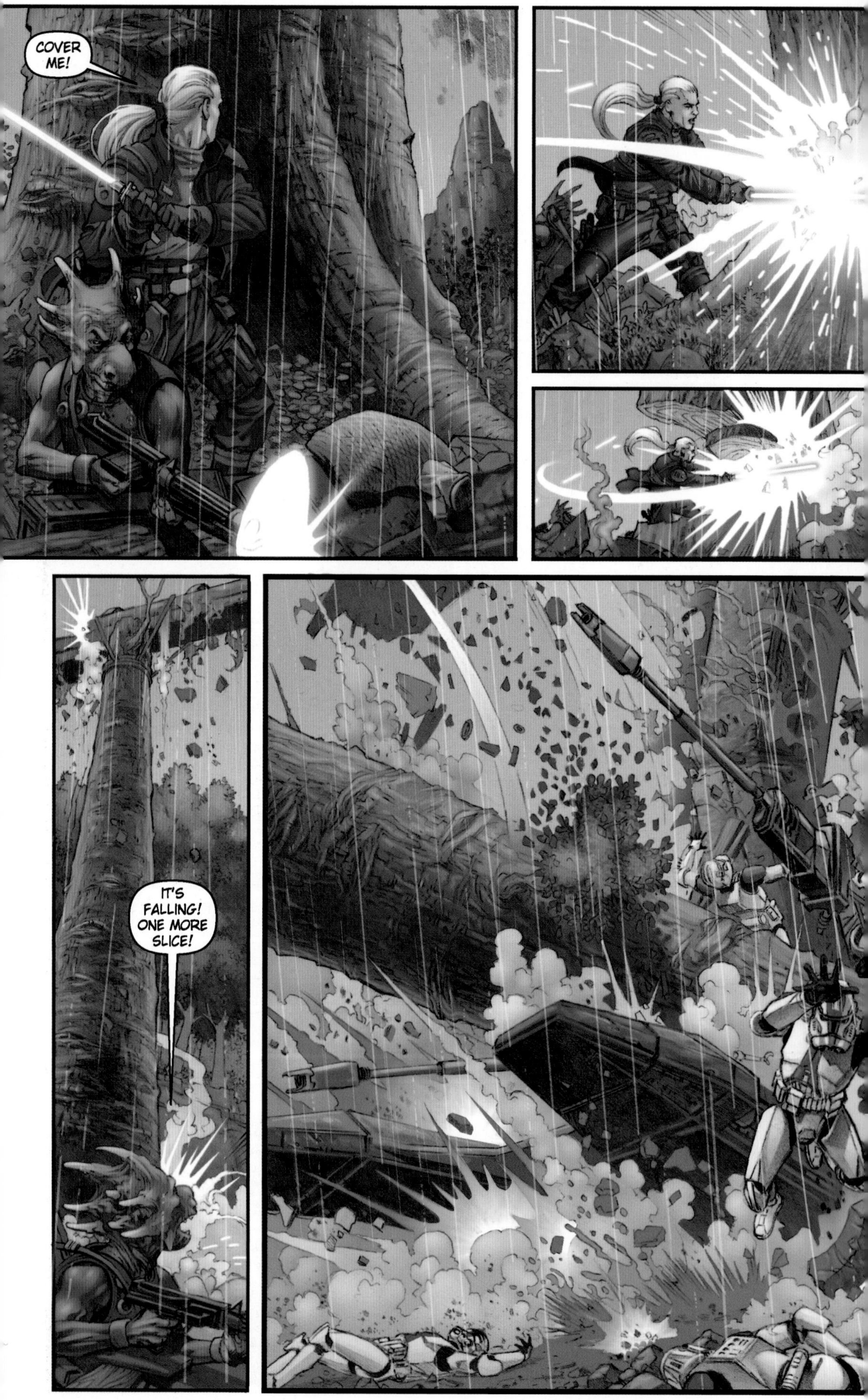
COVER ME!
IT'S FALLING! ONE MORE SLICE!

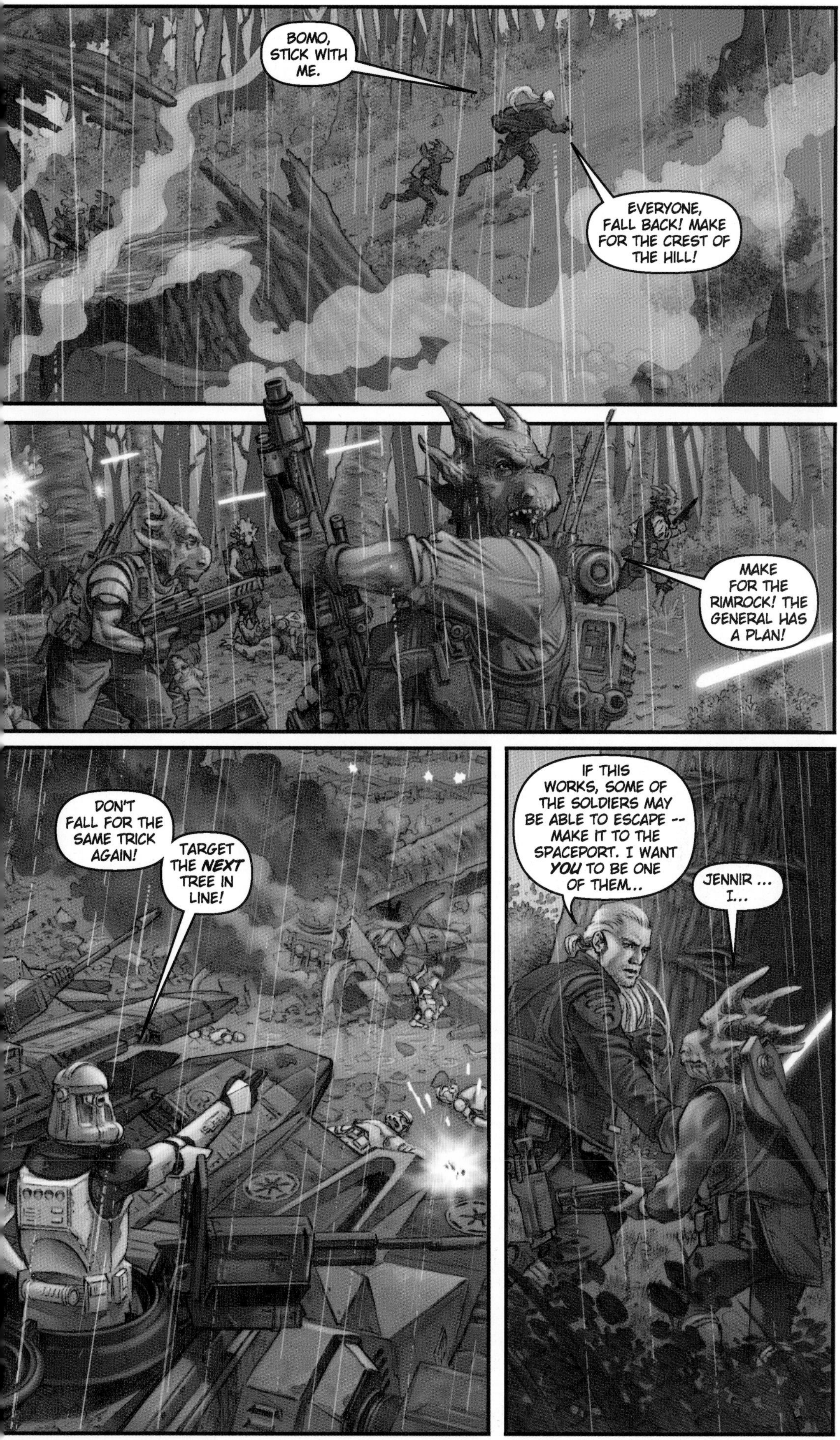
BOMO, STICK WITH ME.
EVERYONE, FALL BACK! MAKE FOR THE CREST OF THE HILL!
MAKE FOR THE RIMROCK! THE GENERAL HAS A PLAN!
DON'T FALL FOR THE SAME TRICK AGAIN!
TARGET THE *NEXT* TREE IN LINE!
IF THIS WORKS, SOME OF THE SOLDIERS MAY BE ABLE TO ESCAPE -- MAKE IT TO THE SPACEPORT. I WANT *YOU* TO BE ONE OF THEM...
JENNIR ... I...

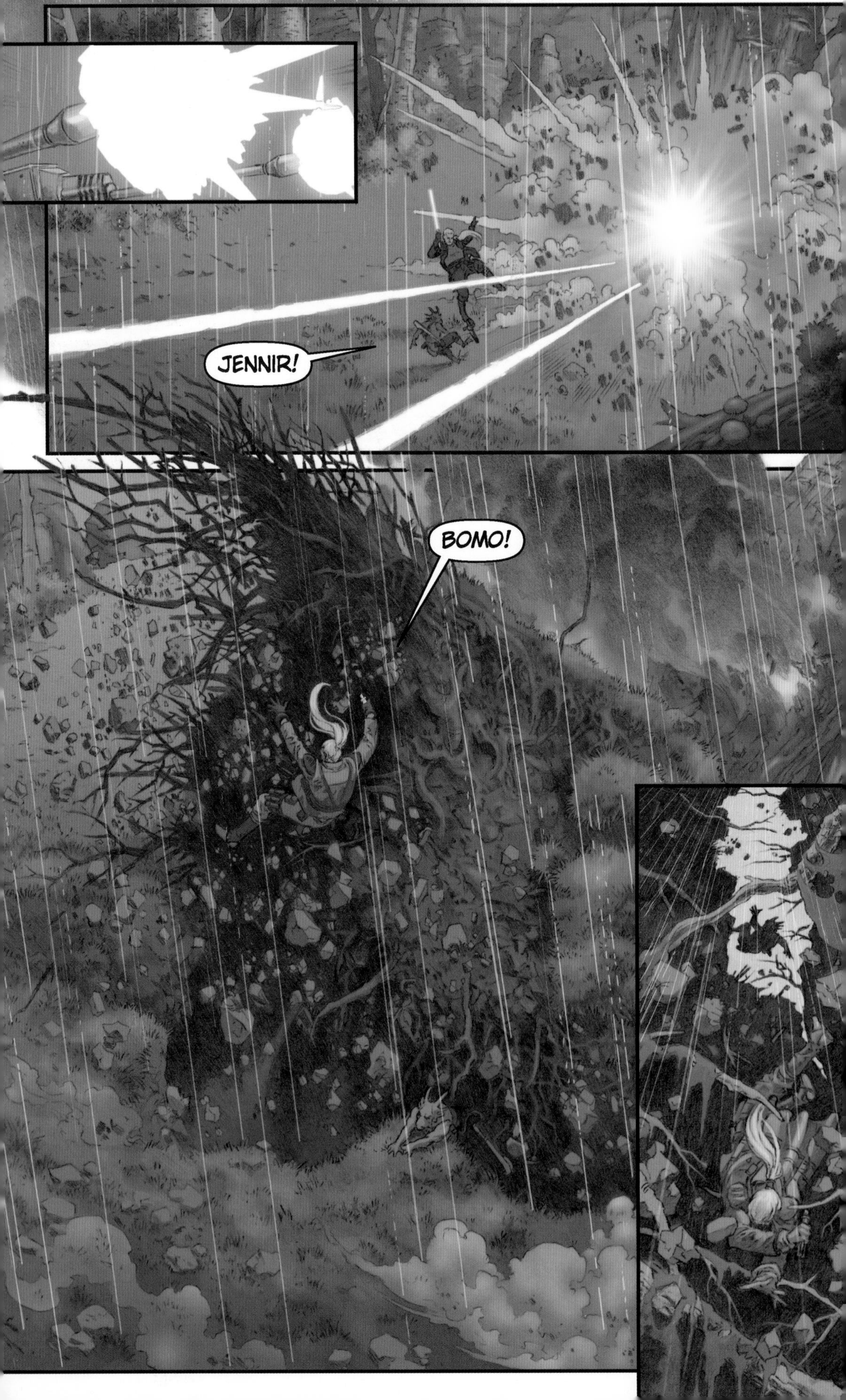
JENNIR!
BOMO!

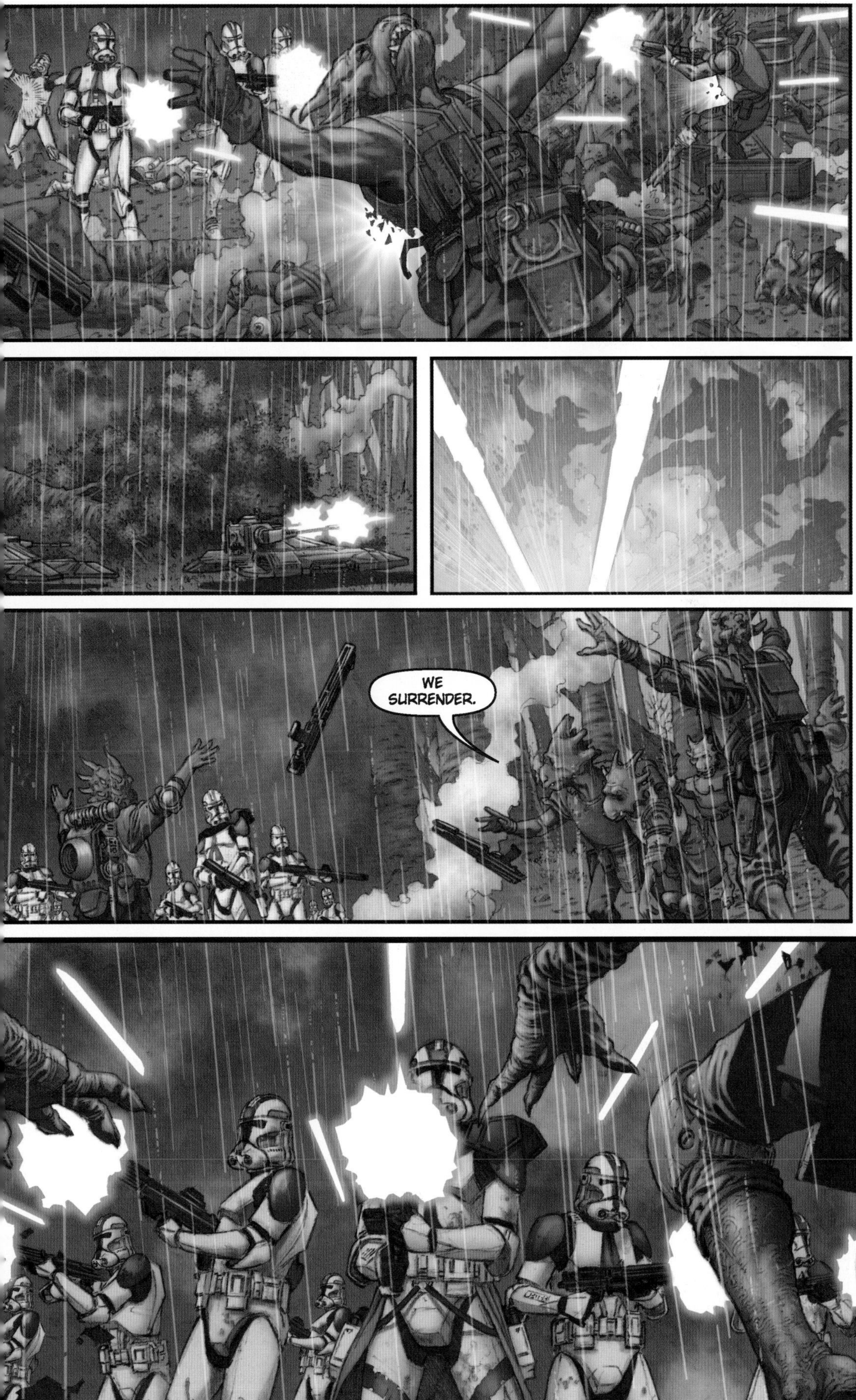
WE SURRENDER.

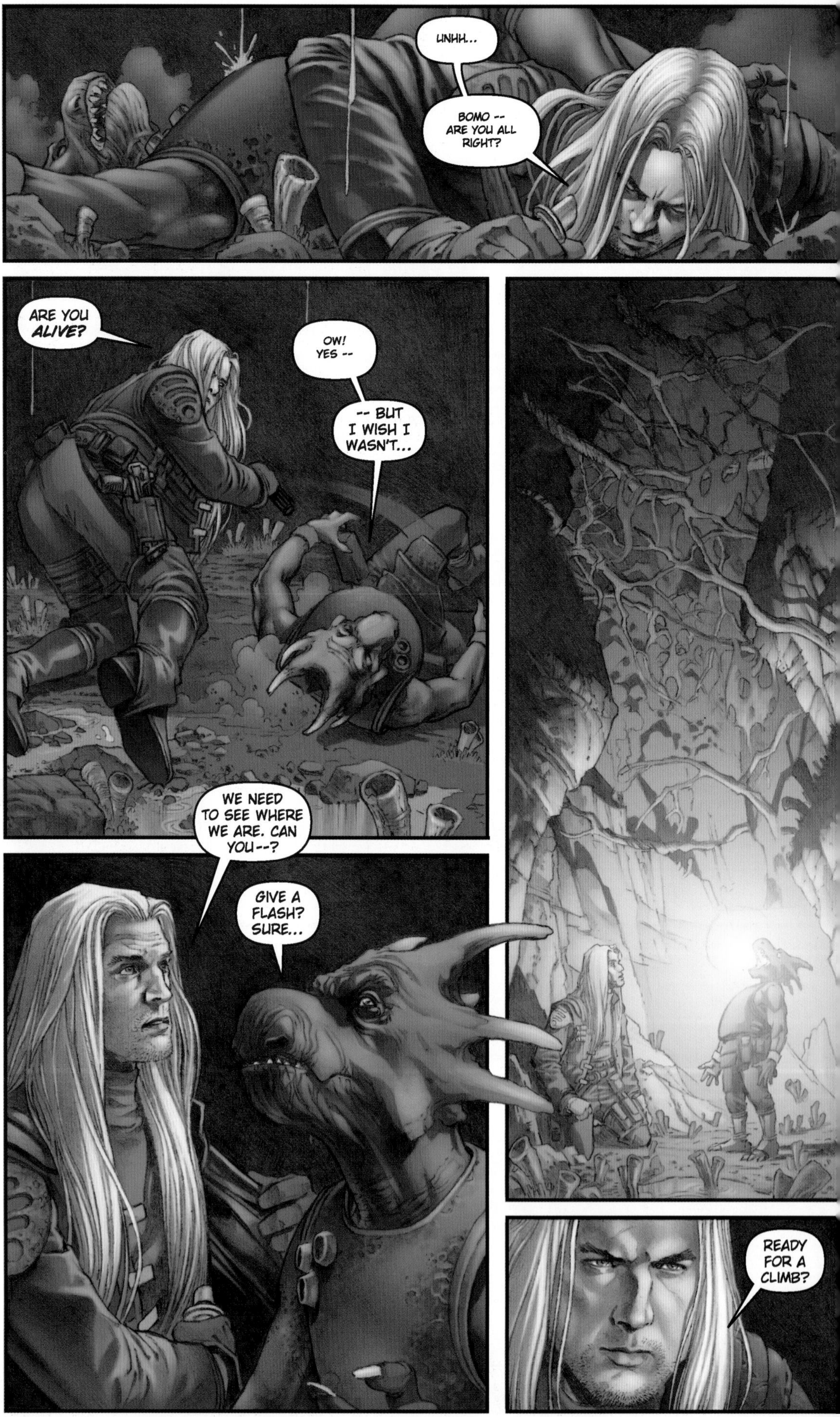
UNHH...
BOMO -- ARE YOU ALL RIGHT?
ARE YOU *ALIVE?*
OW! YES --
-- BUT I WISH I WASN'T...
WE NEED TO SEE WHERE WE ARE. CAN YOU--?
GIVE A FLASH? SURE...
READY FOR A CLIMB?

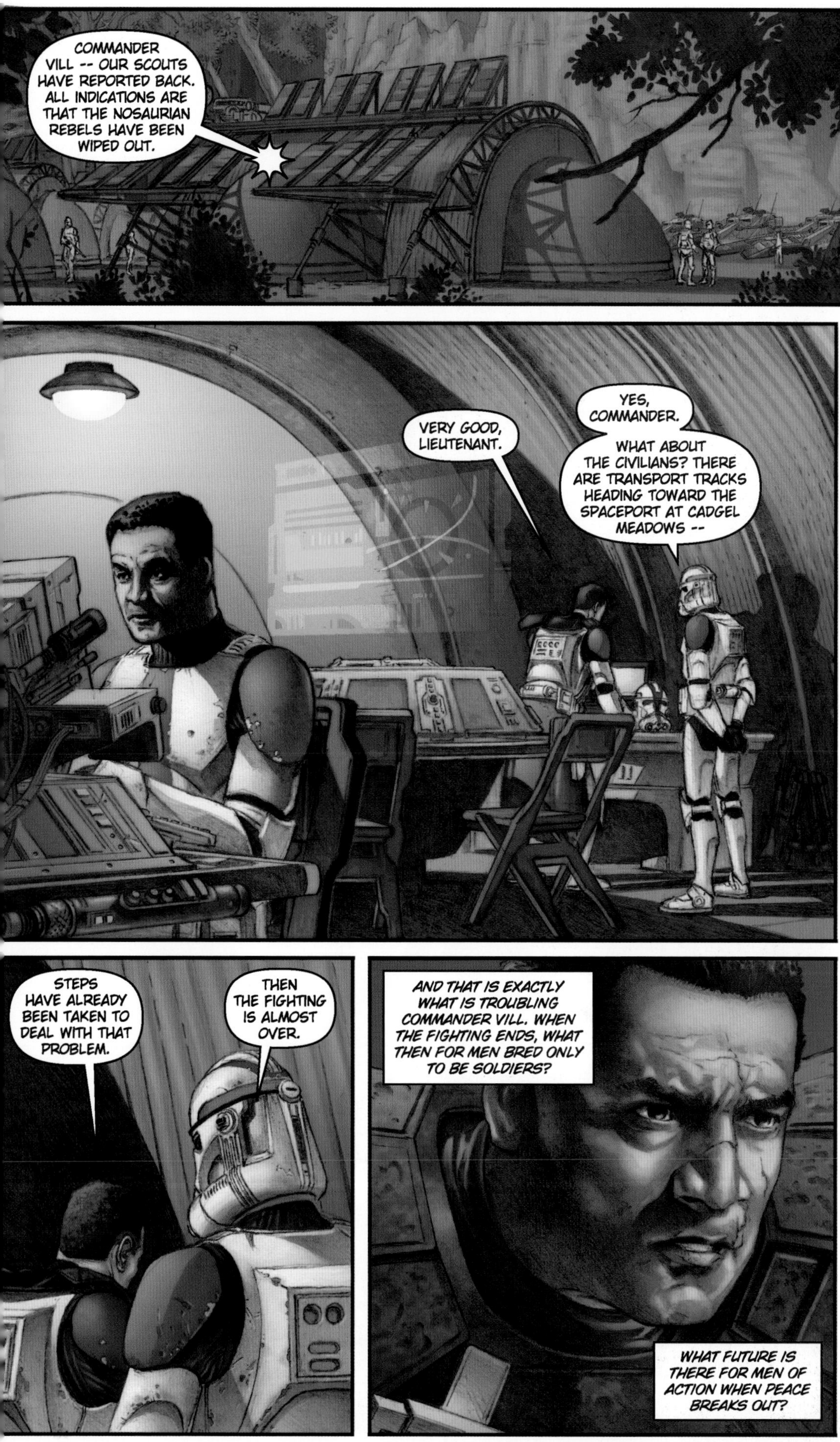

COMMANDER VILL -- OUR SCOUTS HAVE REPORTED BACK. ALL INDICATIONS ARE THAT THE NOSAURIAN REBELS HAVE BEEN WIPED OUT.
VERY GOOD, LIEUTENANT.
YES, COMMANDER.
WHAT ABOUT THE CIVILIANS? THERE ARE TRANSPORT TRACKS HEADING TOWARD THE SPACEPORT AT CADGEL MEADOWS --
STEPS HAVE ALREADY BEEN TAKEN TO DEAL WITH THAT PROBLEM.
THEN THE FIGHTING IS ALMOST OVER.
AND THAT IS EXACTLY WHAT IS TROUBLING COMMANDER VILL. WHEN THE FIGHTING ENDS, WHAT THEN FOR MEN BRED ONLY TO BE SOLDIERS?
WHAT FUTURE IS THERE FOR MEN OF ACTION WHEN PEACE BREAKS OUT?

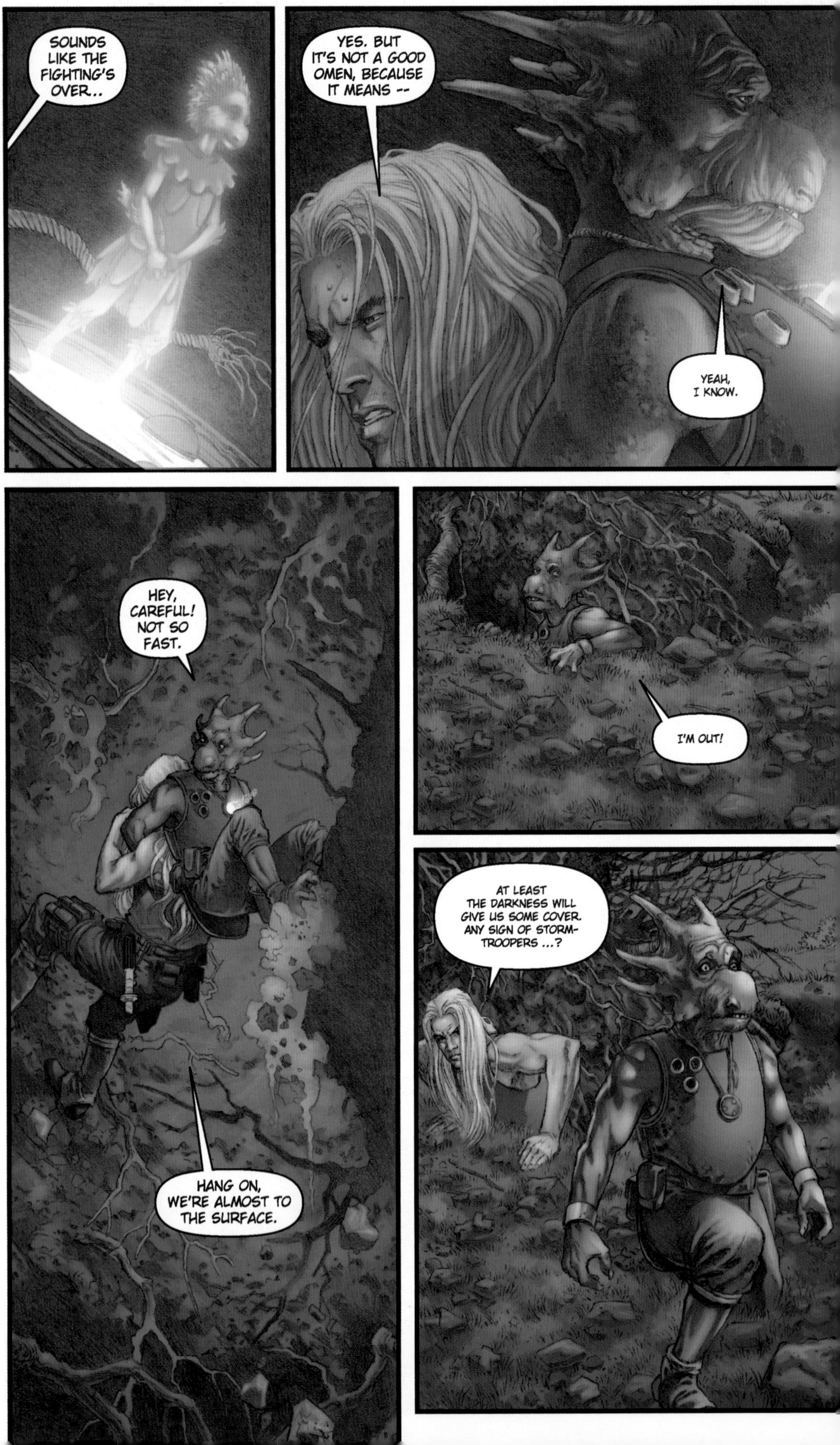
SOUNDS LIKE THE FIGHTING'S OVER...
YES. BUT IT'S NOT A GOOD OMEN, BECAUSE IT MEANS --
YEAH, I KNOW.
HEY, CAREFUL! NOT SO FAST.
HANG ON, WE'RE ALMOST TO THE SURFACE.
I'M OUT!
AT LEAST THE DARKNESS WILL GIVE US SOME COVER. ANY SIGN OF STORM-TROOPERS ...?

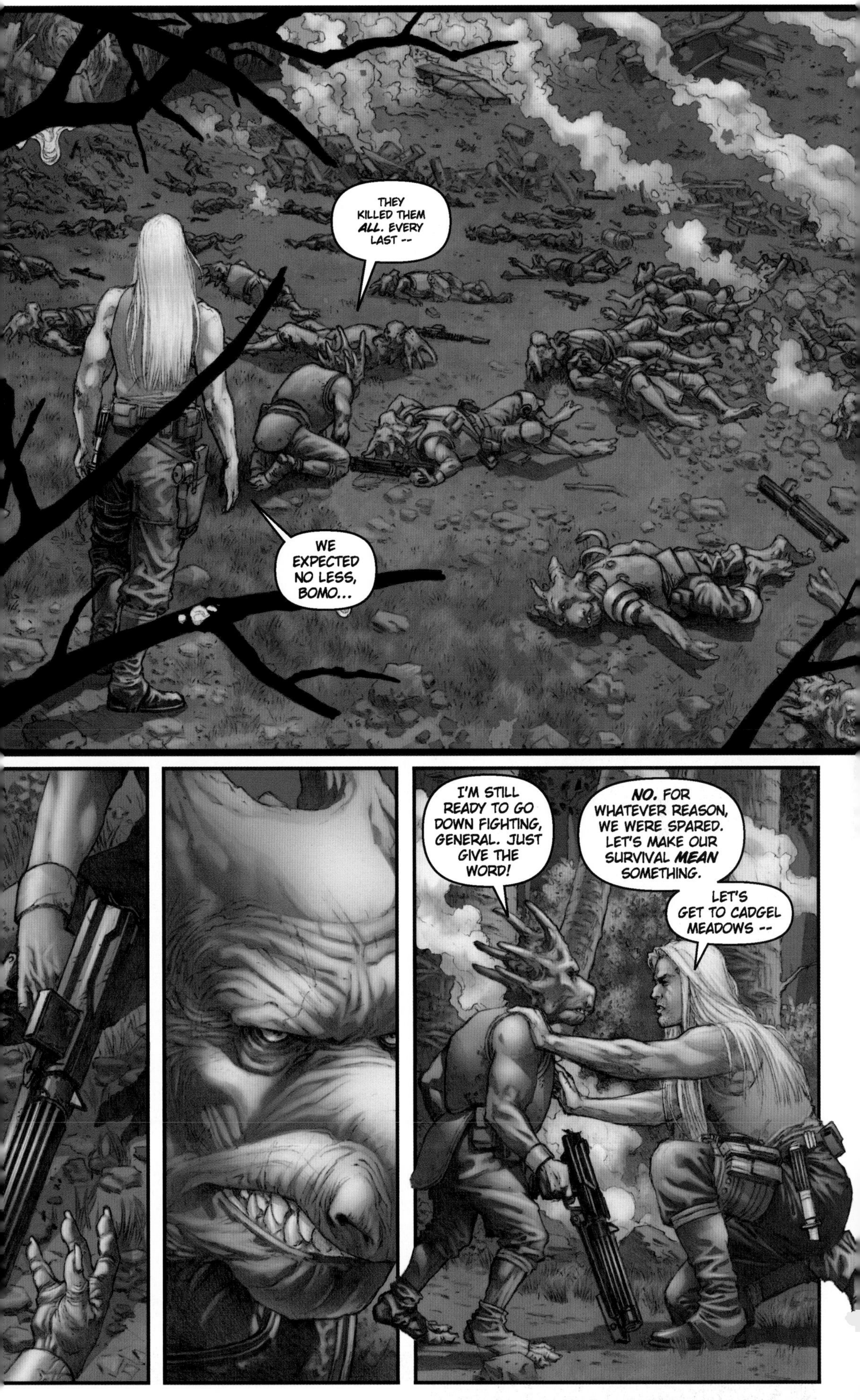

THEY KILLED THEM ALL. EVERY LAST --
WE EXPECTED NO LESS, BOMO...
I'M STILL READY TO GO DOWN FIGHTING, GENERAL. JUST GIVE THE WORD!
NO. FOR WHATEVER REASON, WE WERE SPARED. LET'S MAKE OUR SURVIVAL MEAN SOMETHING.
LET'S GET TO CADGEL MEADOWS --

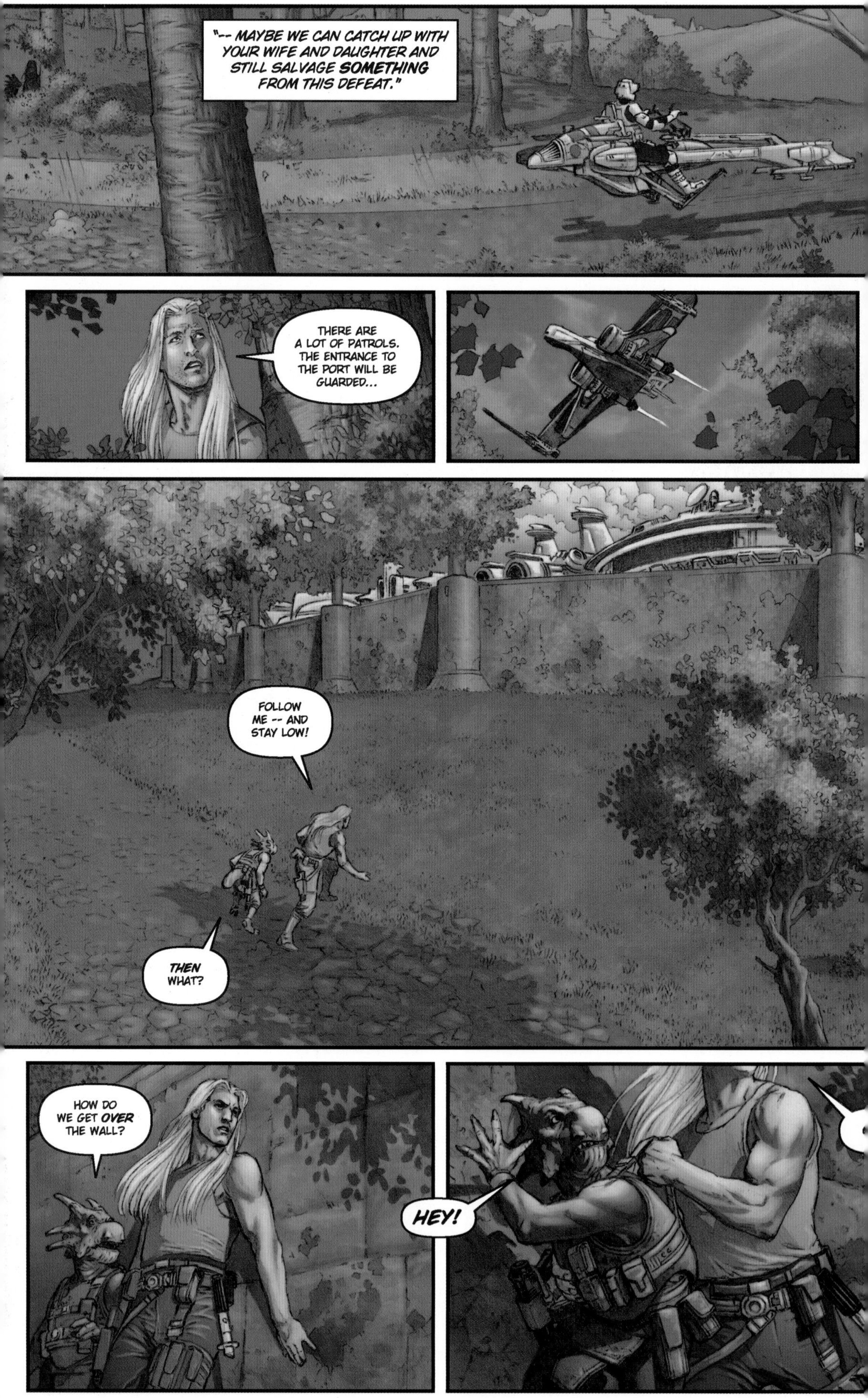
"-- MAYBE WE CAN CATCH UP WITH YOUR WIFE AND DAUGHTER AND STILL SALVAGE SOMETHING FROM THIS DEFEAT."
THERE ARE A LOT OF PATROLS. THE ENTRANCE TO THE PORT WILL BE GUARDED...
FOLLOW ME -- AND STAY LOW!
THEN WHAT?
HOW DO WE GET OVER THE WALL?
HEY!

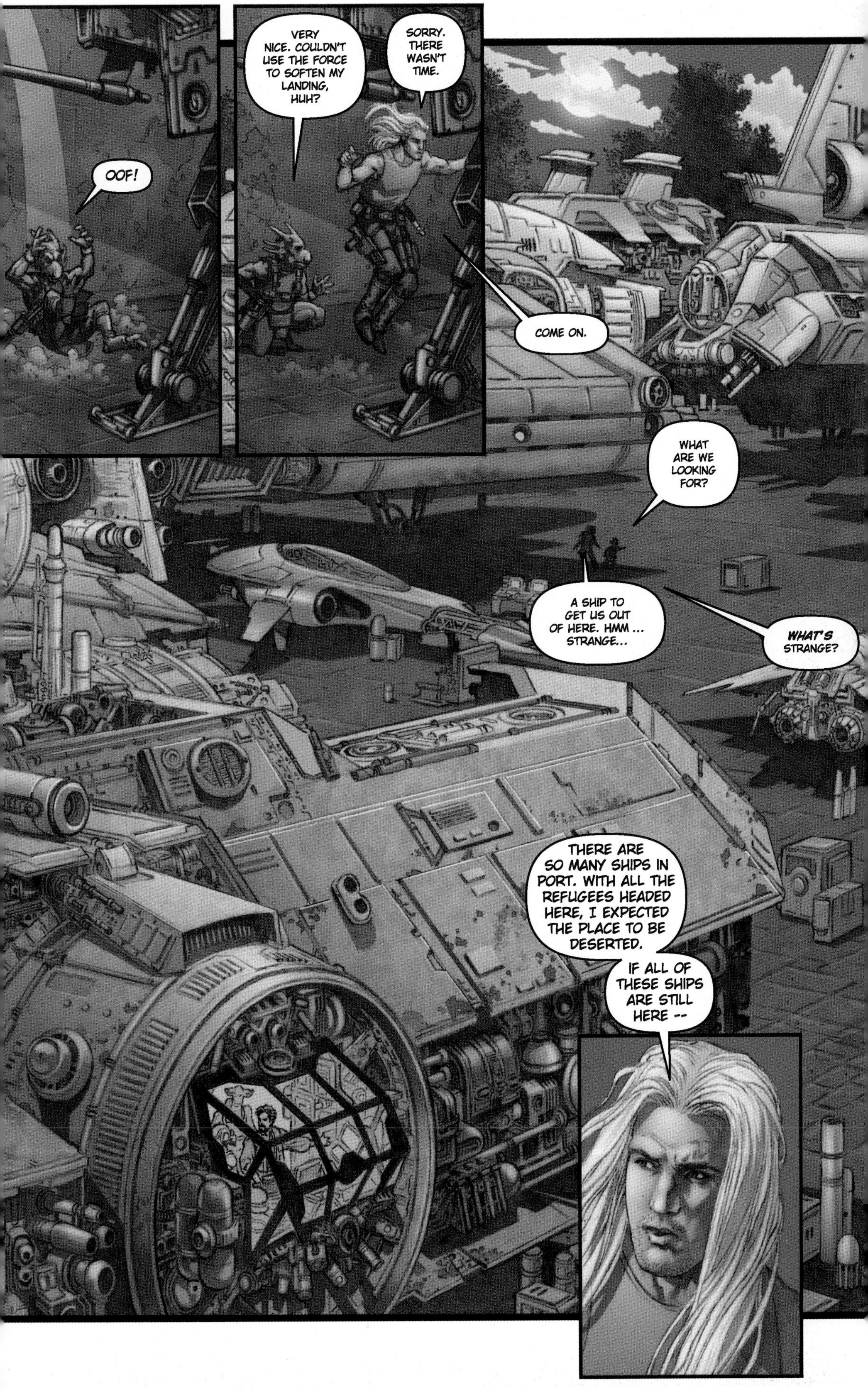
OOF!
VERY NICE. COULDN'T USE THE FORCE TO SOFTEN MY LANDING, HUH?
SORRY. THERE WASN'T TIME.
COME ON.
WHAT ARE WE LOOKING FOR?
A SHIP TO GET US OUT OF HERE. HMM ... STRANGE...
WHAT'S STRANGE?
THERE ARE SO MANY SHIPS IN PORT. WITH ALL THE REFUGEES HEADED HERE, I EXPECTED THE PLACE TO BE DESERTED.
IF ALL OF THESE SHIPS ARE STILL HERE --

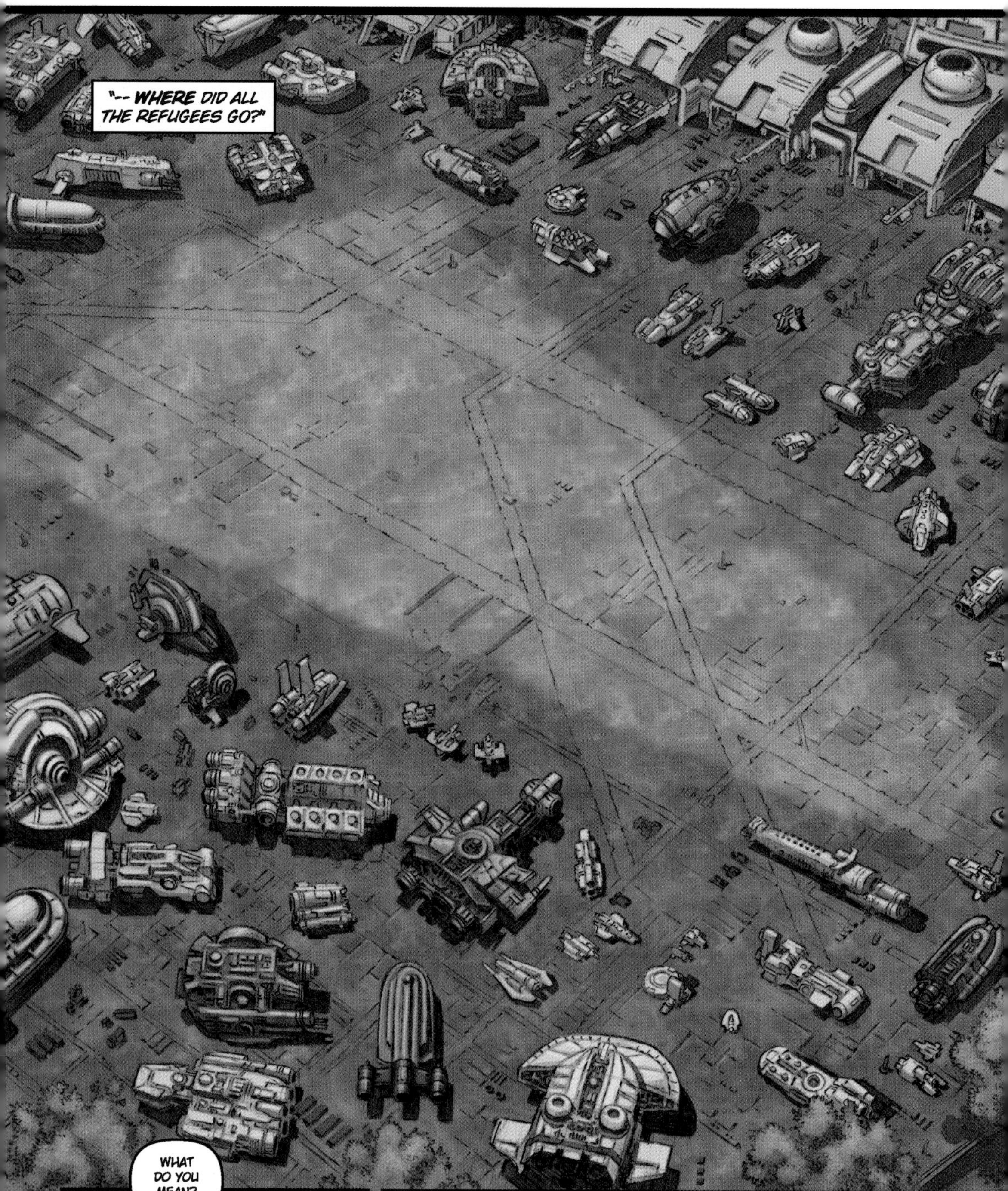
"-- WHERE DID ALL THE REFUGEES GO?"

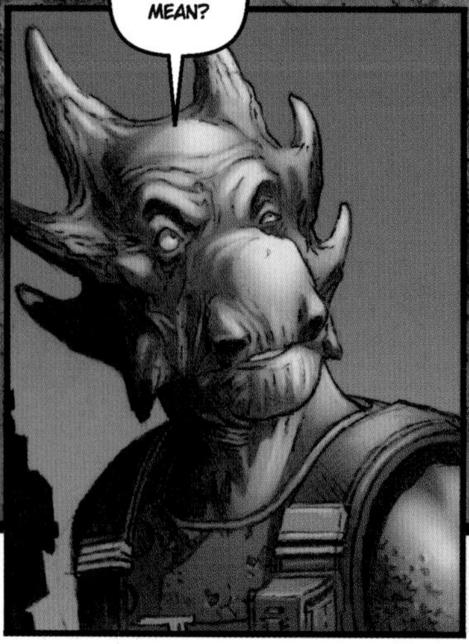
WHAT DO YOU MEAN?

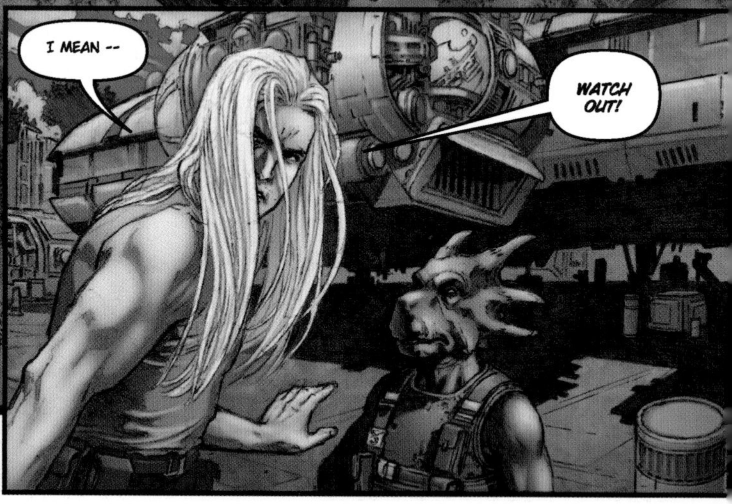
I MEAN --
WATCH OUT!

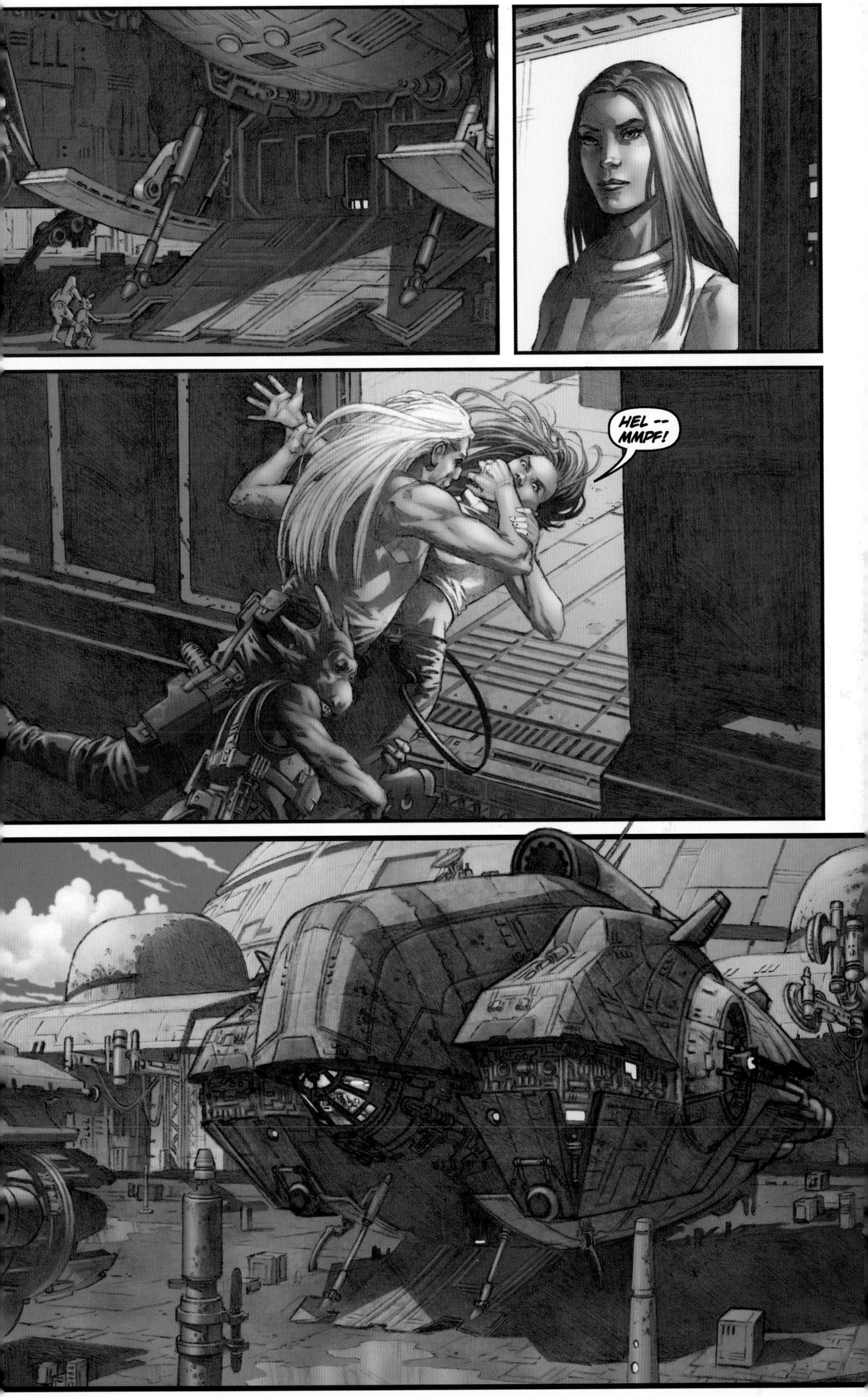
HEL --
MMPF!

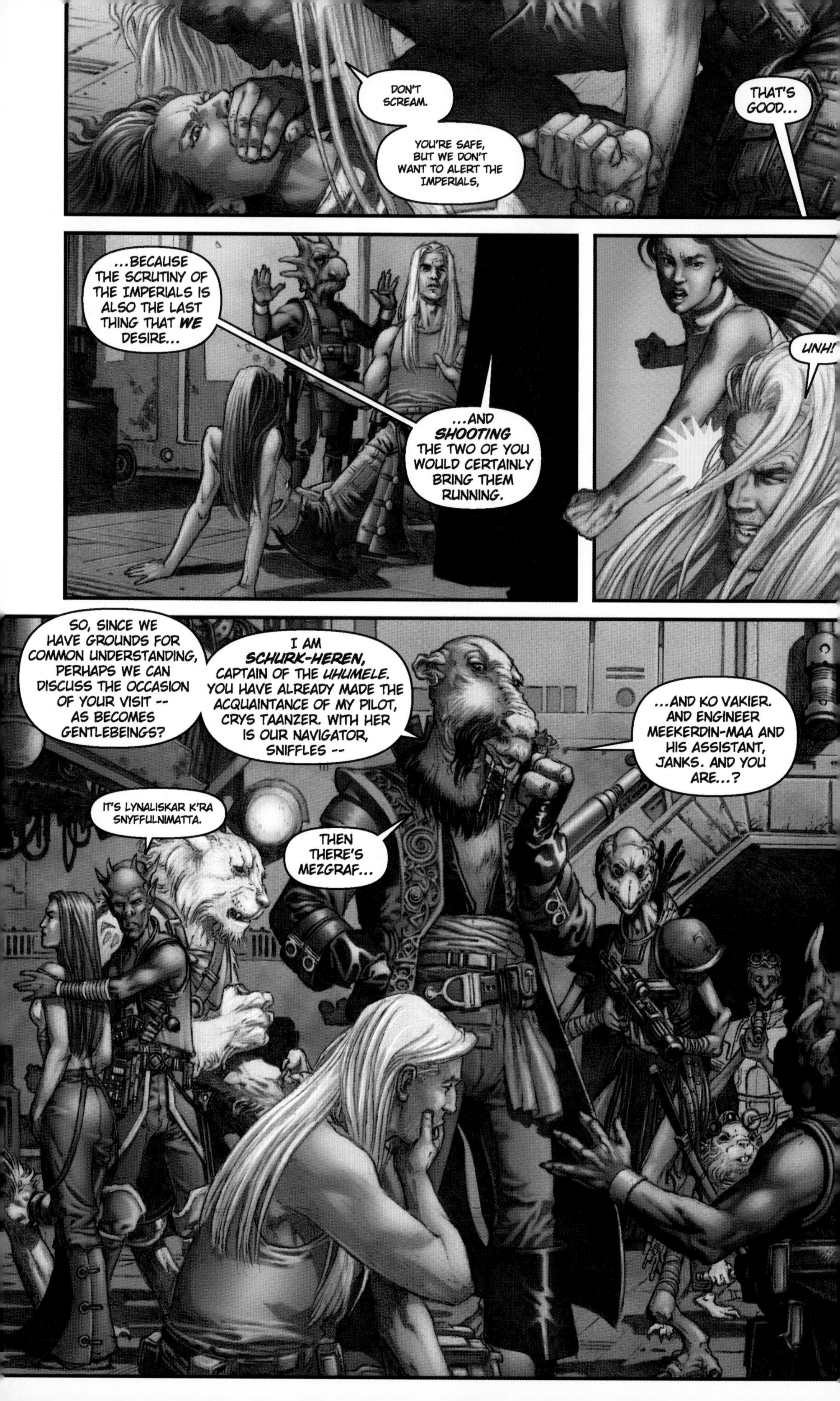
DON'T SCREAM.
YOU'RE SAFE, BUT WE DON'T WANT TO ALERT THE IMPERIALS,
THAT'S GOOD...
...BECAUSE THE SCRUTINY OF THE IMPERIALS IS ALSO THE LAST THING THAT WE DESIRE...
...AND SHOOTING THE TWO OF YOU WOULD CERTAINLY BRING THEM RUNNING.
UNH!
SO, SINCE WE HAVE GROUNDS FOR COMMON UNDERSTANDING, PERHAPS WE CAN DISCUSS THE OCCASION OF YOUR VISIT -- AS BECOMES GENTLEBEINGS?
I AM SCHURK-HEREN, CAPTAIN OF THE UHUMELE. YOU HAVE ALREADY MADE THE ACQUAINTANCE OF MY PILOT, CRYS TAANZER. WITH HER IS OUR NAVIGATOR, SNIFFLES --
IT'S LYNALISKAR K'RA SNYFFULNIMATTA.
THEN THERE'S MEZGRAF...
...AND KO VAKIER. AND ENGINEER MEEKERDIN-MAA AND HIS ASSISTANT, JANKS. AND YOU ARE...?

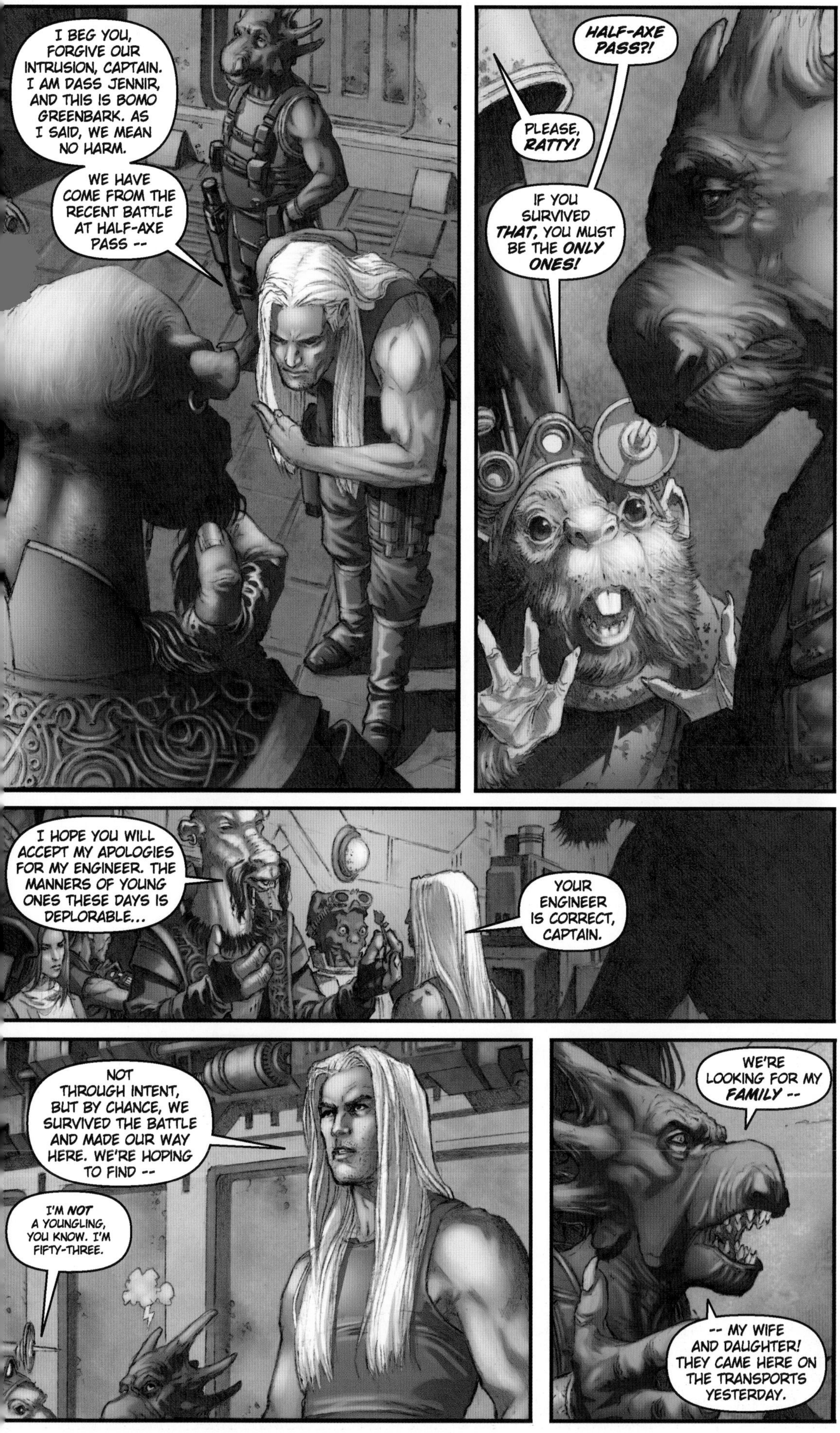
I BEG YOU, FORGIVE OUR INTRUSION, CAPTAIN. I AM DASS JENNIR, AND THIS IS BOMO GREENBARK. AS I SAID, WE MEAN NO HARM.
WE HAVE COME FROM THE RECENT BATTLE AT HALF-AXE PASS --
HALF-AXE PASS?!
PLEASE, RATTY!
IF YOU SURVIVED THAT, YOU MUST BE THE ONLY ONES!
I HOPE YOU WILL ACCEPT MY APOLOGIES FOR MY ENGINEER. THE MANNERS OF YOUNG ONES THESE DAYS IS DEPLORABLE...
YOUR ENGINEER IS CORRECT, CAPTAIN.
NOT THROUGH INTENT, BUT BY CHANCE, WE SURVIVED THE BATTLE AND MADE OUR WAY HERE. WE'RE HOPING TO FIND --
I'M NOT A YOUNGLING, YOU KNOW. I'M FIFTY-THREE.
WE'RE LOOKING FOR MY FAMILY --
-- MY WIFE AND DAUGHTER! THEY CAME HERE ON THE TRANSPORTS YESTERDAY.

BOMO...

I TOLD THEM TO GO TO SULLUST, SO THAT'S WHERE *WE* WANT TO GO. CAN YOU HELP US, OR NOT?

WELL?

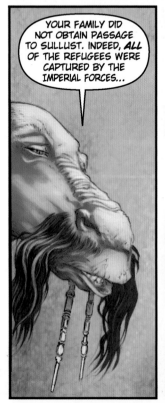

YOUR FAMILY DID NOT OBTAIN PASSAGE TO SULLUST. INDEED, *ALL* OF THE REFUGEES WERE CAPTURED BY THE IMPERIAL FORCES...

THEY WERE ALL ROUNDED UP AND LOADED ON A SHIP. THE EMPIRE IS GOING TO *SELL* THEM TO *SLAVERS!*

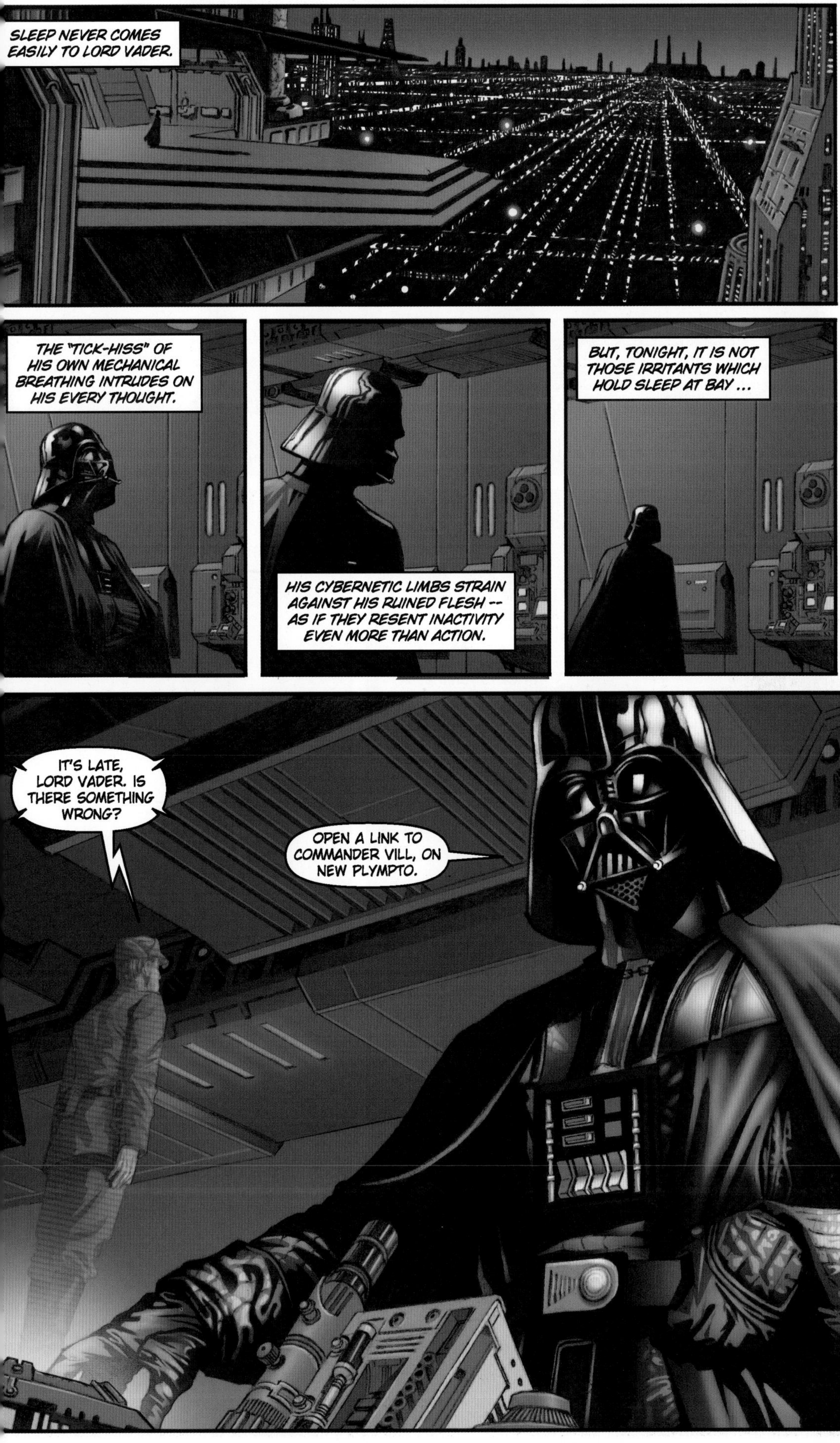
SLEEP NEVER COMES EASILY TO LORD VADER.
THE "TICK-HISS" OF HIS OWN MECHANICAL BREATHING INTRUDES ON HIS EVERY THOUGHT.
HIS CYBERNETIC LIMBS STRAIN AGAINST HIS RUINED FLESH -- AS IF THEY RESENT INACTIVITY EVEN MORE THAN ACTION.
BUT, TONIGHT, IT IS NOT THOSE IRRITANTS WHICH HOLD SLEEP AT BAY ...
IT'S LATE, LORD VADER. IS THERE SOMETHING WRONG?
OPEN A LINK TO COMMANDER VILL, ON NEW PLYMPTO.

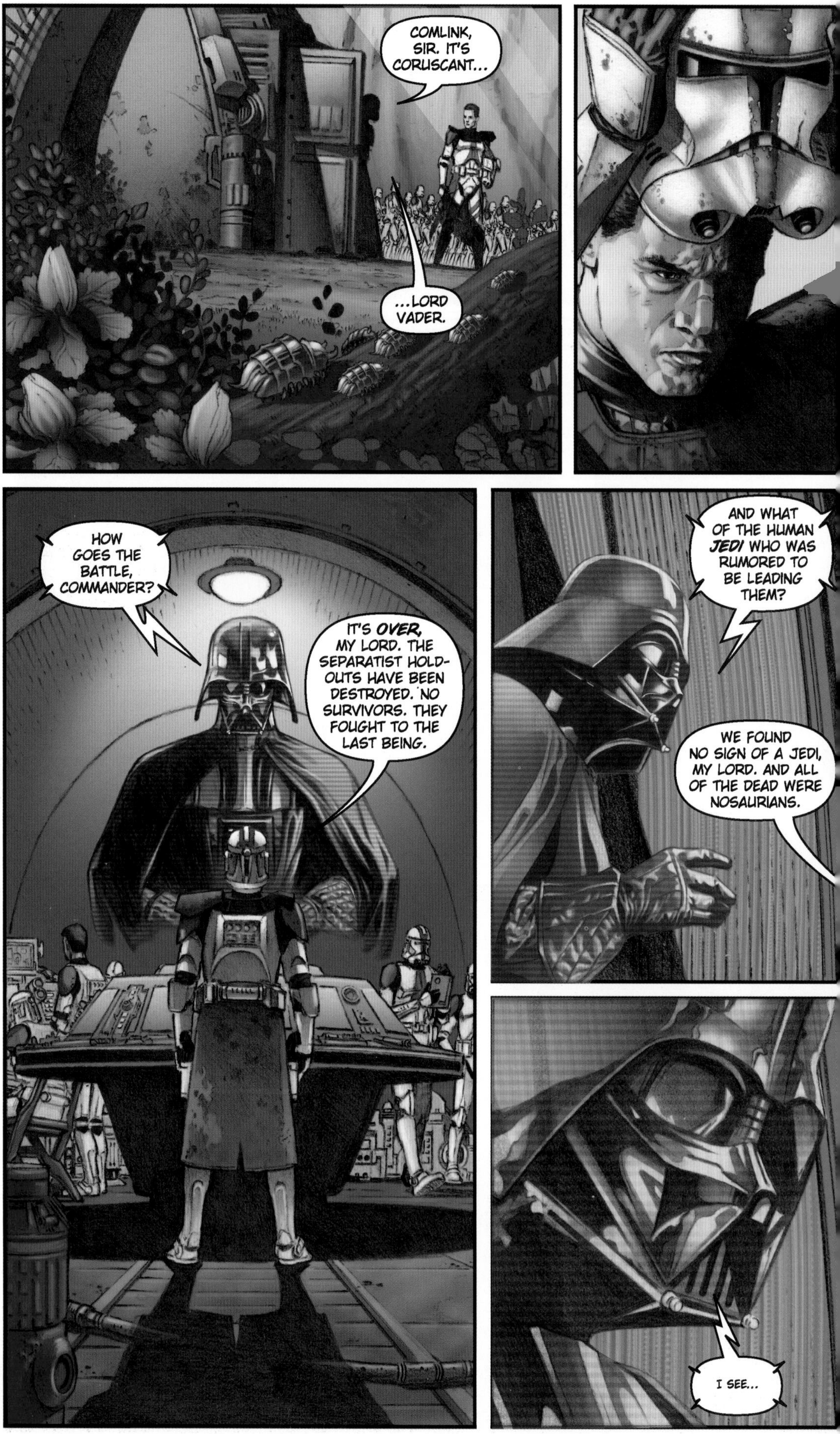
COMLINK, SIR. IT'S CORUSCANT...
...LORD VADER.
HOW GOES THE BATTLE, COMMANDER?
IT'S OVER, MY LORD. THE SEPARATIST HOLD-OUTS HAVE BEEN DESTROYED. NO SURVIVORS. THEY FOUGHT TO THE LAST BEING.
AND WHAT OF THE HUMAN JEDI WHO WAS RUMORED TO BE LEADING THEM?
WE FOUND NO SIGN OF A JEDI, MY LORD. AND ALL OF THE DEAD WERE NOSAURIANS.
I SEE...

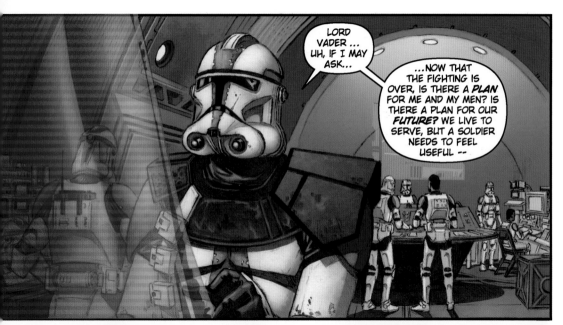

LORD VADER ... UH, IF I MAY ASK...

...NOW THAT THE FIGHTING IS OVER, IS THERE A *PLAN* FOR ME AND MY MEN? IS THERE A PLAN FOR OUR *FUTURE?* WE LIVE TO SERVE, BUT A SOLDIER NEEDS TO FEEL USEFUL --

I ... I'M *CERTAIN* THAT THE EMPEROR HAS A *PLAN,* COMMANDER. WE WILL DISCUSS IT UPON YOUR RETURN TO CORUSCANT...

YES, MY LORD. BUT I'M NOT SURE OF *WHEN* THE REGIMENT AND I WILL BE BACK -- OUR TRANSPORT WAS *RE-TASKED,* BY ORDER OF THE EMPEROR.

*WHERE* WAS IT SENT? HAS *NEW FIGHTING* BROKEN OUT SOMEWHERE?

NO, SIR. THE SHIP IS TRANSPORTING CAPTURED NOSAURIAN CIVILIANS TO THE *SLAVE MARKET* ON ORVAX IV.

THE PRISONERS WERE MOSTLY FEMALES AND YOUNGLINGS, SO IT WAS DECIDED THAT THEY WOULD BE SOLD FOR *PROFIT* RATHER THAN ADDED TO THE IMPERIAL WORKFORCE...

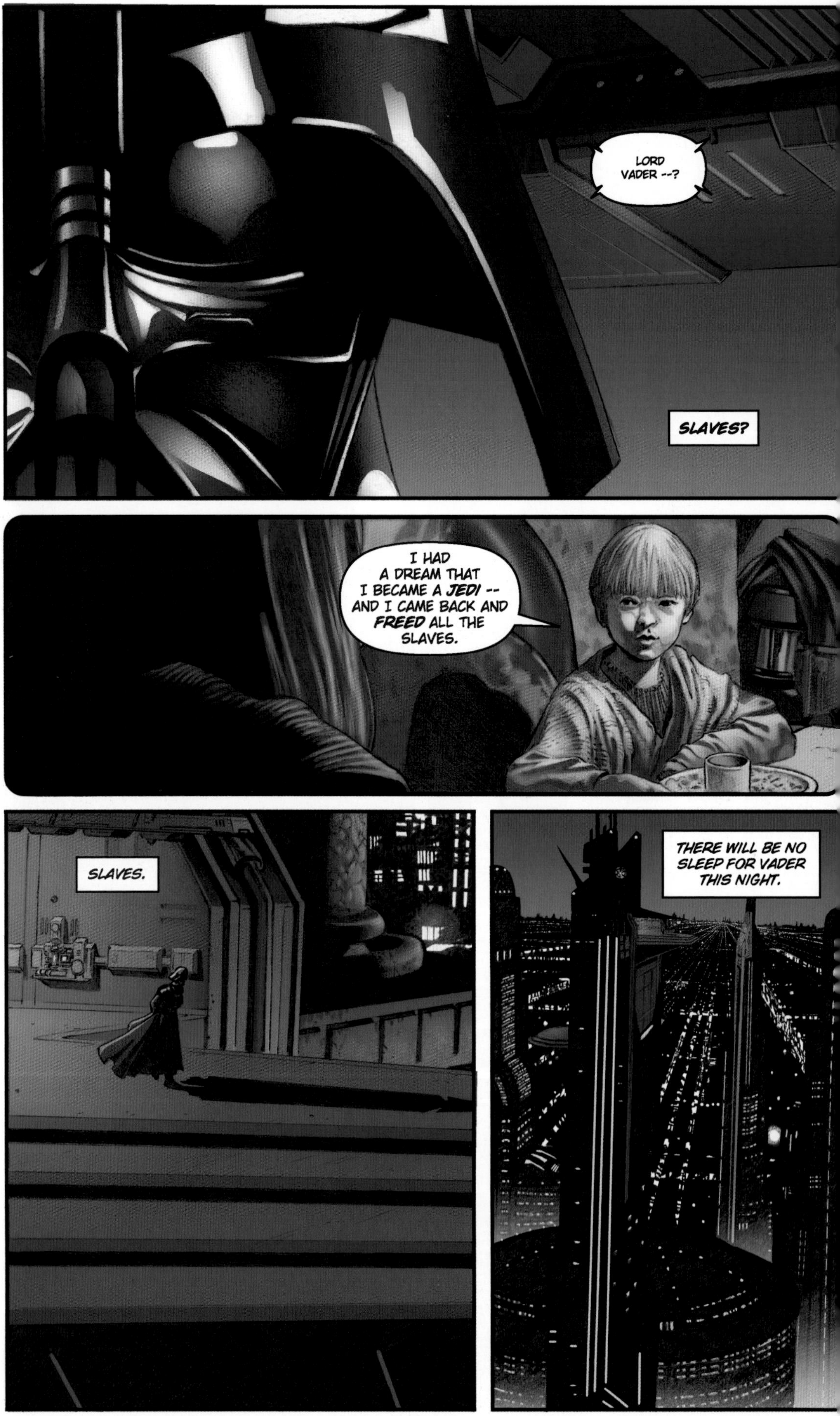
LORD VADER --?
SLAVES?
I HAD A DREAM THAT I BECAME A JEDI -- AND I CAME BACK AND FREED ALL THE SLAVES.
SLAVES.
THERE WILL BE NO SLEEP FOR VADER THIS NIGHT.

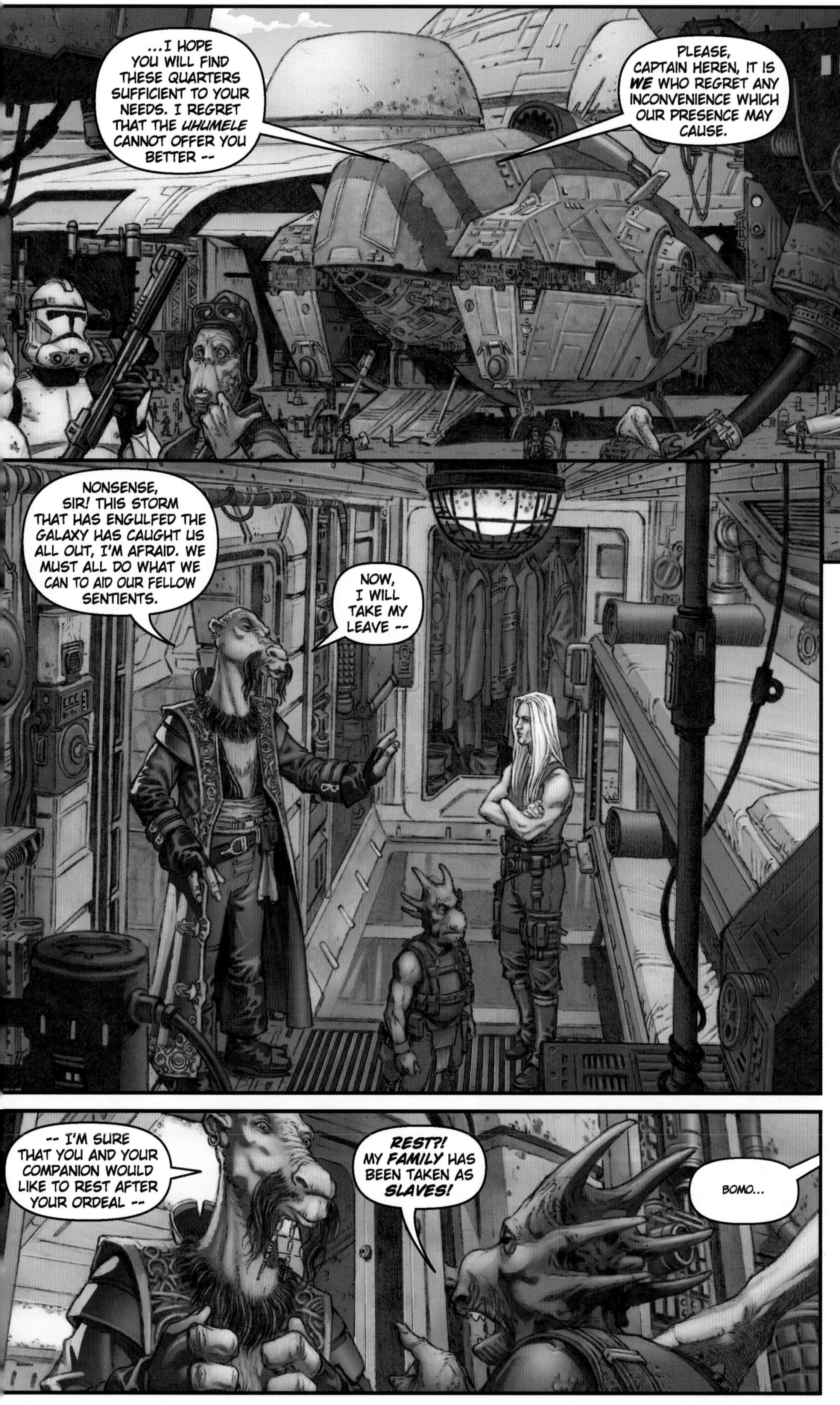
...I HOPE YOU WILL FIND THESE QUARTERS SUFFICIENT TO YOUR NEEDS. I REGRET THAT THE *UHUMELE* CANNOT OFFER YOU BETTER --
PLEASE, CAPTAIN HEREN, IT IS ***WE*** WHO REGRET ANY INCONVENIENCE WHICH OUR PRESENCE MAY CAUSE.
NONSENSE, SIR! THIS STORM THAT HAS ENGULFED THE GALAXY HAS CAUGHT US ALL OUT, I'M AFRAID. WE MUST ALL DO WHAT WE CAN TO AID OUR FELLOW SENTIENTS.
NOW, I WILL TAKE MY LEAVE --
-- I'M SURE THAT YOU AND YOUR COMPANION WOULD LIKE TO REST AFTER YOUR ORDEAL --
***REST?!*** MY ***FAMILY*** HAS BEEN TAKEN AS ***SLAVES!***
BOMO...

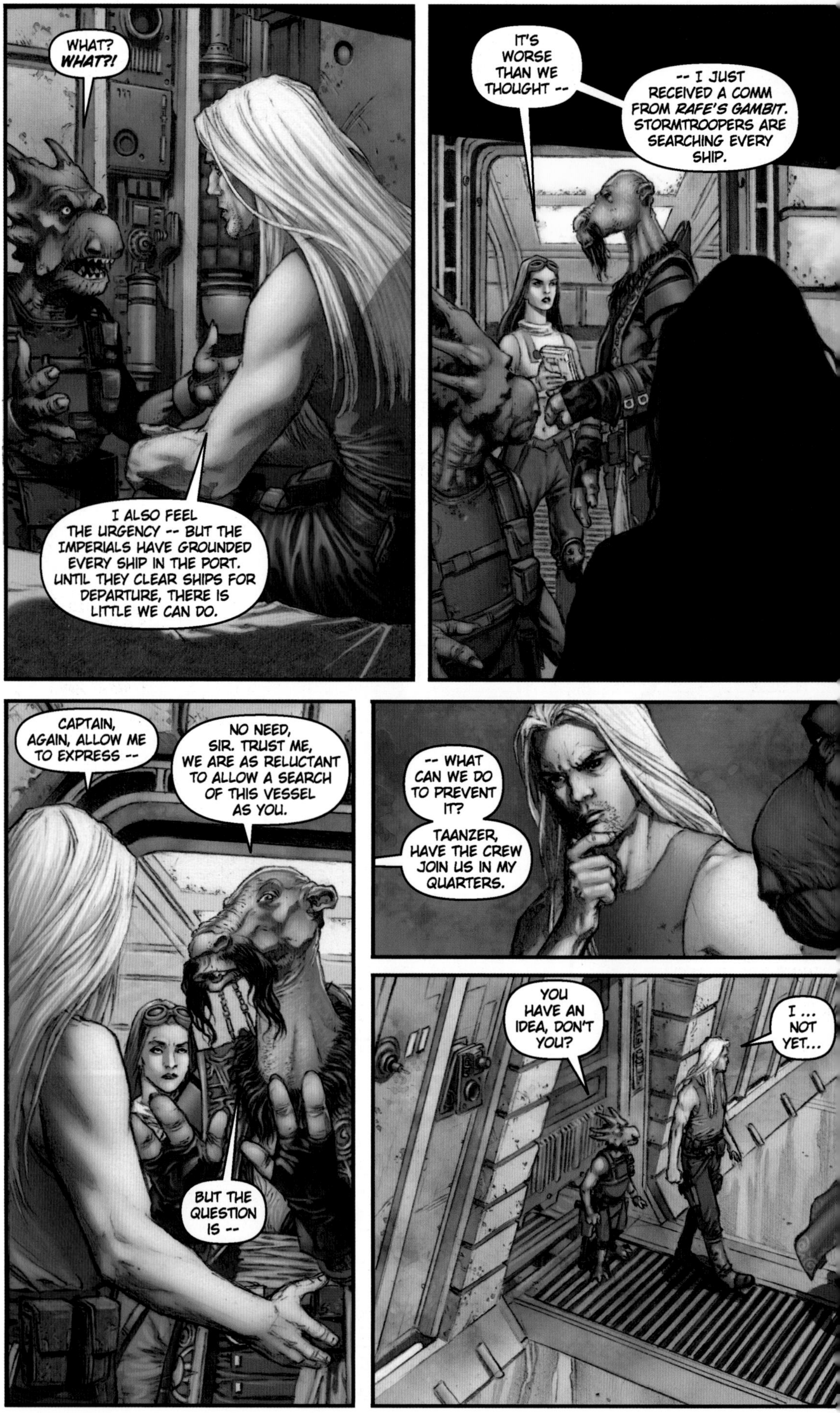
WHAT? *WHAT?!*
I ALSO FEEL THE URGENCY -- BUT THE IMPERIALS HAVE GROUNDED EVERY SHIP IN THE PORT. UNTIL THEY CLEAR SHIPS FOR DEPARTURE, THERE IS LITTLE WE CAN DO.
IT'S WORSE THAN WE THOUGHT --
-- I JUST RECEIVED A COMM FROM *RAFE'S GAMBIT*. STORMTROOPERS ARE SEARCHING EVERY SHIP.
CAPTAIN, AGAIN, ALLOW ME TO EXPRESS --
NO NEED, SIR. TRUST ME, WE ARE AS RELUCTANT TO ALLOW A SEARCH OF THIS VESSEL AS YOU.
BUT THE QUESTION IS --
-- WHAT CAN WE DO TO PREVENT IT?
TAANZER, HAVE THE CREW JOIN US IN MY QUARTERS.
YOU HAVE AN IDEA, DON'T YOU?
I ... NOT YET...

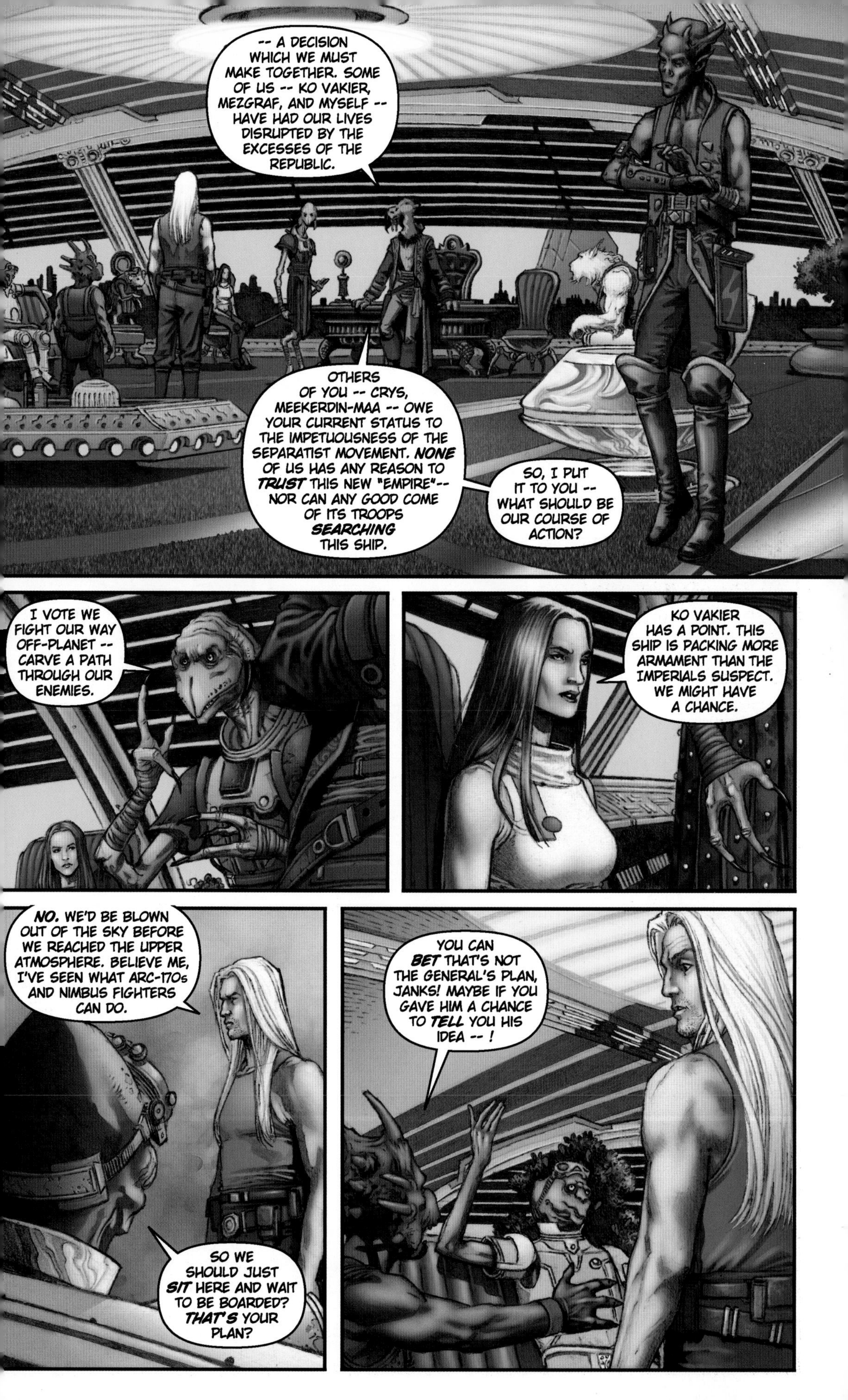
-- A DECISION WHICH WE MUST MAKE TOGETHER. SOME OF US -- KO VAKIER, MEZGRAF, AND MYSELF -- HAVE HAD OUR LIVES DISRUPTED BY THE EXCESSES OF THE REPUBLIC.
OTHERS OF YOU -- CRYS, MEEKERDIN-MAA -- OWE YOUR CURRENT STATUS TO THE IMPETUOUSNESS OF THE SEPARATIST MOVEMENT. NONE OF US HAS ANY REASON TO TRUST THIS NEW "EMPIRE"-- NOR CAN ANY GOOD COME OF ITS TROOPS SEARCHING THIS SHIP.
SO, I PUT IT TO YOU -- WHAT SHOULD BE OUR COURSE OF ACTION?
I VOTE WE FIGHT OUR WAY OFF-PLANET -- CARVE A PATH THROUGH OUR ENEMIES.
KO VAKIER HAS A POINT. THIS SHIP IS PACKING MORE ARMAMENT THAN THE IMPERIALS SUSPECT. WE MIGHT HAVE A CHANCE.
NO. WE'D BE BLOWN OUT OF THE SKY BEFORE WE REACHED THE UPPER ATMOSPHERE. BELIEVE ME, I'VE SEEN WHAT ARC-170s AND NIMBUS FIGHTERS CAN DO.
SO WE SHOULD JUST SIT HERE AND WAIT TO BE BOARDED? THAT'S YOUR PLAN?
YOU CAN BET THAT'S NOT THE GENERAL'S PLAN, JANKS! MAYBE IF YOU GAVE HIM A CHANCE TO TELL YOU HIS IDEA -- !

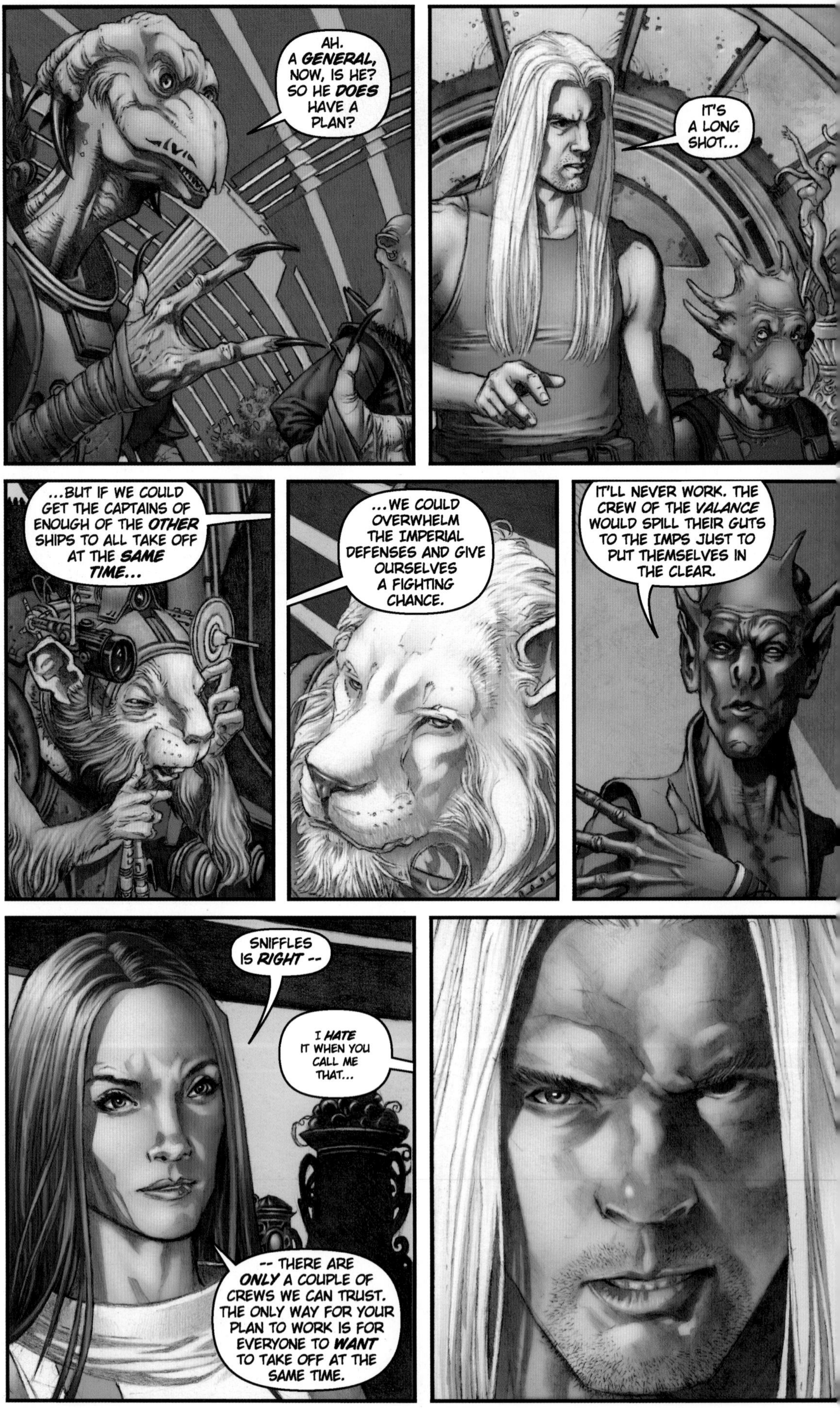
AH. A *GENERAL,* NOW, IS HE? SO HE *DOES* HAVE A PLAN?
IT'S A LONG SHOT...
...BUT IF WE COULD GET THE CAPTAINS OF ENOUGH OF THE *OTHER* SHIPS TO ALL TAKE OFF AT THE *SAME TIME...*
...WE COULD OVERWHELM THE IMPERIAL DEFENSES AND GIVE OURSELVES A FIGHTING CHANCE.
IT'LL NEVER WORK. THE CREW OF THE *VALANCE* WOULD SPILL THEIR GUTS TO THE IMPS JUST TO PUT THEMSELVES IN THE CLEAR.
SNIFFLES IS *RIGHT* --
I *HATE* IT WHEN YOU CALL ME THAT...
-- THERE ARE *ONLY* A COUPLE OF CREWS WE CAN TRUST. THE ONLY WAY FOR YOUR PLAN TO WORK IS FOR EVERYONE TO *WANT* TO TAKE OFF AT THE SAME TIME.

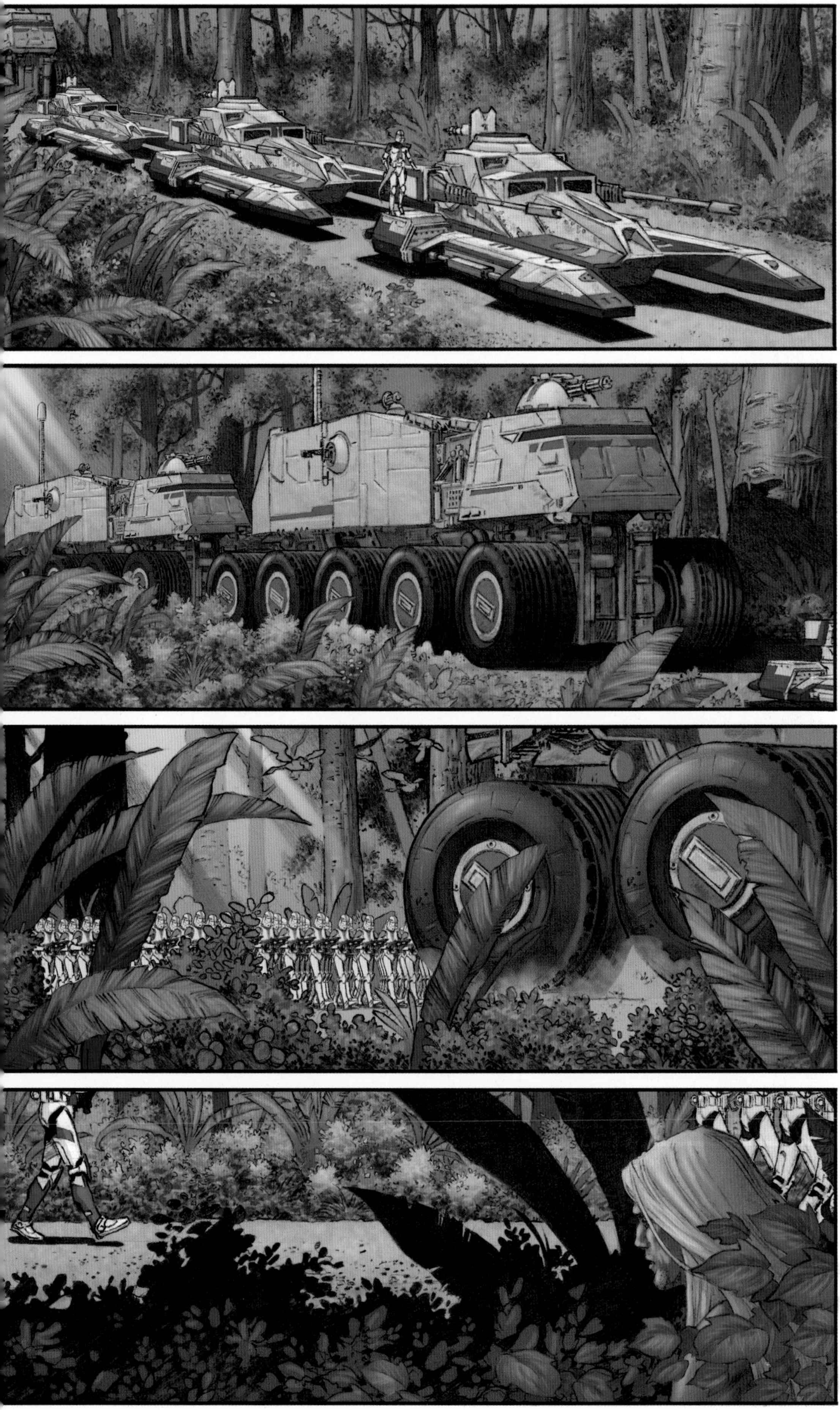

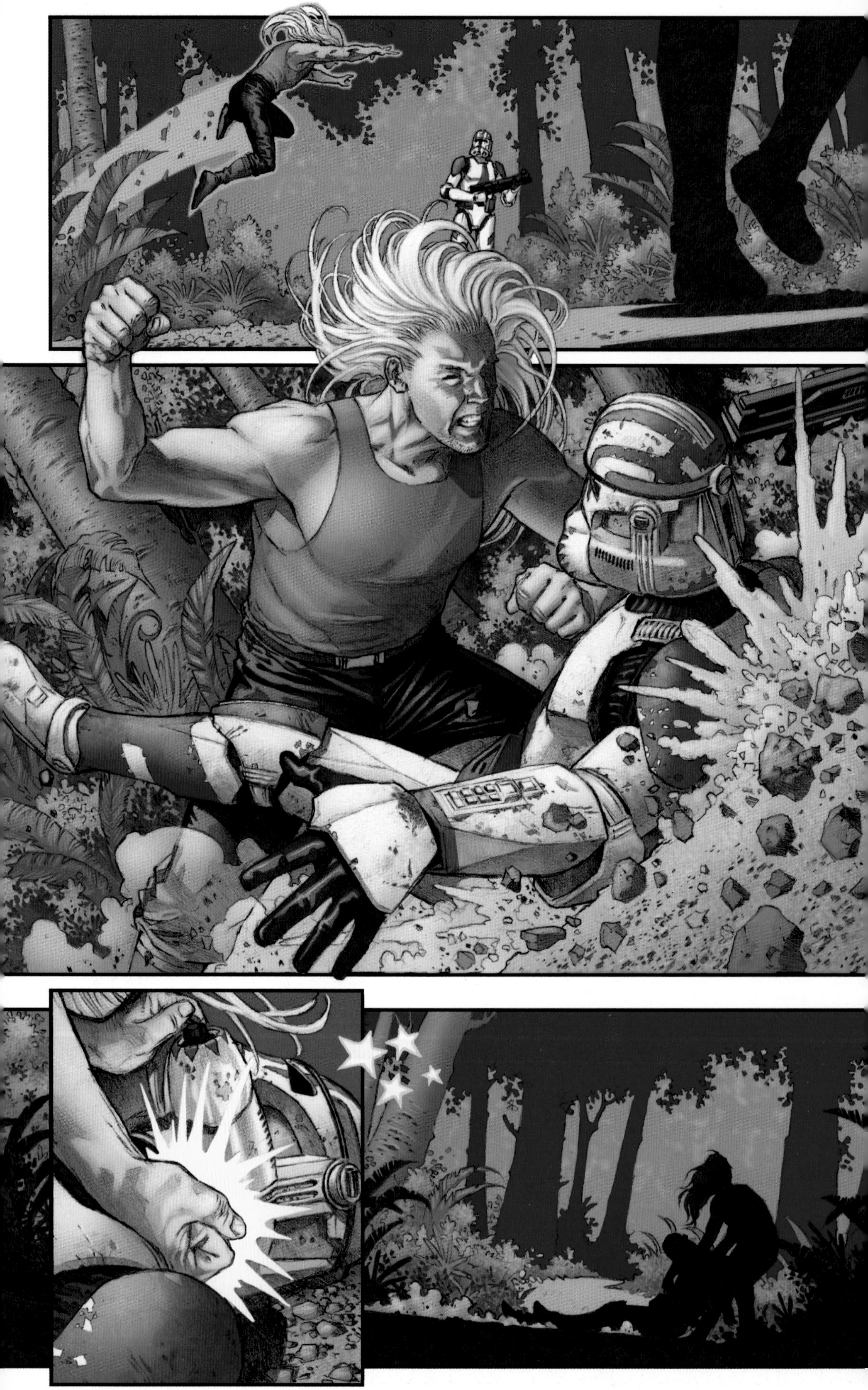

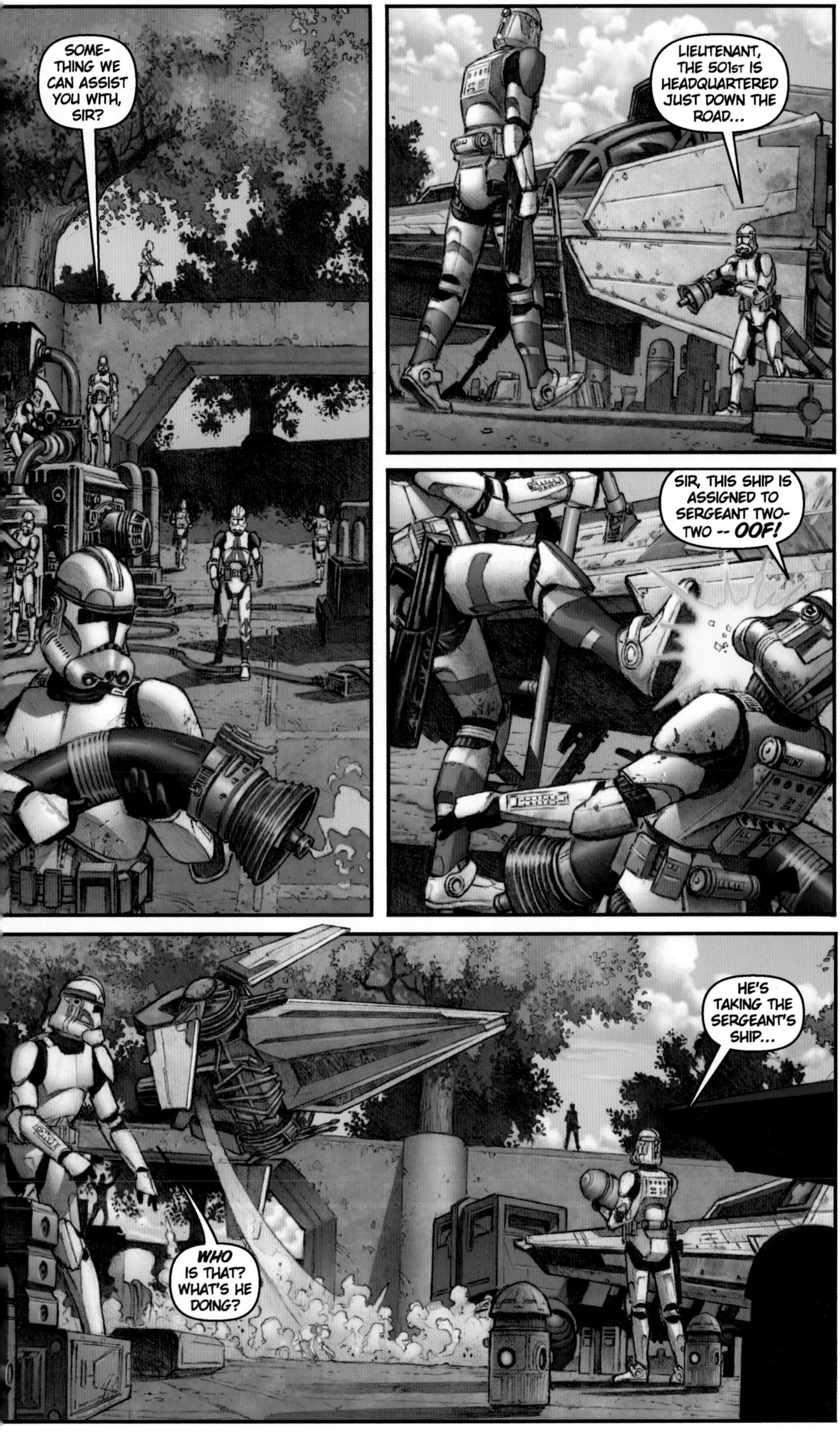
SOME-THING WE CAN ASSIST YOU WITH, SIR?
LIEUTENANT, THE 501st IS HEADQUARTERED JUST DOWN THE ROAD...
SIR, THIS SHIP IS ASSIGNED TO SERGEANT TWO-TWO -- OOF!
HE'S TAKING THE SERGEANT'S SHIP...
WHO IS THAT? WHAT'S HE DOING?

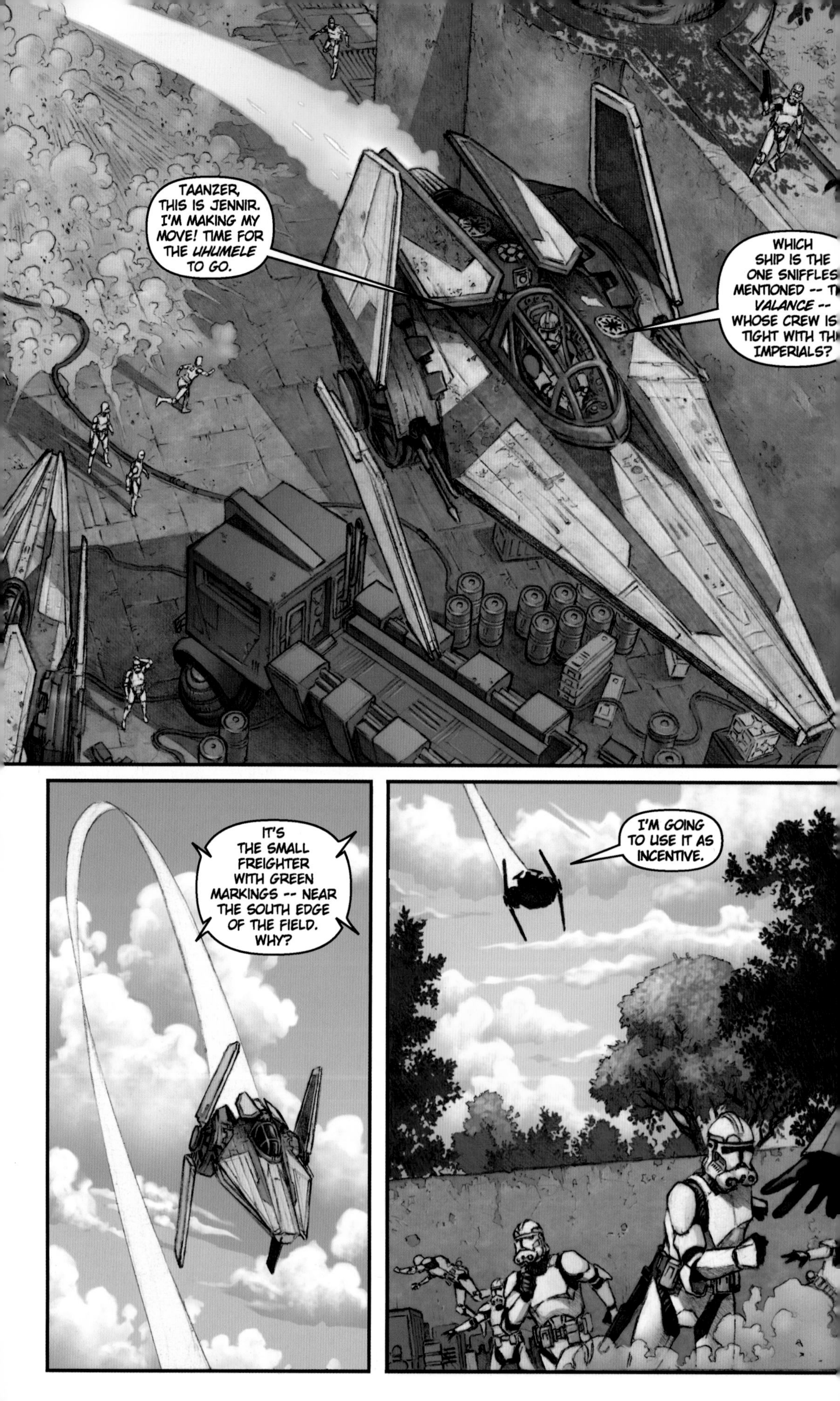

TAANZER, THIS IS JENNIR. I'M MAKING MY MOVE! TIME FOR THE *UHUMELE* TO GO.
WHICH SHIP IS THE ONE SNIFFLES MENTIONED -- TH *VALANCE* -- WHOSE CREW IS TIGHT WITH TH IMPERIALS?
IT'S THE SMALL FREIGHTER WITH GREEN MARKINGS -- NEAR THE SOUTH EDGE OF THE FIELD. WHY?
I'M GOING TO USE IT AS INCENTIVE.

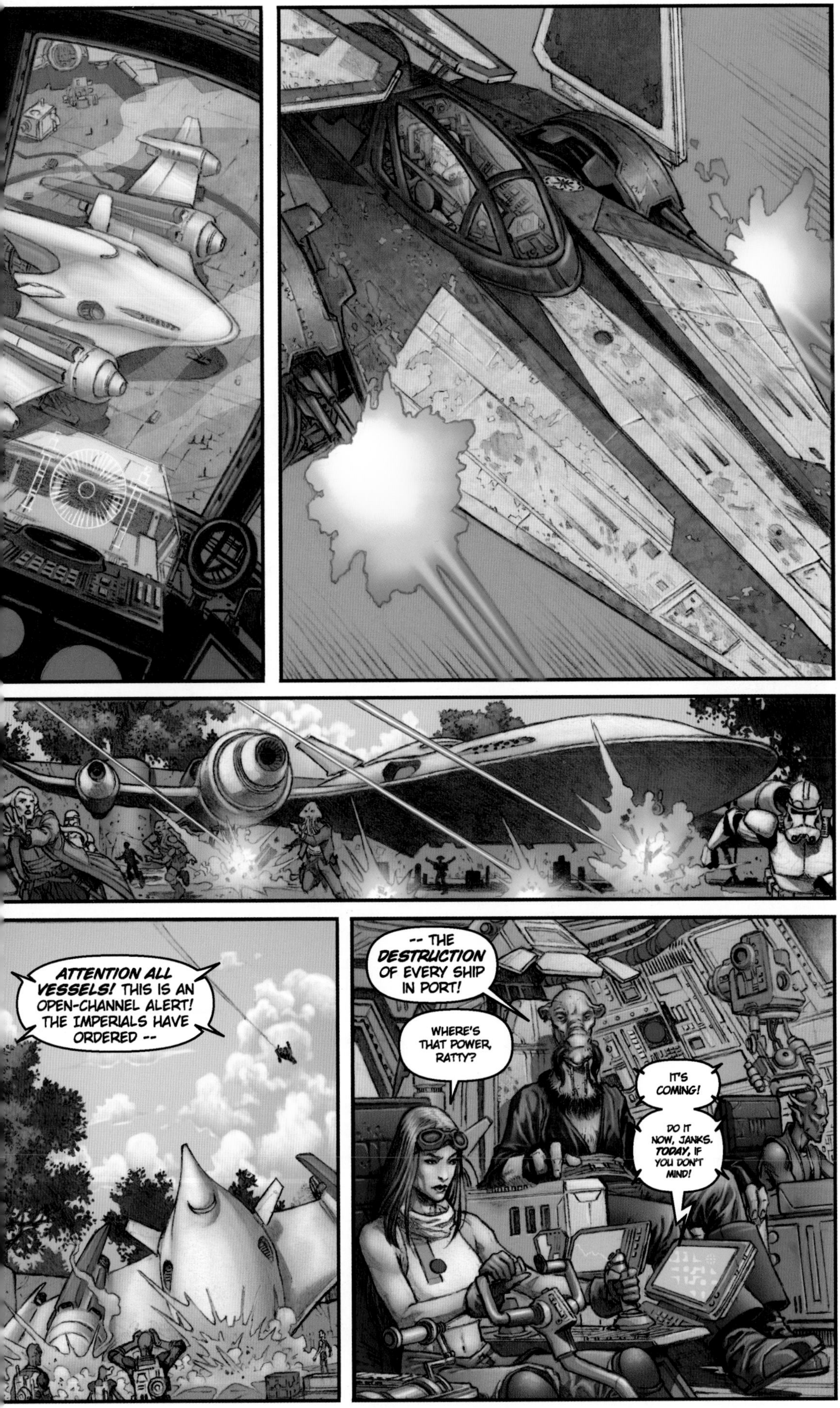
ATTENTION ALL VESSELS! THIS IS AN OPEN-CHANNEL ALERT! THE IMPERIALS HAVE ORDERED --
-- THE DESTRUCTION OF EVERY SHIP IN PORT!
WHERE'S THAT POWER, RATTY?
IT'S COMING!
DO IT NOW, JANKS. TODAY, IF YOU DON'T MIND!

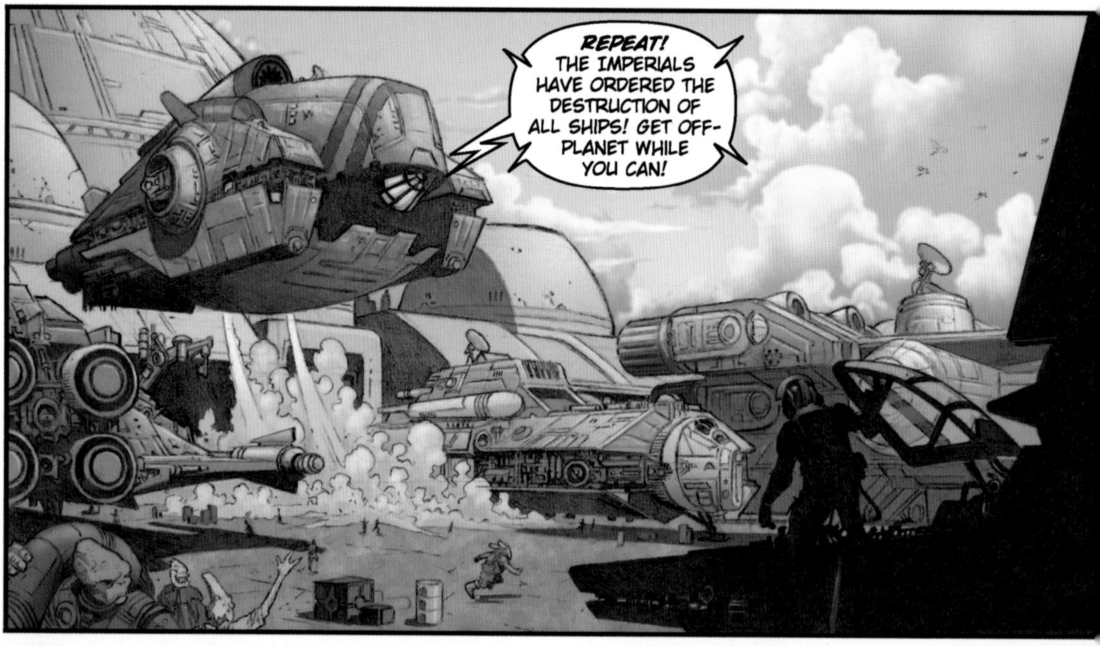
REPEAT! THE IMPERIALS HAVE ORDERED THE DESTRUCTION OF ALL SHIPS! GET OFF-PLANET WHILE YOU CAN!

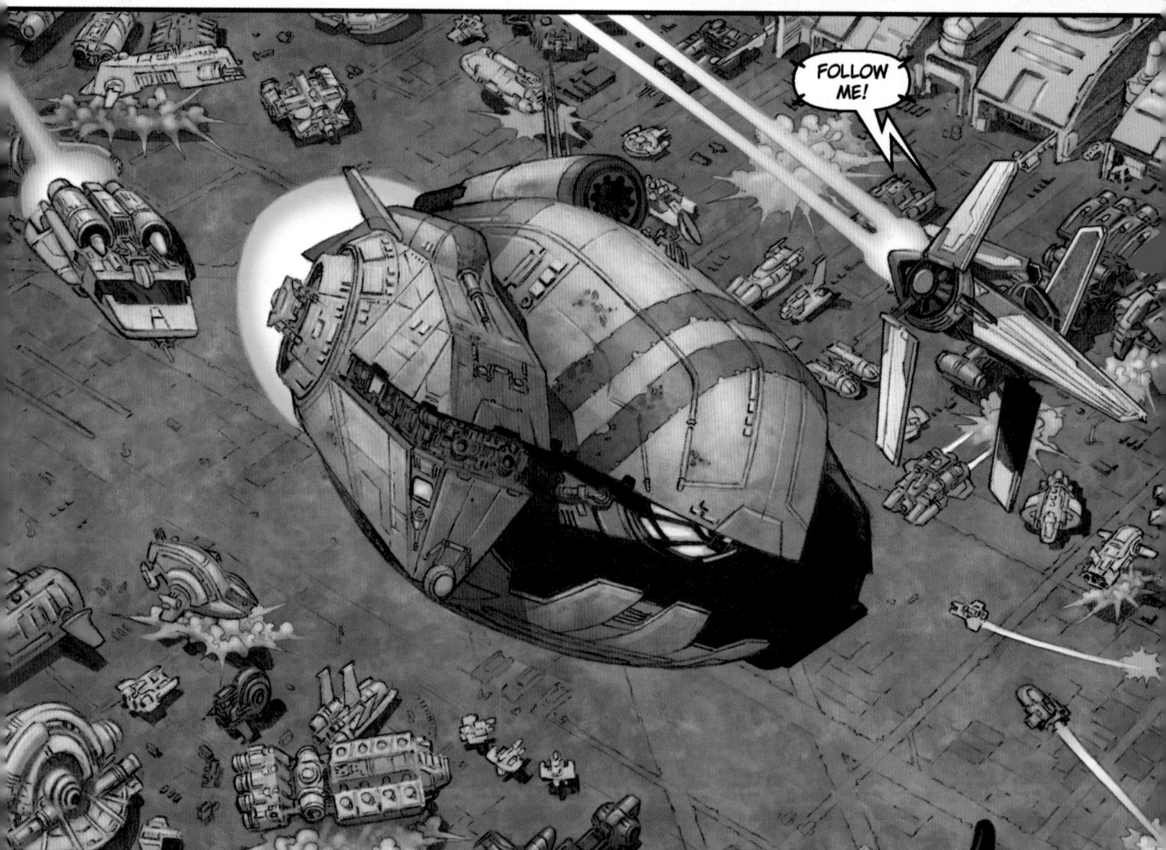
FOLLOW ME!

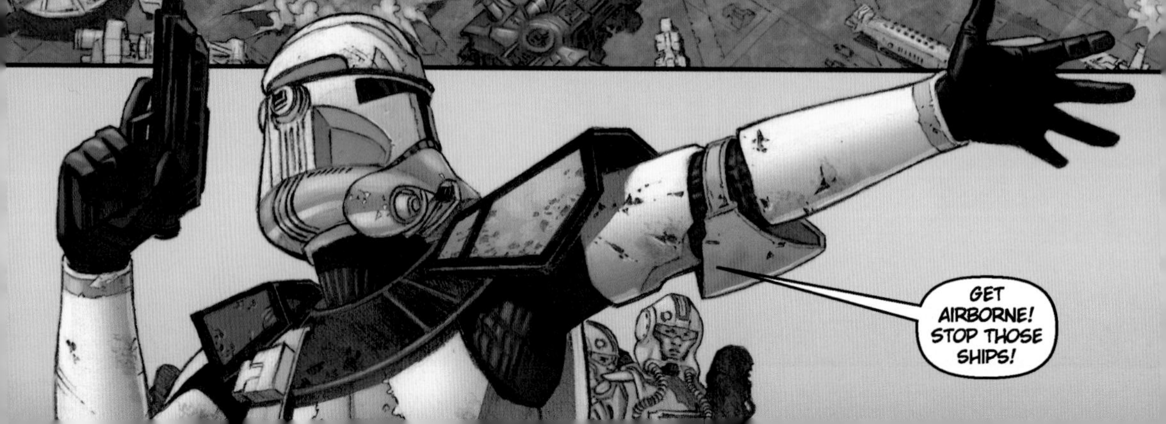
GET AIRBORNE! STOP THOSE SHIPS!

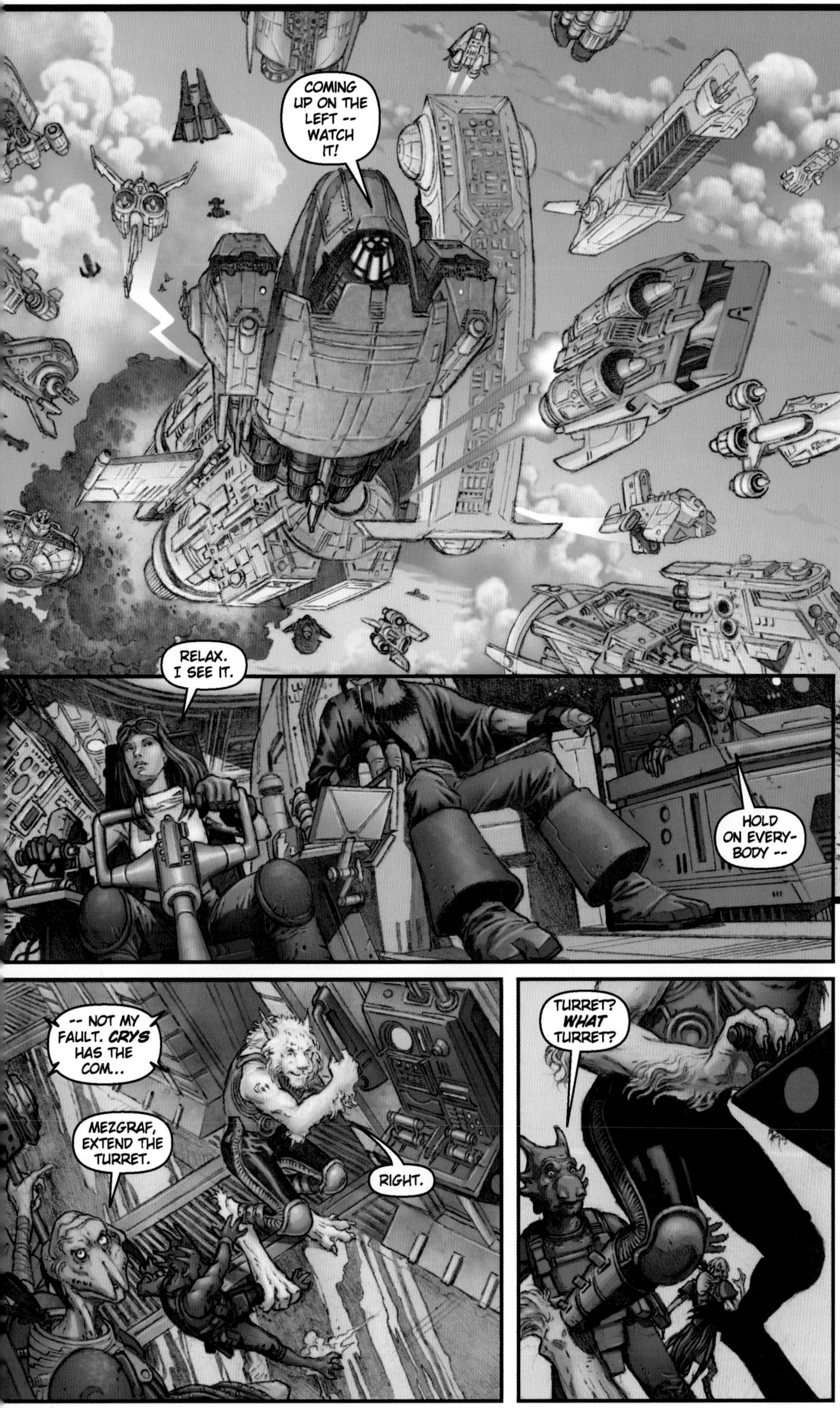

COMING UP ON THE LEFT -- WATCH IT!
RELAX. I SEE IT.
HOLD ON EVERY-BODY --
-- NOT MY FAULT. CRYS HAS THE COM...
MEZGRAF, EXTEND THE TURRET.
RIGHT.
TURRET? WHAT TURRET?

"YOU'LL SEE."

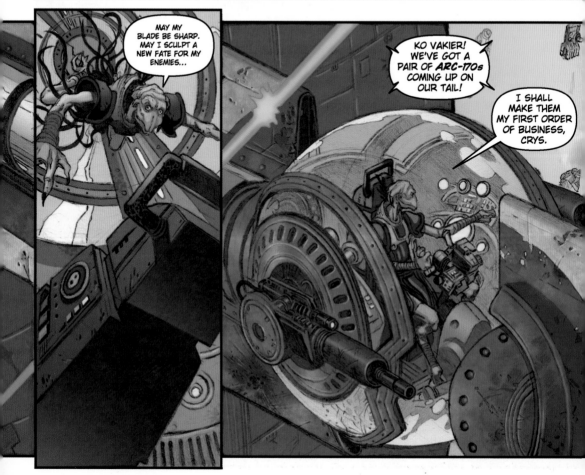

MAY MY BLADE BE SHARP. MAY I SCULPT A NEW FATE FOR MY ENEMIES...

KO VAKIER! WE'VE GOT A PAIR OF *ARC-170s* COMING UP ON OUR TAIL!

I SHALL MAKE THEM MY FIRST ORDER OF BUSINESS, CRYS.

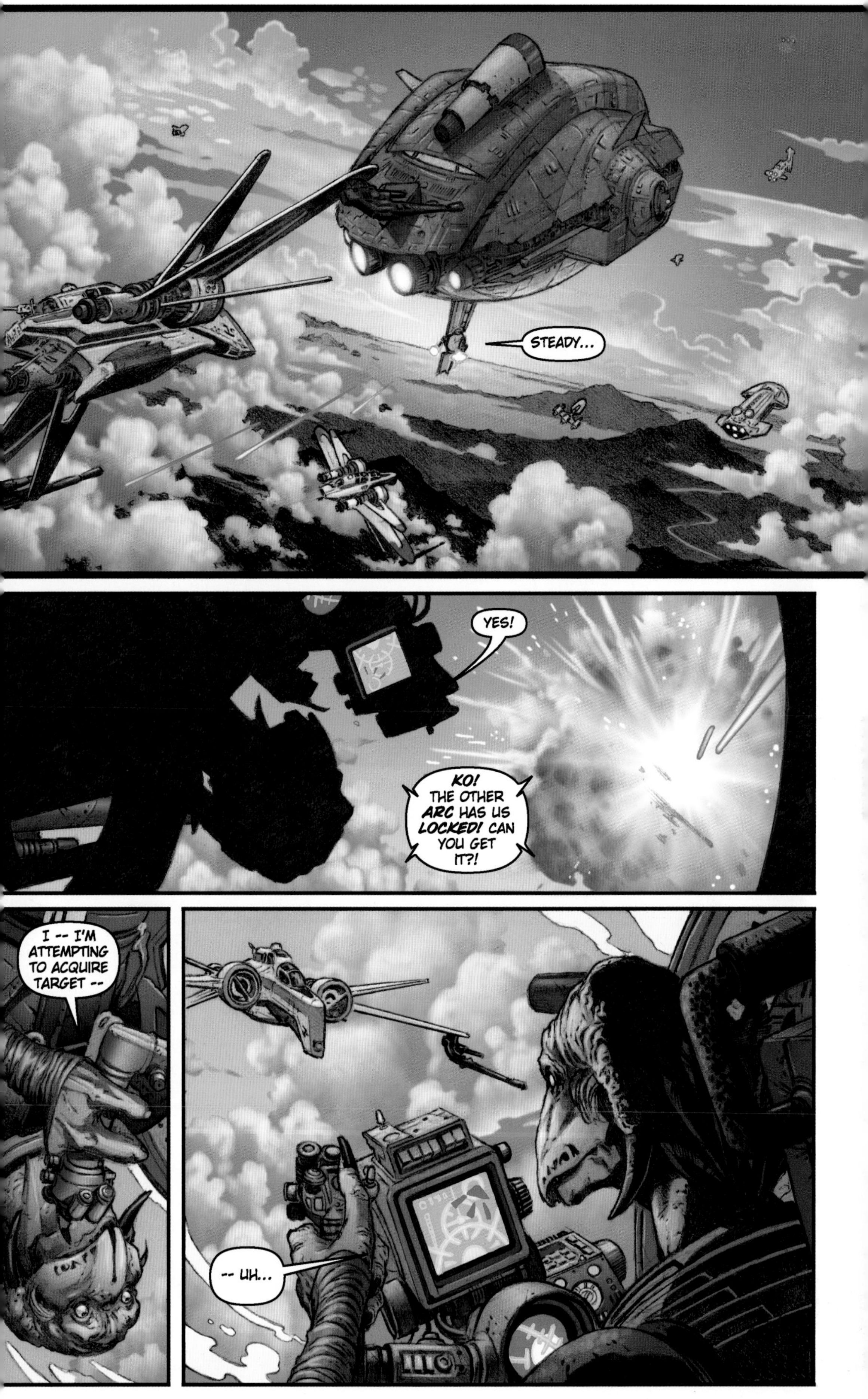
STEADY...
YES!
KO! THE OTHER ARC HAS US LOCKED! CAN YOU GET IT?!
I -- I'M ATTEMPTING TO ACQUIRE TARGET --
-- UH...

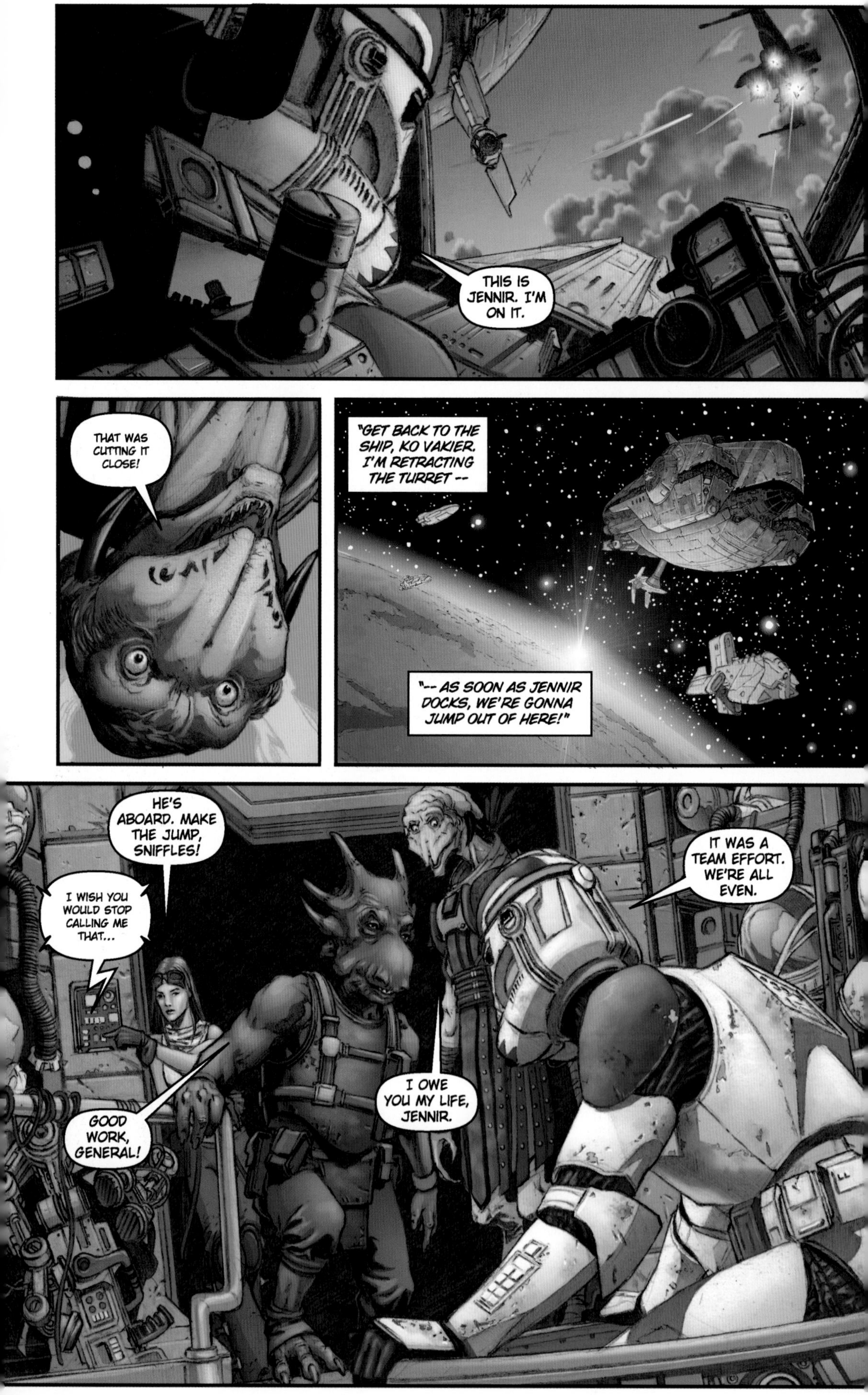
THIS IS JENNIR. I'M ON IT.
THAT WAS CUTTING IT CLOSE!
"GET BACK TO THE SHIP, KO VAKIER. I'M RETRACTING THE TURRET --
"-- AS SOON AS JENNIR DOCKS, WE'RE GONNA JUMP OUT OF HERE!"
HE'S ABOARD. MAKE THE JUMP, SNIFFLES!
I WISH YOU WOULD STOP CALLING ME THAT...
GOOD WORK, GENERAL!
I OWE YOU MY LIFE, JENNIR.
IT WAS A TEAM EFFORT. WE'RE ALL EVEN.

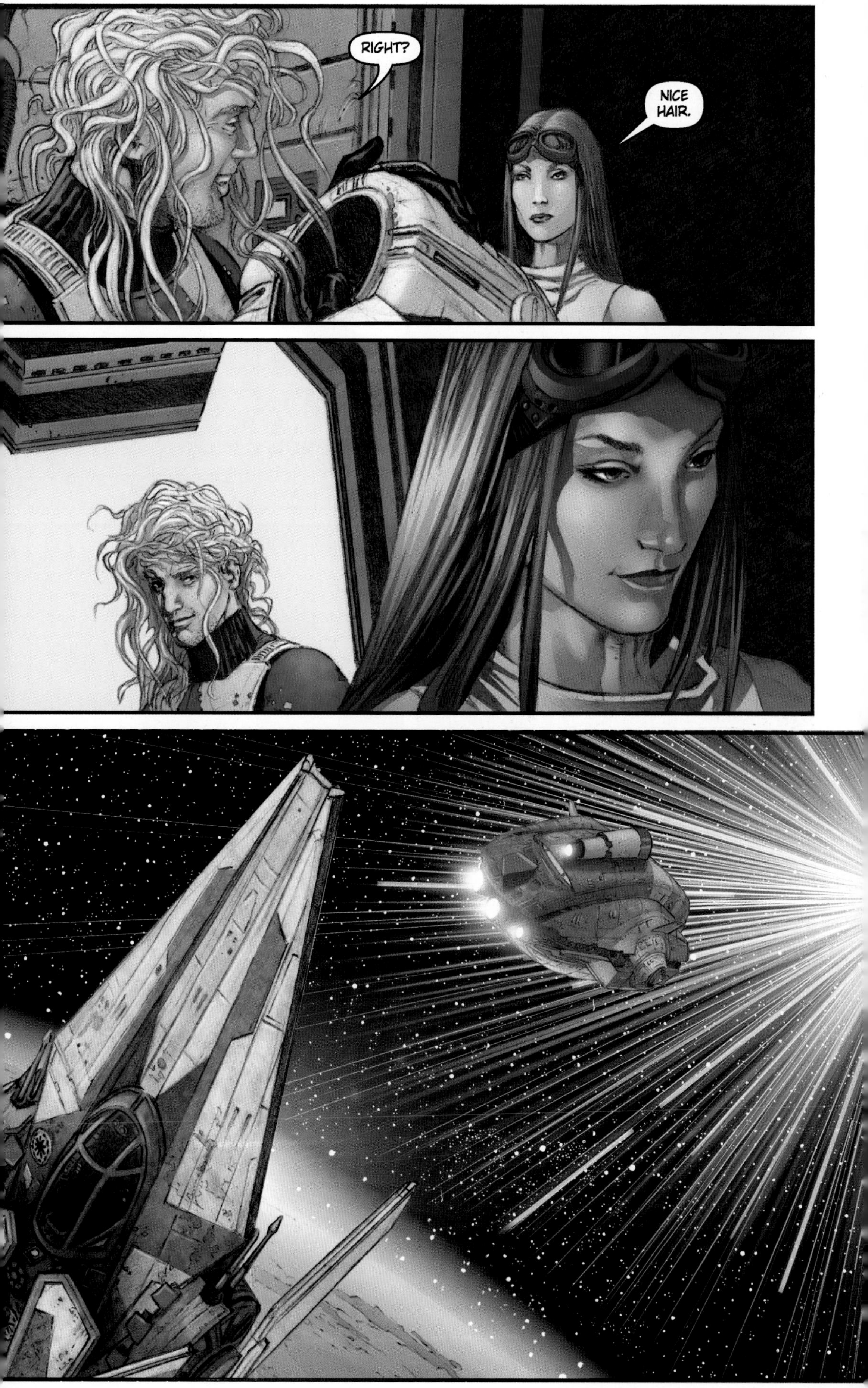
RIGHT?
NICE HAIR.

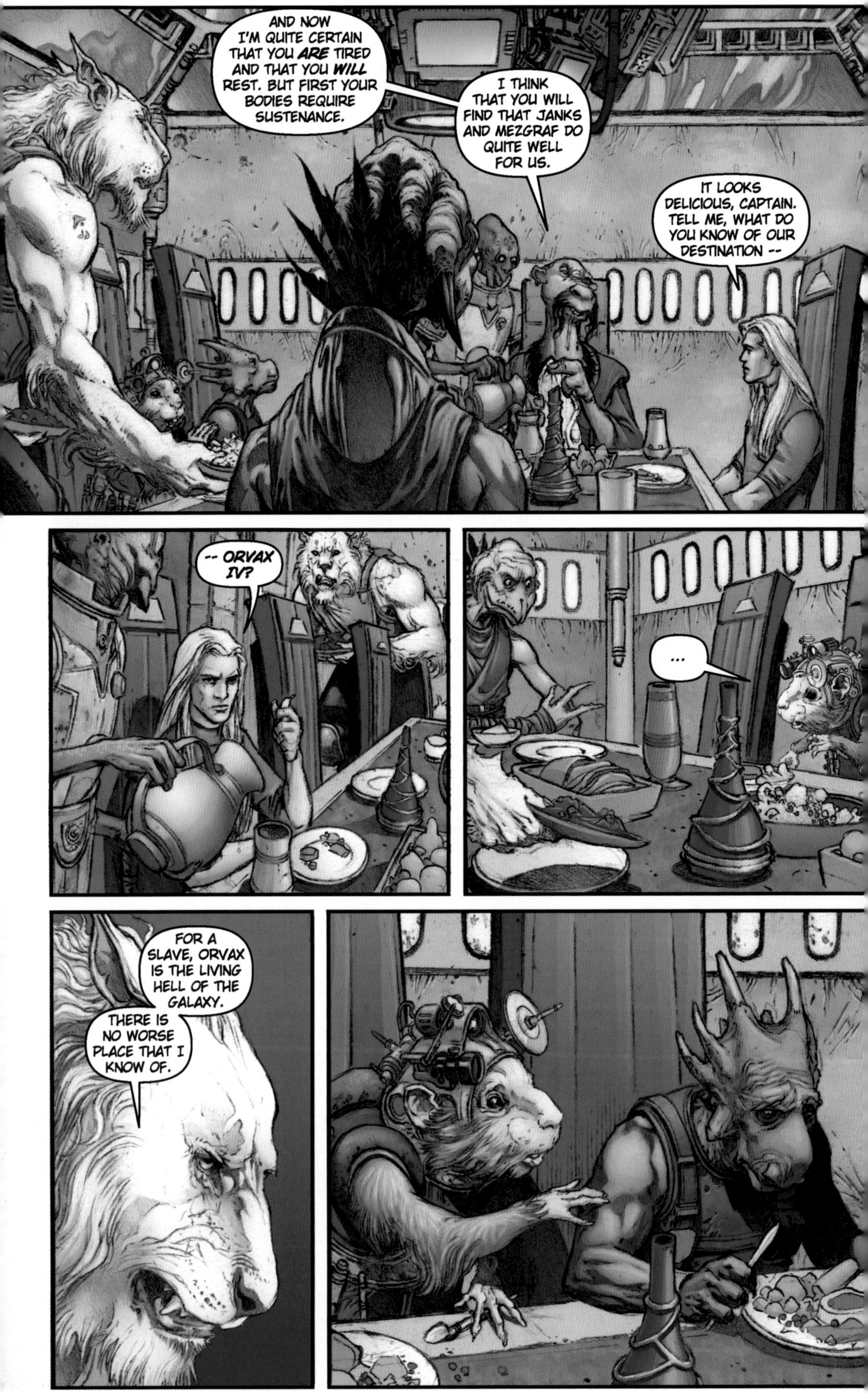
AND NOW I'M QUITE CERTAIN THAT YOU *ARE* TIRED AND THAT YOU *WILL* REST. BUT FIRST YOUR BODIES REQUIRE SUSTENANCE.
I THINK THAT YOU WILL FIND THAT JANKS AND MEZGRAF DO QUITE WELL FOR US.
IT LOOKS DELICIOUS, CAPTAIN. TELL ME, WHAT DO YOU KNOW OF OUR DESTINATION --
-- *ORVAX IV?*
...
FOR A SLAVE, ORVAX IS THE LIVING HELL OF THE GALAXY.
THERE IS NO WORSE PLACE THAT I KNOW OF.

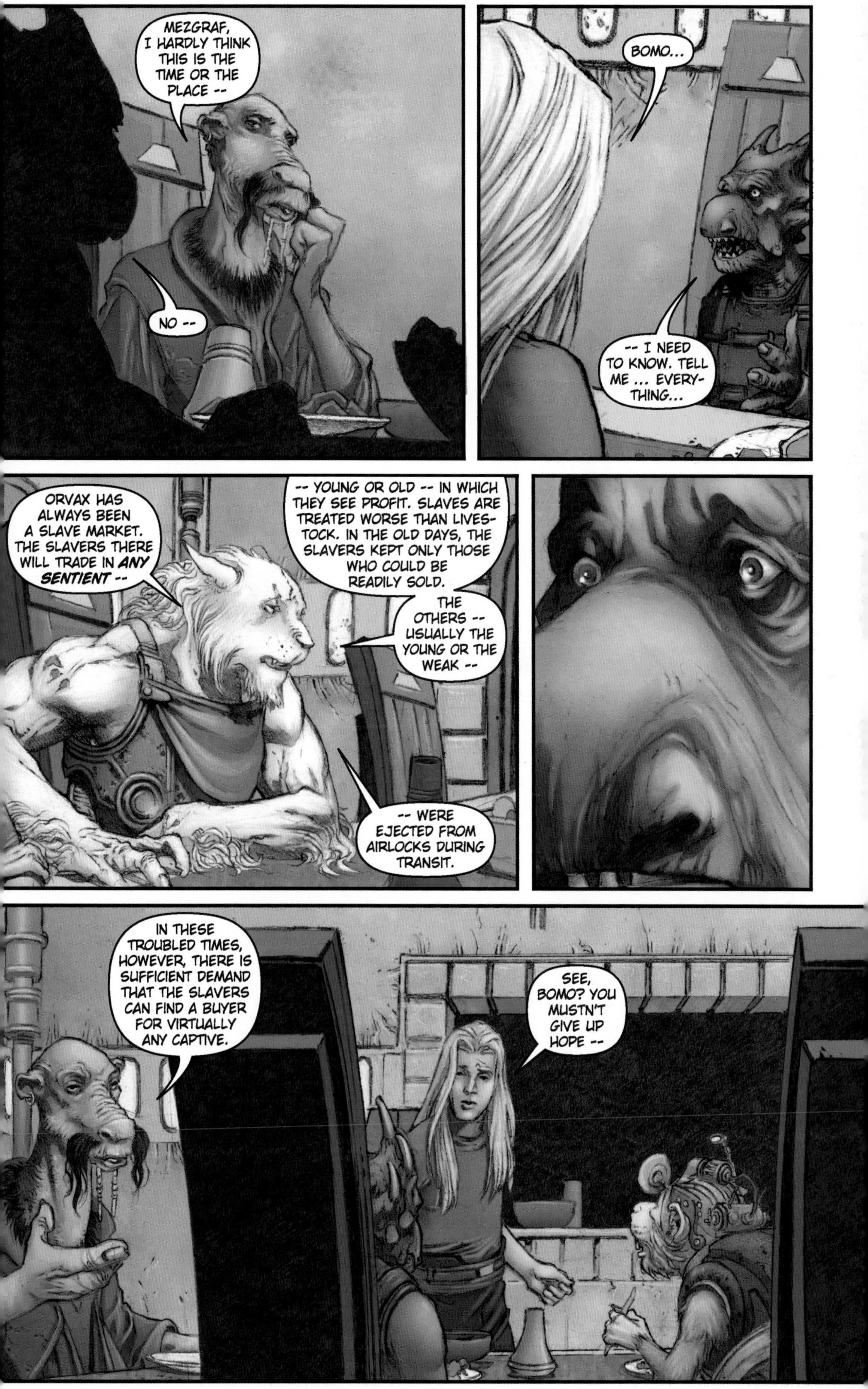
MEZGRAF, I HARDLY THINK THIS IS THE TIME OR THE PLACE --
NO --
BOMO...
-- I NEED TO KNOW. TELL ME ... EVERY-THING...
ORVAX HAS ALWAYS BEEN A SLAVE MARKET. THE SLAVERS THERE WILL TRADE IN ANY SENTIENT --
-- YOUNG OR OLD -- IN WHICH THEY SEE PROFIT. SLAVES ARE TREATED WORSE THAN LIVES-TOCK. IN THE OLD DAYS, THE SLAVERS KEPT ONLY THOSE WHO COULD BE READILY SOLD.
THE OTHERS -- USUALLY THE YOUNG OR THE WEAK --
-- WERE EJECTED FROM AIRLOCKS DURING TRANSIT.
IN THESE TROUBLED TIMES, HOWEVER, THERE IS SUFFICIENT DEMAND THAT THE SLAVERS CAN FIND A BUYER FOR VIRTUALLY ANY CAPTIVE.
SEE, BOMO? YOU MUSTN'T GIVE UP HOPE --

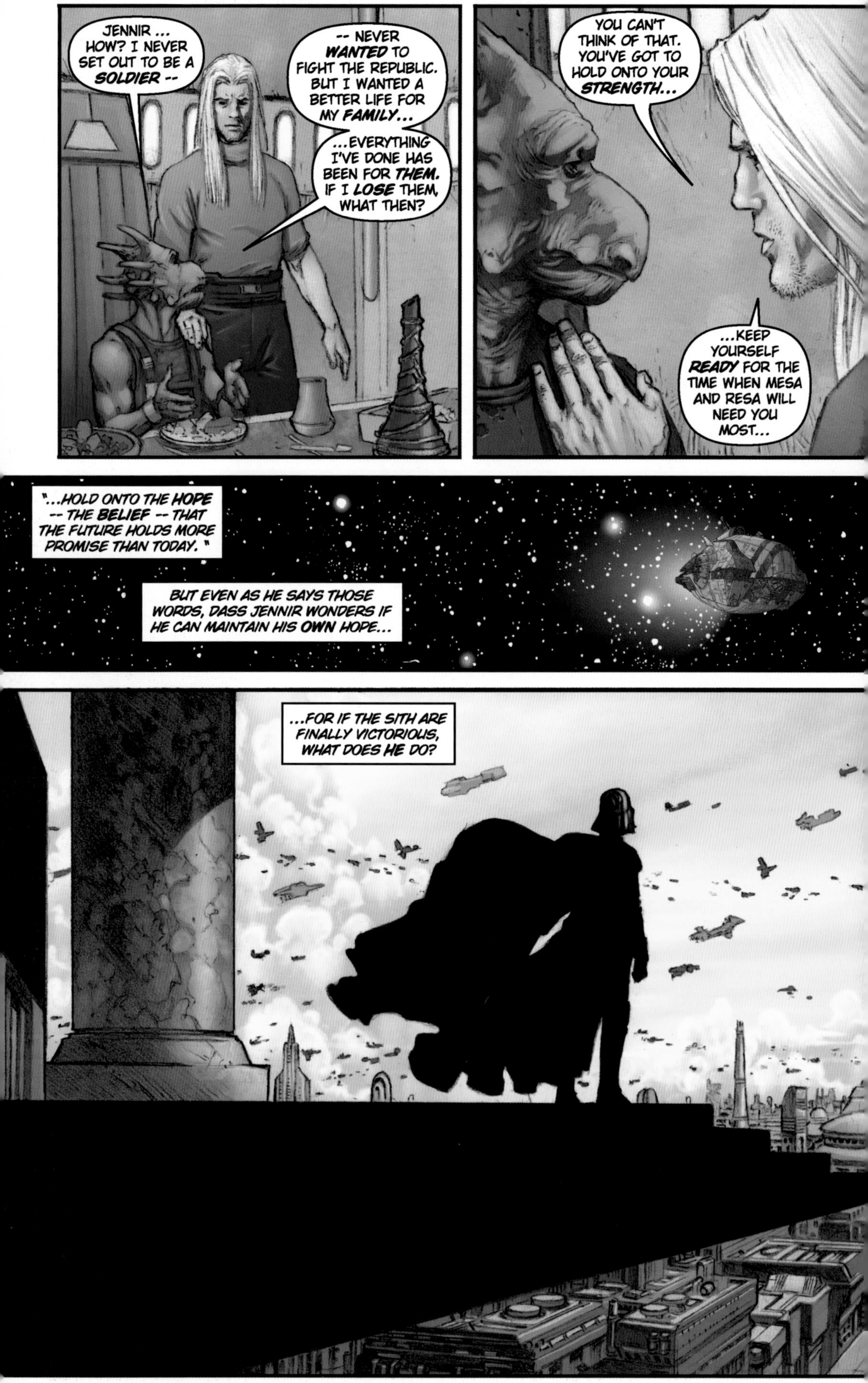
JENNIR ... HOW? I NEVER SET OUT TO BE A SOLDIER --
-- NEVER WANTED TO FIGHT THE REPUBLIC. BUT I WANTED A BETTER LIFE FOR MY FAMILY...
...EVERYTHING I'VE DONE HAS BEEN FOR THEM. IF I LOSE THEM, WHAT THEN?
YOU CAN'T THINK OF THAT. YOU'VE GOT TO HOLD ONTO YOUR STRENGTH...
...KEEP YOURSELF READY FOR THE TIME WHEN MESA AND RESA WILL NEED YOU MOST...
"...HOLD ONTO THE HOPE -- THE BELIEF -- THAT THE FUTURE HOLDS MORE PROMISE THAN TODAY."
BUT EVEN AS HE SAYS THOSE WORDS, DASS JENNIR WONDERS IF HE CAN MAINTAIN HIS OWN HOPE...
...FOR IF THE SITH ARE FINALLY VICTORIOUS, WHAT DOES HE DO?

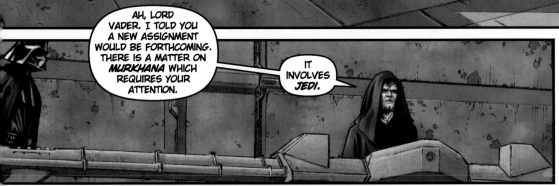

AH, LORD VADER. I TOLD YOU A NEW ASSIGNMENT WOULD BE FORTHCOMING. THERE IS A MATTER ON *MURKHANA* WHICH REQUIRES YOUR ATTENTION.

IT INVOLVES *JEDI.*

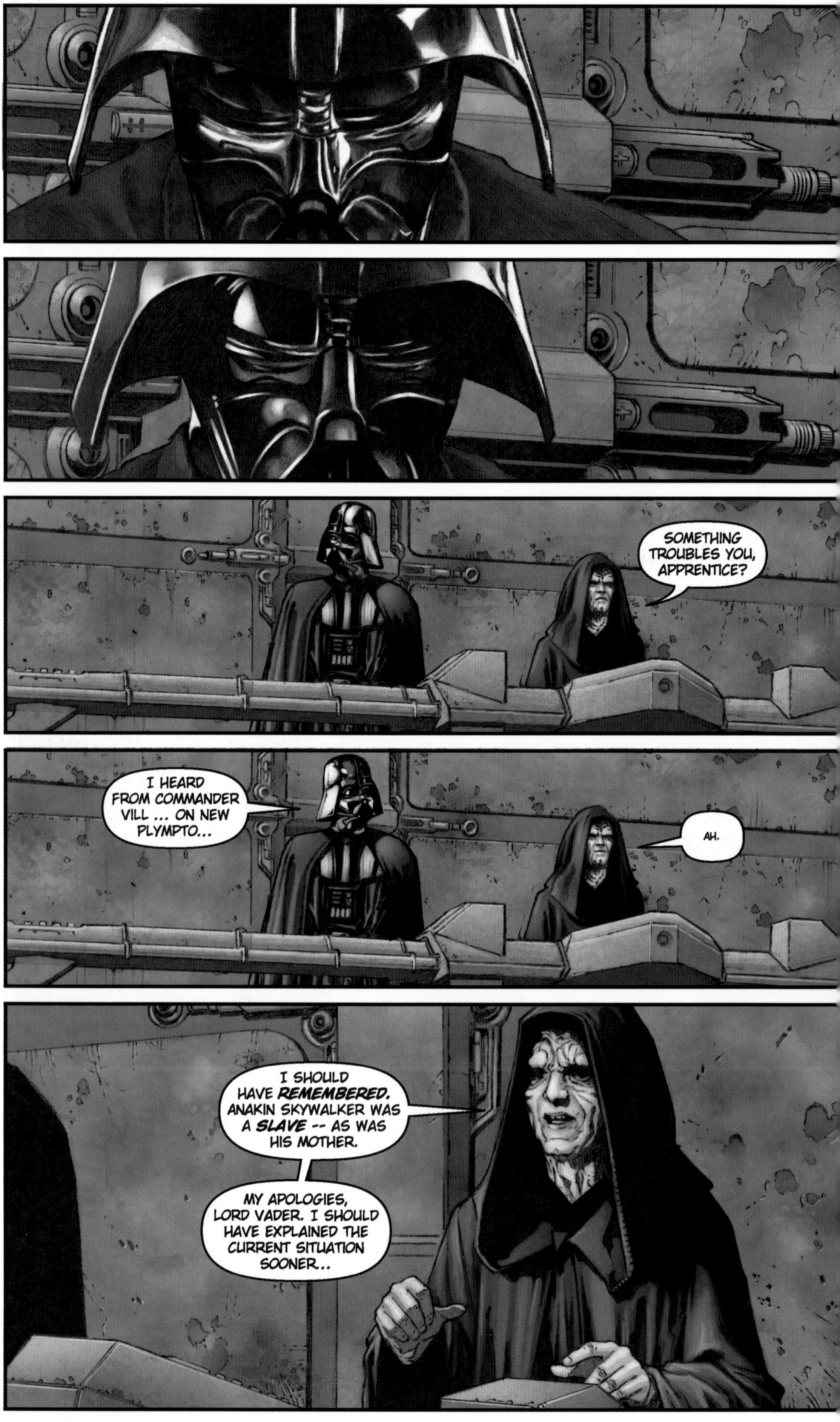
SOMETHING TROUBLES YOU, APPRENTICE?
I HEARD FROM COMMANDER VILL ... ON NEW PLYMPTO...
AH.
I SHOULD HAVE REMEMBERED. ANAKIN SKYWALKER WAS A SLAVE -- AS WAS HIS MOTHER.
MY APOLOGIES, LORD VADER. I SHOULD HAVE EXPLAINED THE CURRENT SITUATION SOONER..

THE SLAVERY THAT EXISTS IN THE LAWLESS REACHES OF THE *OUTER RIM* IS WRONG. THE TRADING IN INDIVIDUALS' LIVES AND FREEDOM FOR PERSONAL GAIN MUST END. AND IT *WILL ...* IN TIME.

BUT WHAT THE EMPIRE IS DOING ON NEW PLYMPTO -- AND ELSEWHERE -- IS *DIFFERENT.*

UNREPENTANT SEPARATISTS LIKE THE NOSAURIANS *MUST* BE DEALT WITH. PUT TO WORK, THEY WILL MAKE A POSITIVE *CONTRIBUTION* TO THE EMPIRE, AND THEIR LIVES WILL BE *SPARED.*

IT IS A MERCIFUL *ALTERNATIVE* TO WHAT WOULD OTHERWISE BE *NECESSARY.*

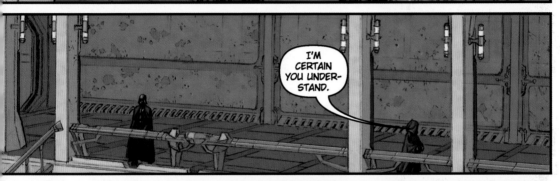

I'M CERTAIN YOU UNDER-STAND.

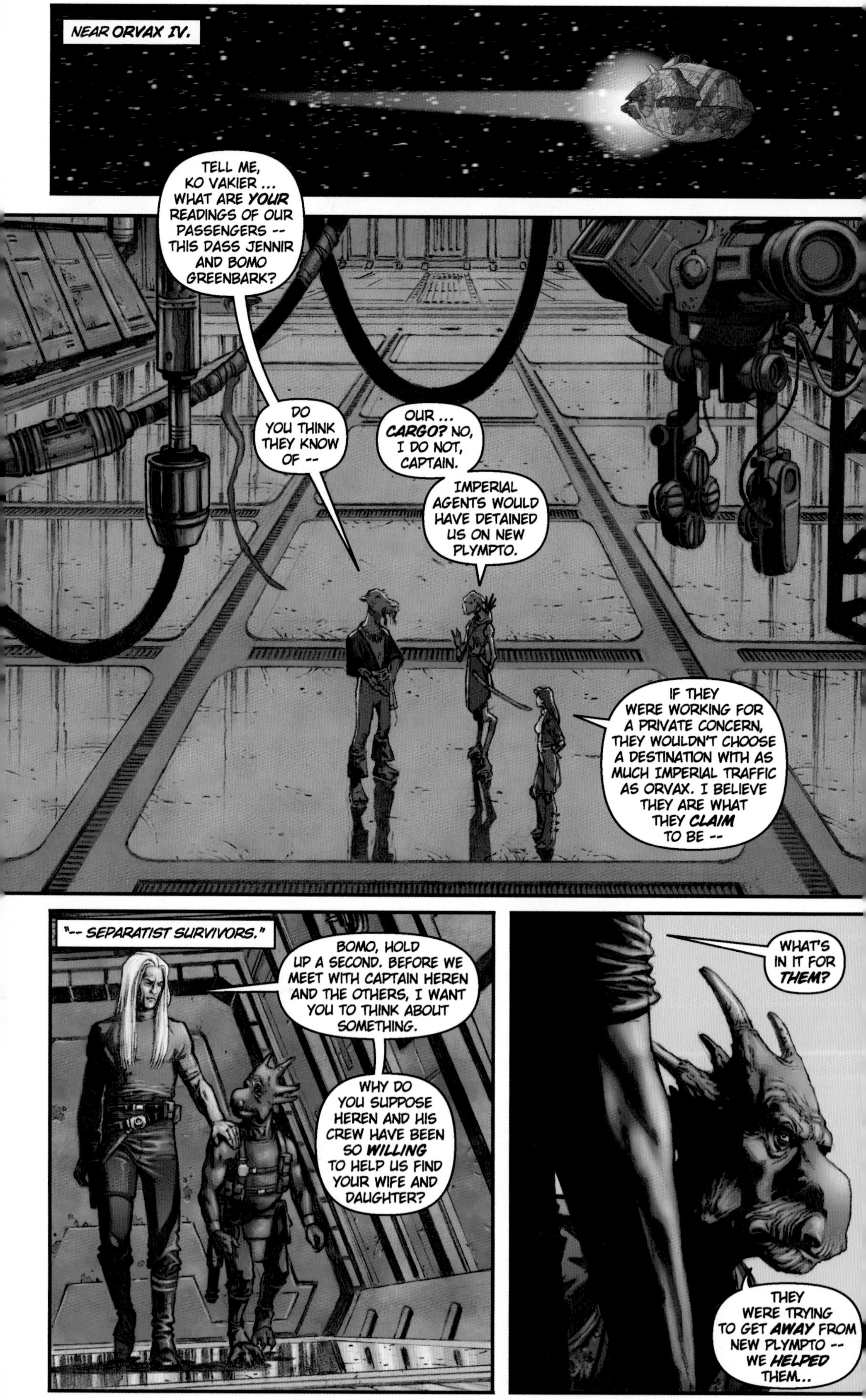
NEAR ORVAX IV.
TELL ME, KO VAKIER ... WHAT ARE YOUR READINGS OF OUR PASSENGERS -- THIS DASS JENNIR AND BOMO GREENBARK?
DO YOU THINK THEY KNOW OF --
OUR ... CARGO? NO, I DO NOT, CAPTAIN.
IMPERIAL AGENTS WOULD HAVE DETAINED US ON NEW PLYMPTO.
IF THEY WERE WORKING FOR A PRIVATE CONCERN, THEY WOULDN'T CHOOSE A DESTINATION WITH AS MUCH IMPERIAL TRAFFIC AS ORVAX. I BELIEVE THEY ARE WHAT THEY CLAIM TO BE --
"-- SEPARATIST SURVIVORS."
BOMO, HOLD UP A SECOND. BEFORE WE MEET WITH CAPTAIN HEREN AND THE OTHERS, I WANT YOU TO THINK ABOUT SOMETHING.
WHY DO YOU SUPPOSE HEREN AND HIS CREW HAVE BEEN SO WILLING TO HELP US FIND YOUR WIFE AND DAUGHTER?
WHAT'S IN IT FOR THEM?
THEY WERE TRYING TO GET AWAY FROM NEW PLYMPTO -- WE HELPED THEM..

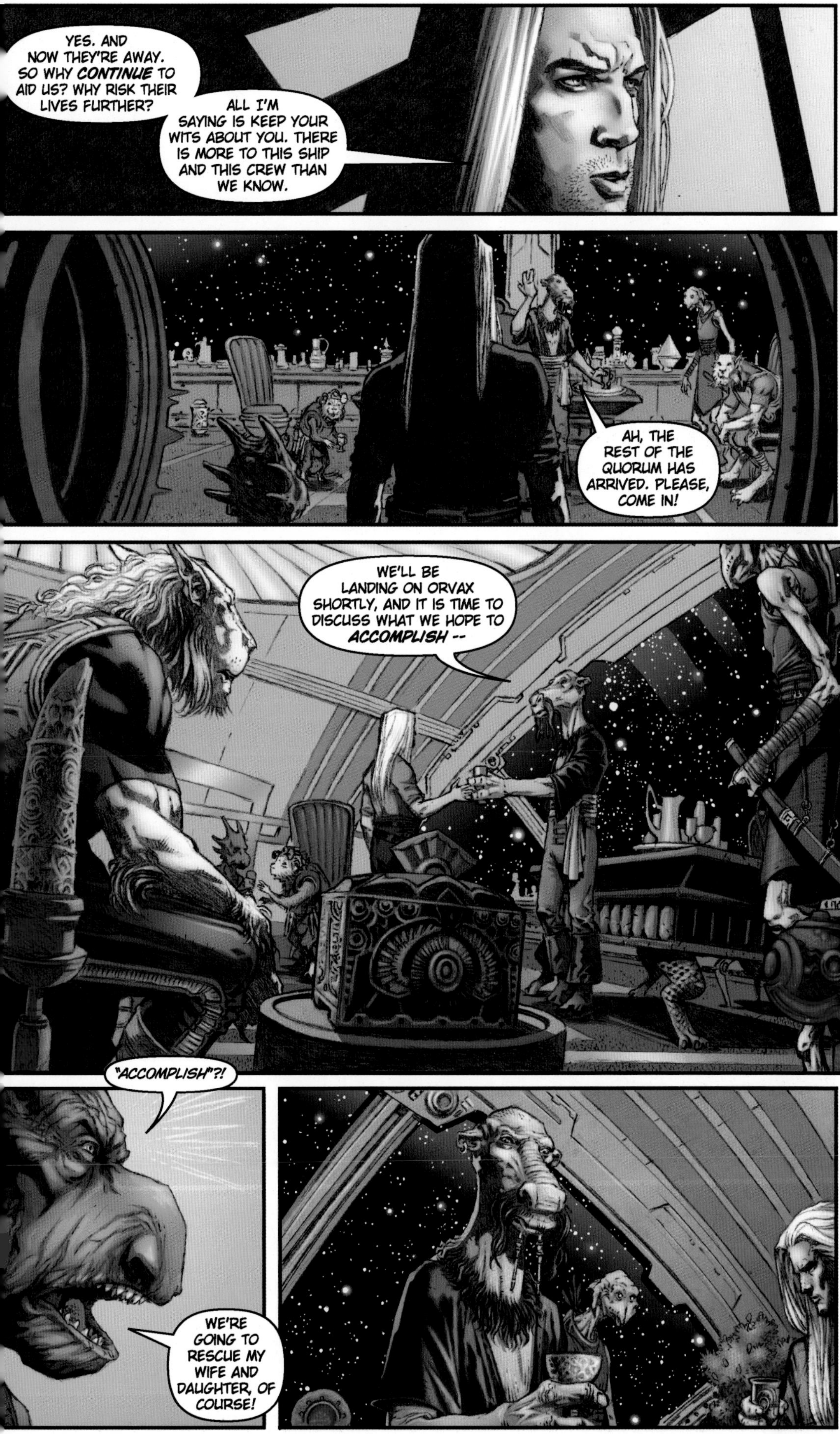
YES. AND NOW THEY'RE AWAY. SO WHY *CONTINUE* TO AID US? WHY RISK THEIR LIVES FURTHER?
ALL I'M SAYING IS KEEP YOUR WITS ABOUT YOU. THERE IS MORE TO THIS SHIP AND THIS CREW THAN WE KNOW.
AH, THE REST OF THE QUORUM HAS ARRIVED. PLEASE, COME IN!
WE'LL BE LANDING ON ORVAX SHORTLY, AND IT IS TIME TO DISCUSS WHAT WE HOPE TO *ACCOMPLISH* --
"ACCOMPLISH"?!
WE'RE GOING TO RESCUE MY WIFE AND DAUGHTER, OF COURSE!

LOOK, IF YOU DON'T WANT TO HELP, JENNIR AND I CAN DO IT OURSELVES. WE CAN BE IN AND OUT BEFORE THE SLAVERS KNOW WHAT HIT THEM!

HAVE YOU BEEN TO ORVAX IV, LITTLE ONE? NO? THEN YOU SHOULD LISTEN TO ONE WHO HAS.

THE SLAVERS ROUTINELY SEPARATE FAMILIES. EVEN IF YOUR WIFE AND DAUGHTER ARE STILL TOGETHER, FINDING THEM AMONG THE THOUSANDS OF PRISONERS WILL BE NO EASY TASK.

ALL OF THIS ASSUMES THEY ARE STILL ON ORVAX. WE ARE RUNNING TWO DAYS BEHIND THE IMPERIALS. IT IS ENTIRELY POSSIBLE ONE OR BOTH OF THE FEMALES HAS ALREADY BEEN SOLD.

WE WILL STILL FIND THEM, BOMO. YOU HAVE MY WORD ON THAT.

BUT THERE ARE TWO ASPECTS TO THIS THAT I DON'T THINK YOU'VE CONSIDERED --

YEAH?

WHAT *ARE* THEY, *"GENERAL"*? HAVE I FORGOTTEN HOW *DANGEROUS* IT WILL BE? MISCALCULATED THE ANGLE OF OUR APPROACH? FAILED TO TAKE INTO ACCOUNT THE PHASES OF ORVAX'S MOONS?

BOMO, YOU'VE BEEN SO FOCUSED ON RESA AND MESA --

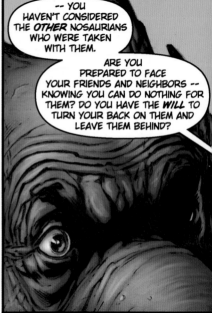

-- YOU HAVEN'T CONSIDERED THE *OTHER* NOSAURIANS WHO WERE TAKEN WITH THEM.

ARE YOU PREPARED TO FACE YOUR FRIENDS AND NEIGHBORS -- KNOWING YOU CAN DO NOTHING FOR THEM? DO YOU HAVE THE *WILL* TO TURN YOUR BACK ON THEM AND LEAVE THEM BEHIND?

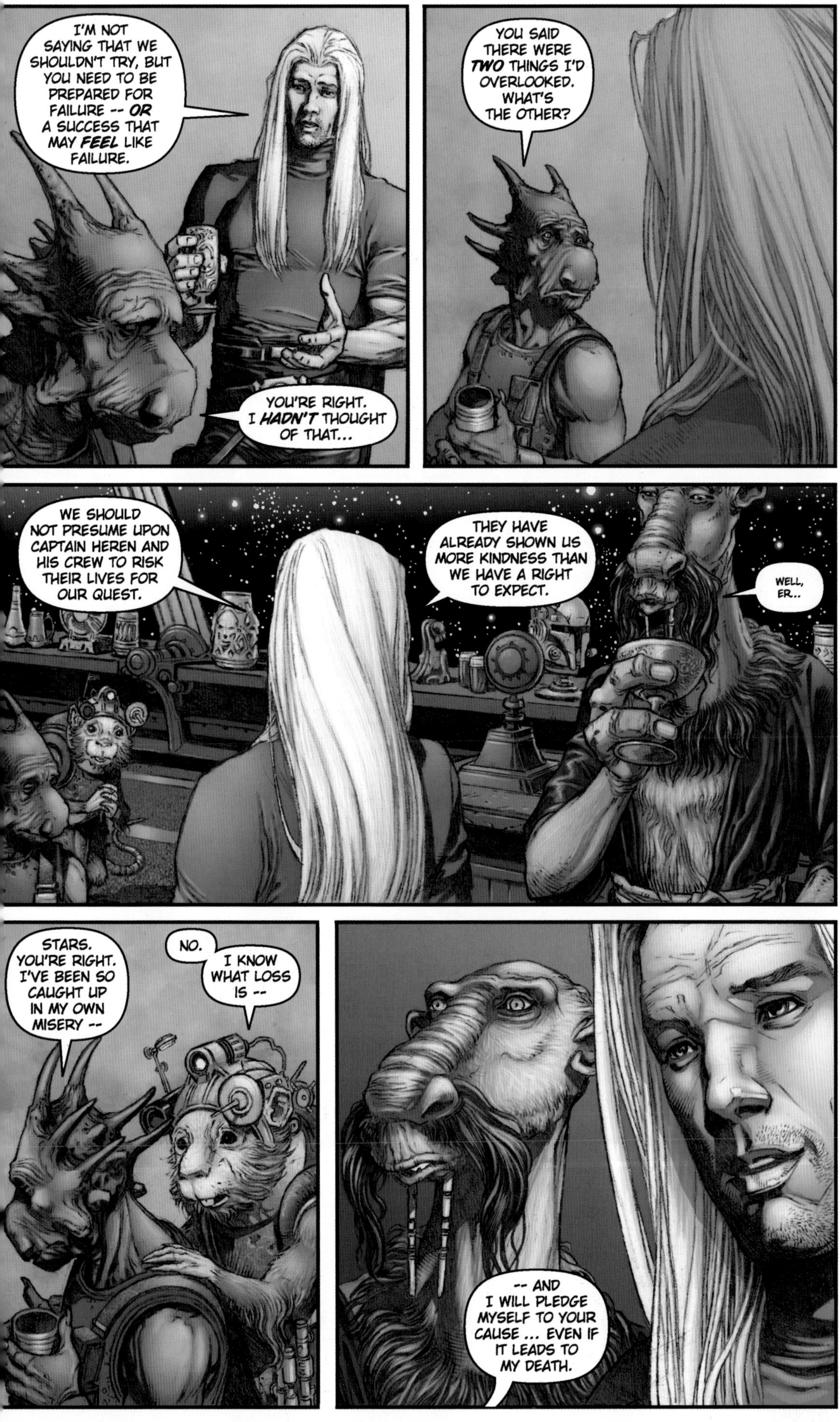
I'M NOT SAYING THAT WE SHOULDN'T TRY, BUT YOU NEED TO BE PREPARED FOR FAILURE -- *OR* A SUCCESS THAT MAY *FEEL* LIKE FAILURE.
YOU'RE RIGHT. I *HADN'T* THOUGHT OF THAT...
YOU SAID THERE WERE *TWO* THINGS I'D OVERLOOKED. WHAT'S THE OTHER?
WE SHOULD NOT PRESUME UPON CAPTAIN HEREN AND HIS CREW TO RISK THEIR LIVES FOR OUR QUEST.
THEY HAVE ALREADY SHOWN US MORE KINDNESS THAN WE HAVE A RIGHT TO EXPECT.
WELL, ER..
STARS. YOU'RE RIGHT. I'VE BEEN SO CAUGHT UP IN MY OWN MISERY --
NO.
I KNOW WHAT LOSS IS --
-- AND I WILL PLEDGE MYSELF TO YOUR CAUSE ... EVEN IF IT LEADS TO MY DEATH.

AND I WOULD FOREGO ALL HONOR IF I DID NOT JOIN RATTY.

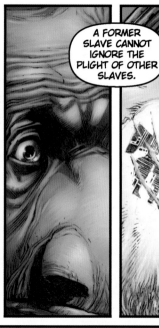

A FORMER SLAVE CANNOT IGNORE THE PLIGHT OF OTHER SLAVES.

AND, WITH THE CAPTAIN'S PERMISSION, I WILL ALSO PLEDGE MY SWORD. DEATH HOLDS NO TERRORS FOR ME.

THE GALAXY COULD DO WITH FEWER IMPERIALS -- AND FEWER SLAVERS.

WELL, THEN --

"-- ALL WE NEED IS A PLAN."

THIS PLAN ISN'T WORKING FOR ME, GENERAL.

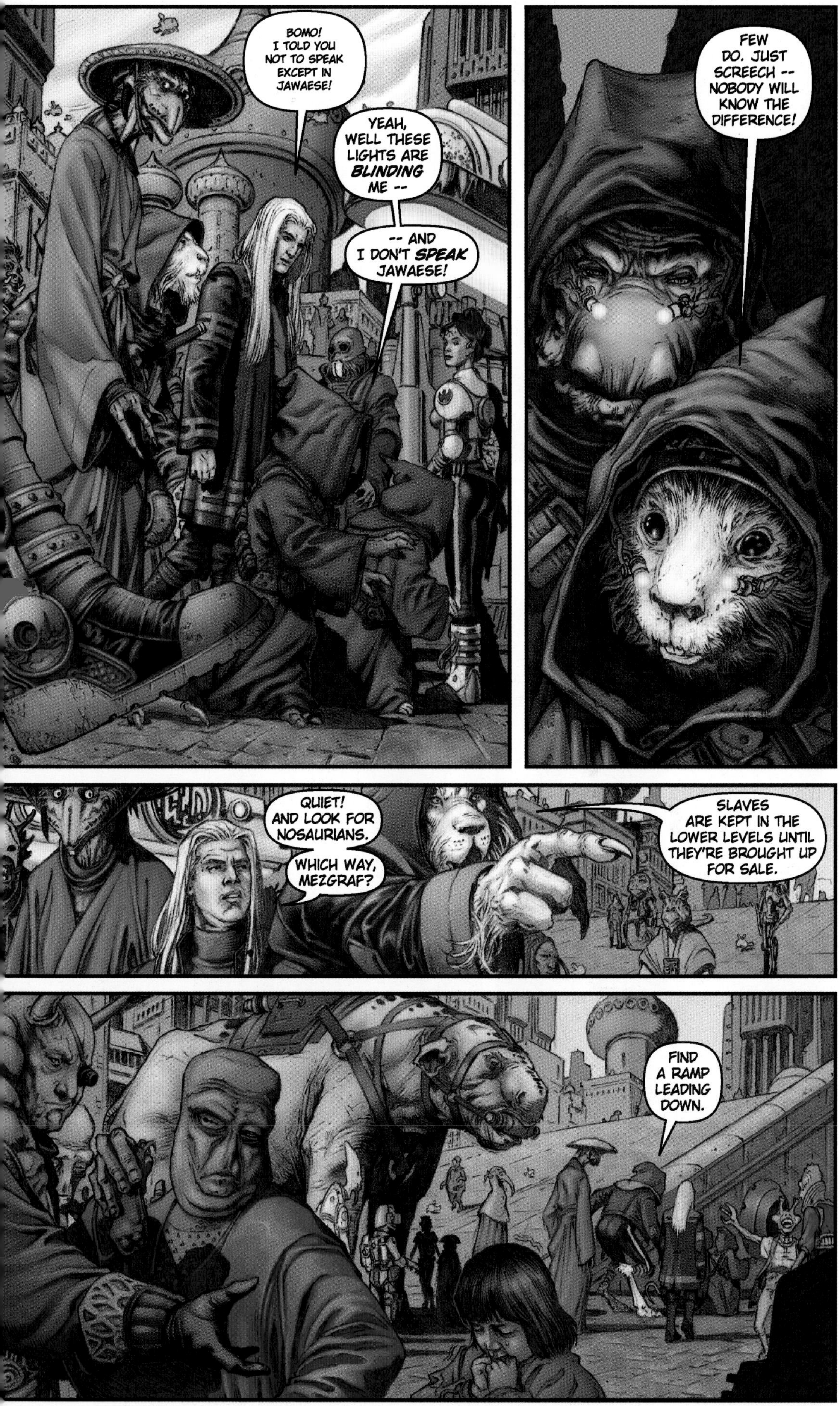

BOMO! I TOLD YOU NOT TO SPEAK EXCEPT IN JAWAESE!
YEAH, WELL THESE LIGHTS ARE BLINDING ME --
-- AND I DON'T SPEAK JAWAESE!
FEW DO. JUST SCREECH -- NOBODY WILL KNOW THE DIFFERENCE!
QUIET! AND LOOK FOR NOSAURIANS.
WHICH WAY, MEZGRAF?
SLAVES ARE KEPT IN THE LOWER LEVELS UNTIL THEY'RE BROUGHT UP FOR SALE.
FIND A RAMP LEADING DOWN.

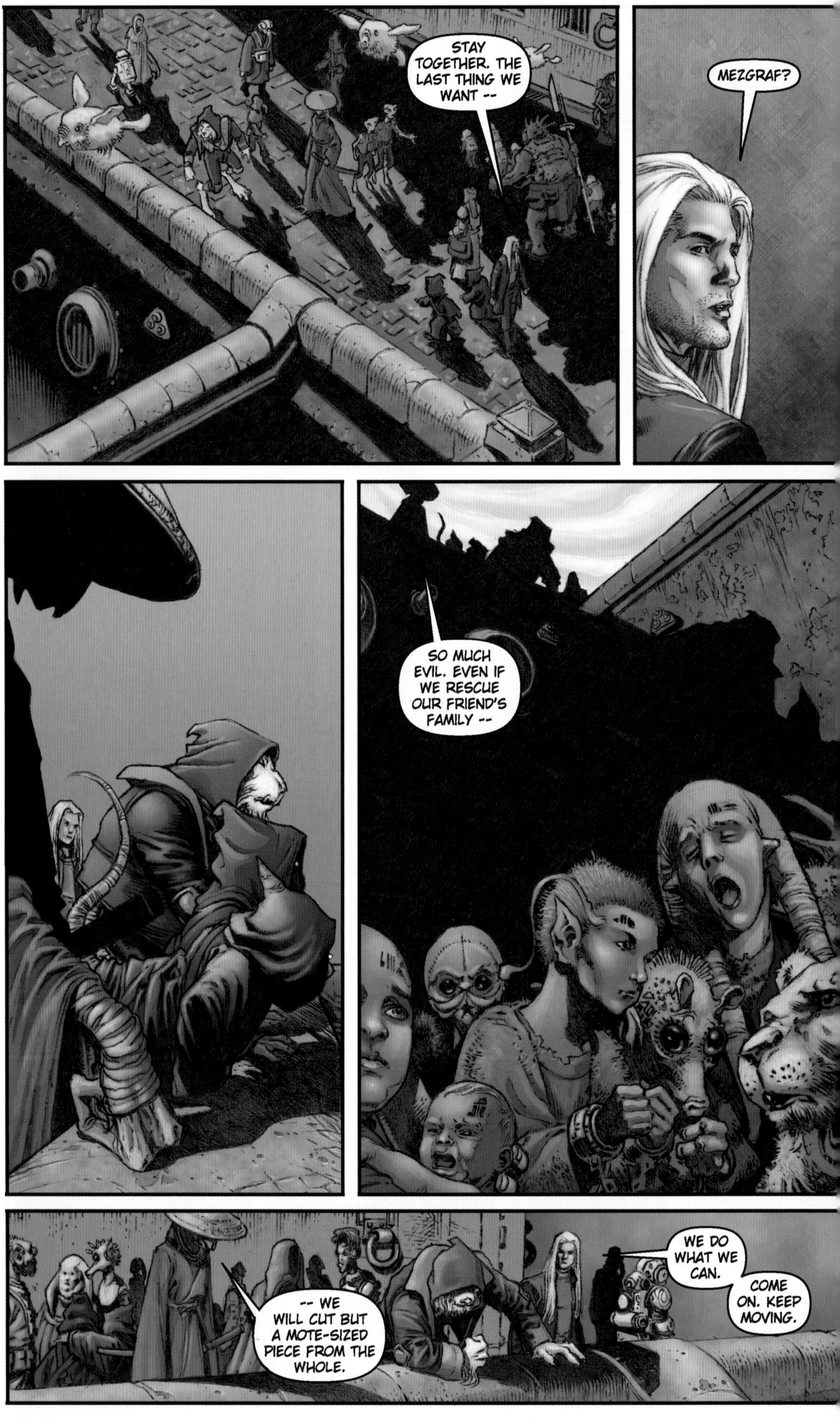
STAY TOGETHER. THE LAST THING WE WANT --
MEZGRAF?
SO MUCH EVIL. EVEN IF WE RESCUE OUR FRIEND'S FAMILY --
-- WE WILL CUT BUT A MOTE-SIZED PIECE FROM THE WHOLE.
WE DO WHAT WE CAN.
COME ON. KEEP MOVING.

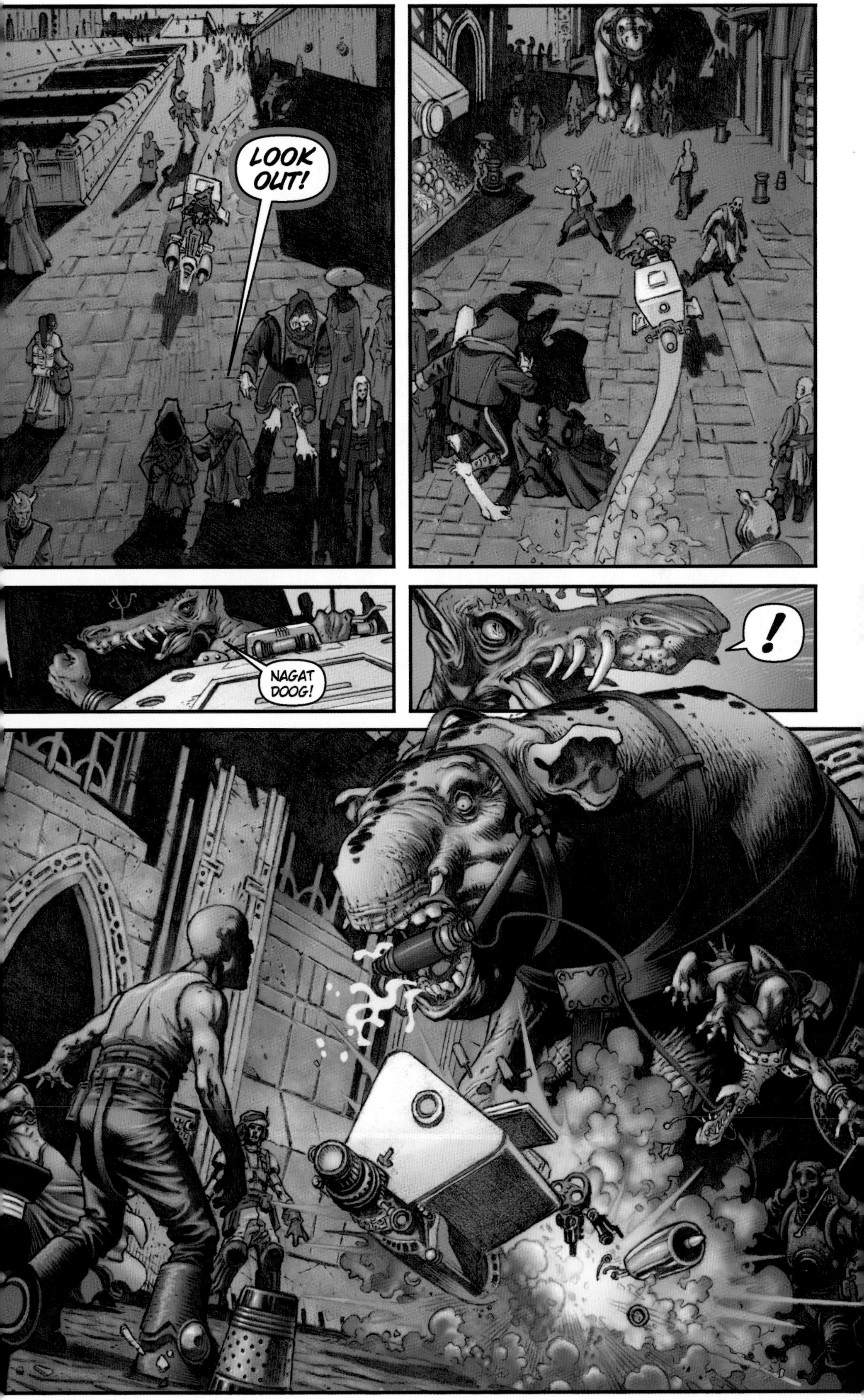
LOOK OUT!
NAGAT DOOG!
!

MEZGRAF ... STAY OUT OF THAT THING'S PATH -- !

WHY? DO YOU THINK IT WILL BE SWAYED BY YOUR BLASTER?

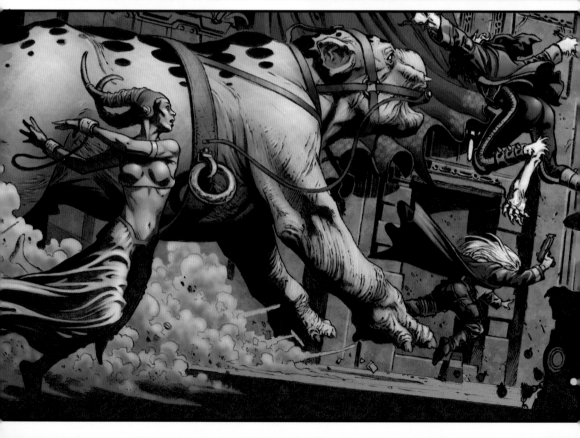

MEZGRAF!

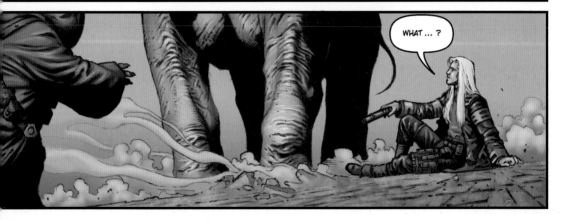

WHAT ... ?

INTERESTING. I WOULD NEVER HAVE THOUGHT OF IT!

IT'S ALL RIGHT, GIRL...NOTHING TO FEAR. CALM YOURSELF...

MANY THANKS! MANY THANKS!

THERE'S NO TELLING WHAT MIGHT HAVE HAP-- ~GASP!~

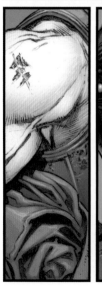

ESCAPEE!

GUARDS-- ESCAPEE!

I'LL TAKE CARE OF THIS.

ALL OF YOU GET CLEAR. AND, MEZGRAF... KEEP YOUR COAT ON.

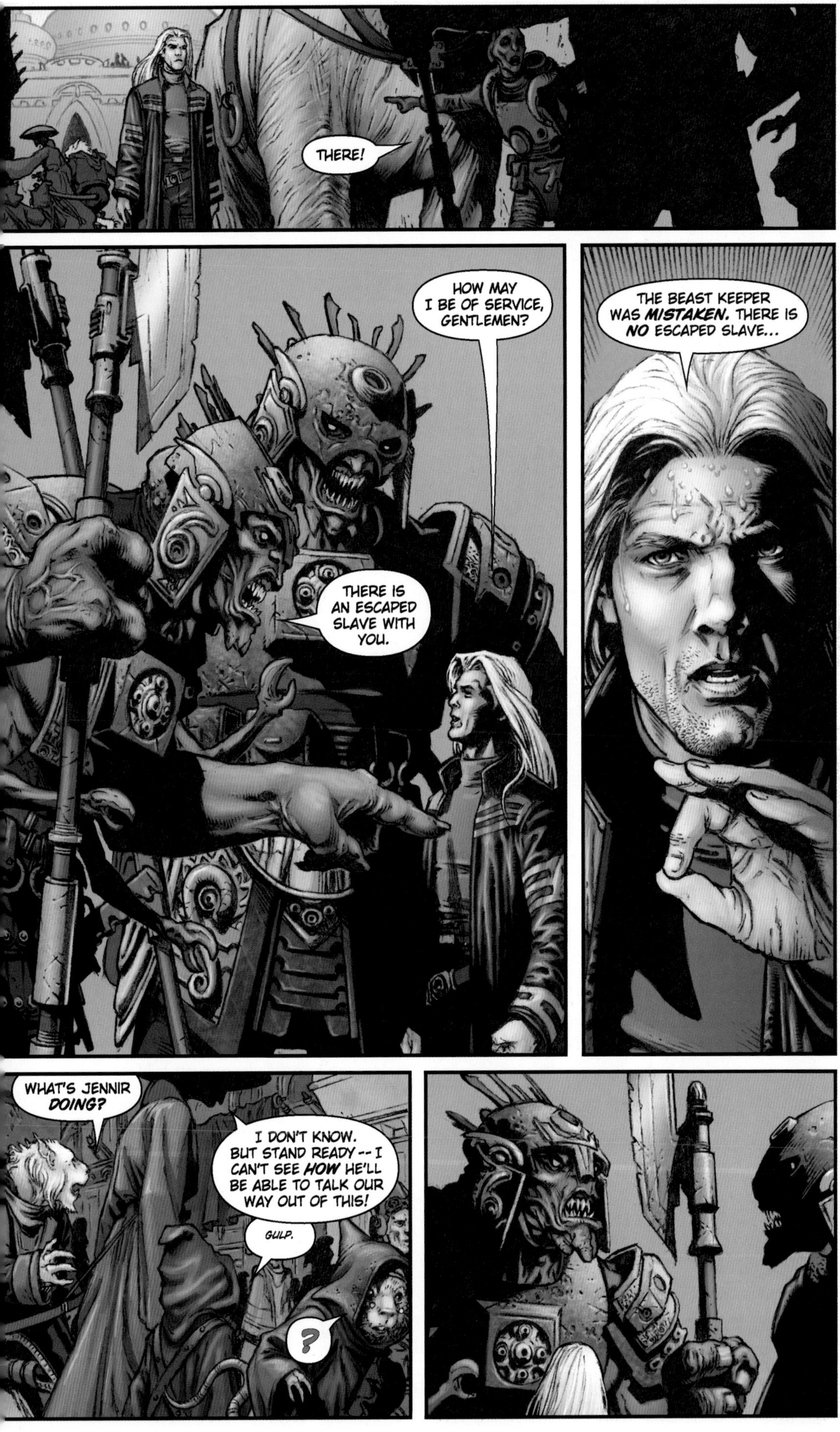

THERE!
HOW MAY I BE OF SERVICE, GENTLEMEN?
THERE IS AN ESCAPED SLAVE WITH YOU.
THE BEAST KEEPER WAS **MISTAKEN.** THERE IS **NO** ESCAPED SLAVE...
WHAT'S JENNIR **DOING?**
I DON'T KNOW. BUT STAND READY -- I CAN'T SEE **HOW** HE'LL BE ABLE TO TALK OUR WAY OUT OF THIS!
GULP.
?

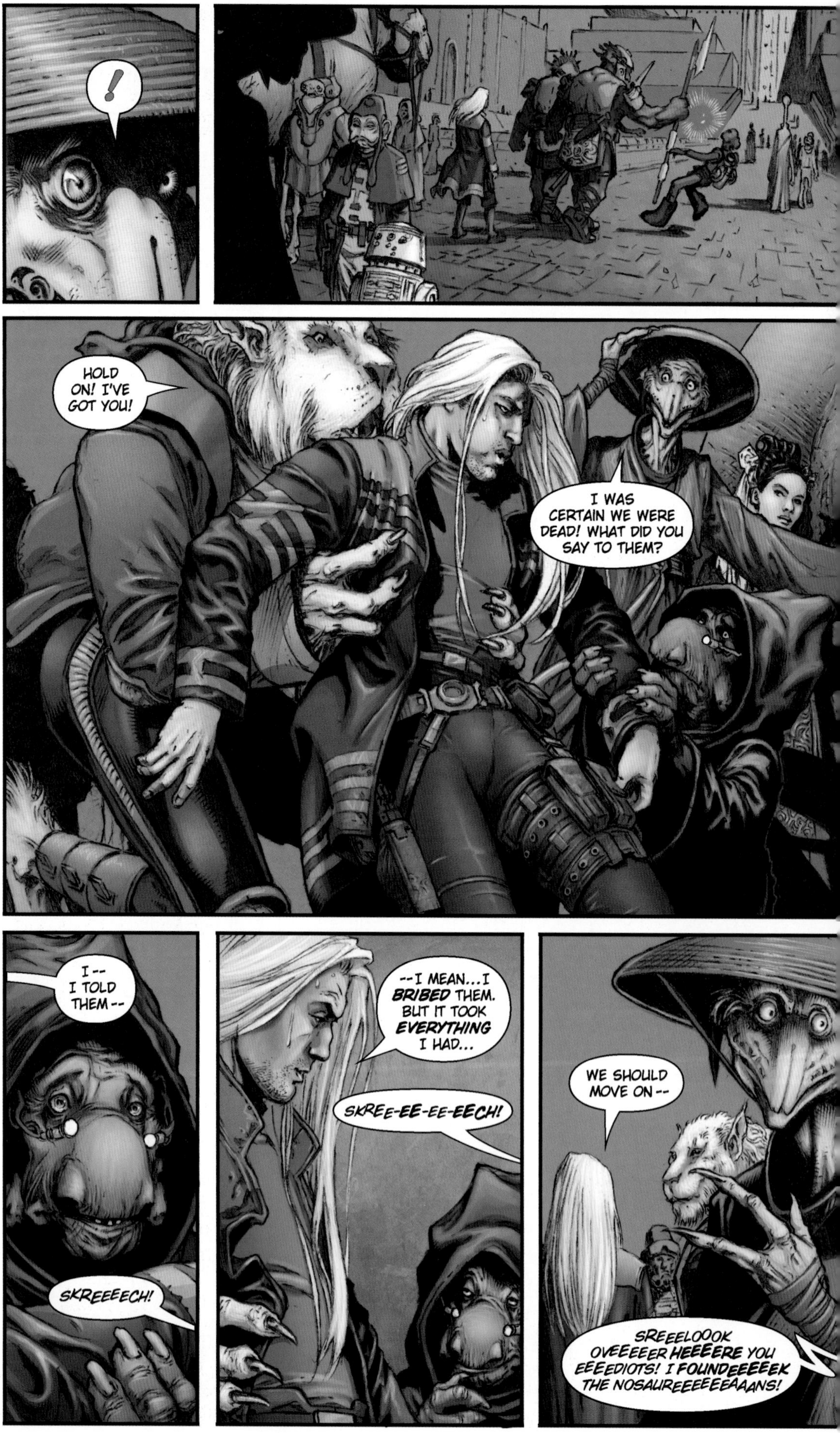
!
HOLD ON! I'VE GOT YOU!
I WAS CERTAIN WE WERE DEAD! WHAT DID YOU SAY TO THEM?
I -- I TOLD THEM --
SKREEEECH!
--I MEAN...I BRIBED THEM. BUT IT TOOK EVERYTHING I HAD...
SKREE-EE-EE-EECH!
WE SHOULD MOVE ON --
SREEELOOOK OVEEEEER HEEEERE YOU EEEEDIOTS! I FOUNDEEEEEK THE NOSAUREEEEEEAAANS!

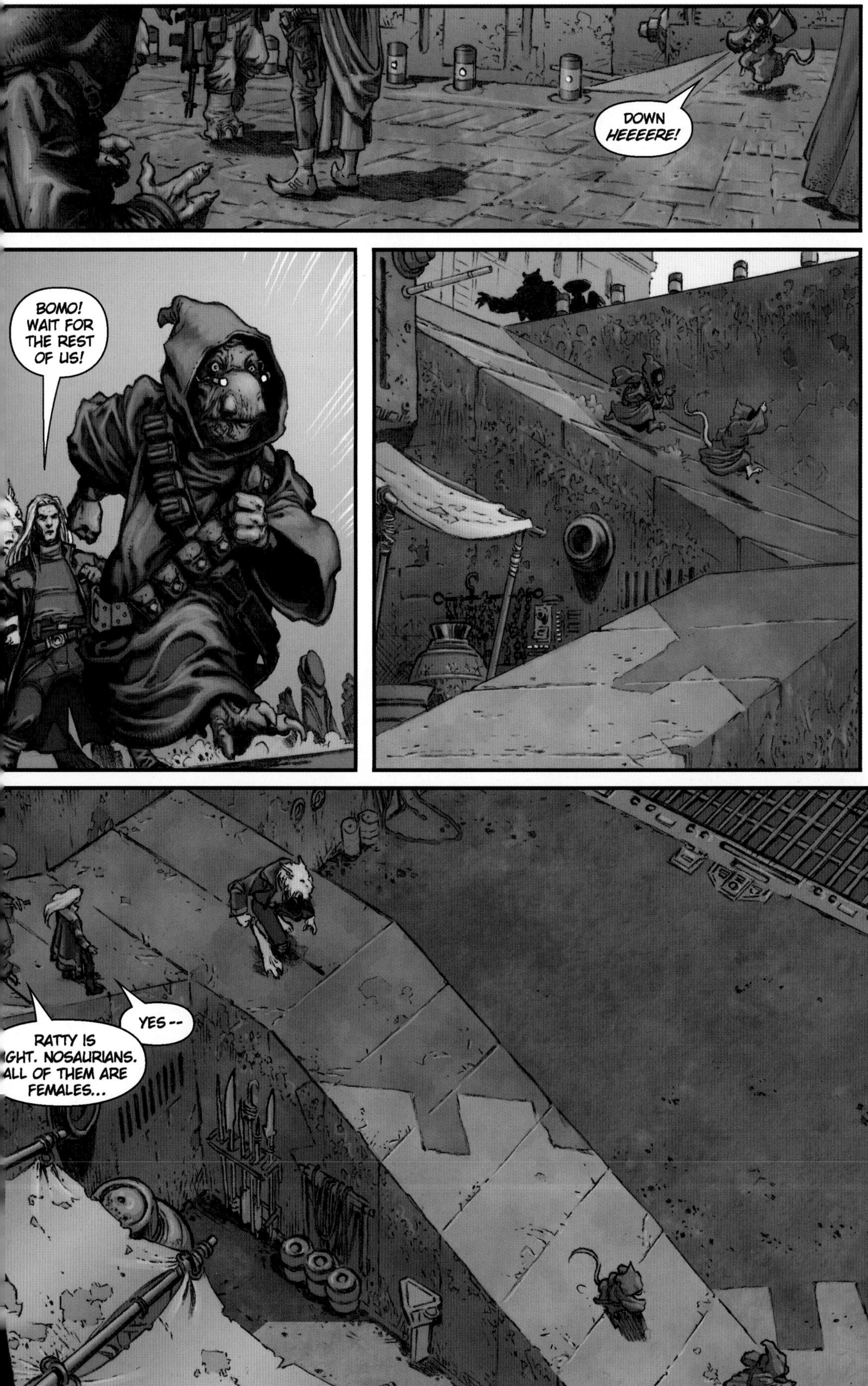
DOWN HEEEERE!
BOMO! WAIT FOR THE REST OF US!
RATTY IS GHT. NOSAURIANS. ALL OF THEM ARE FEMALES...
YES --

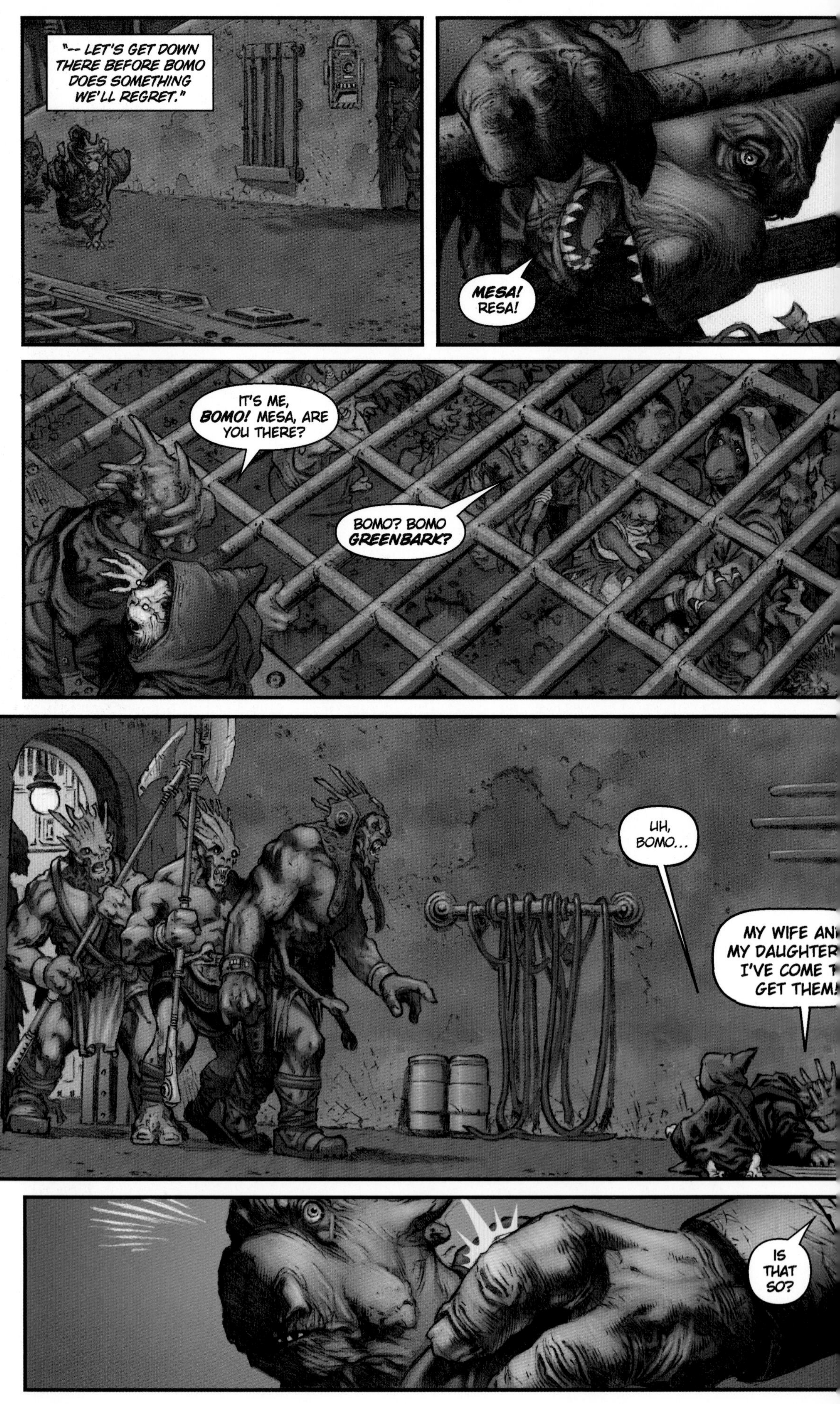
"-- LET'S GET DOWN THERE BEFORE BOMO DOES SOMETHING WE'LL REGRET."
MESA! RESA!
IT'S ME, BOMO! MESA, ARE YOU THERE?
BOMO? BOMO GREENBARK?
UH, BOMO...
MY WIFE AN MY DAUGHTER I'VE COME T GET THEM!
IS THAT SO?

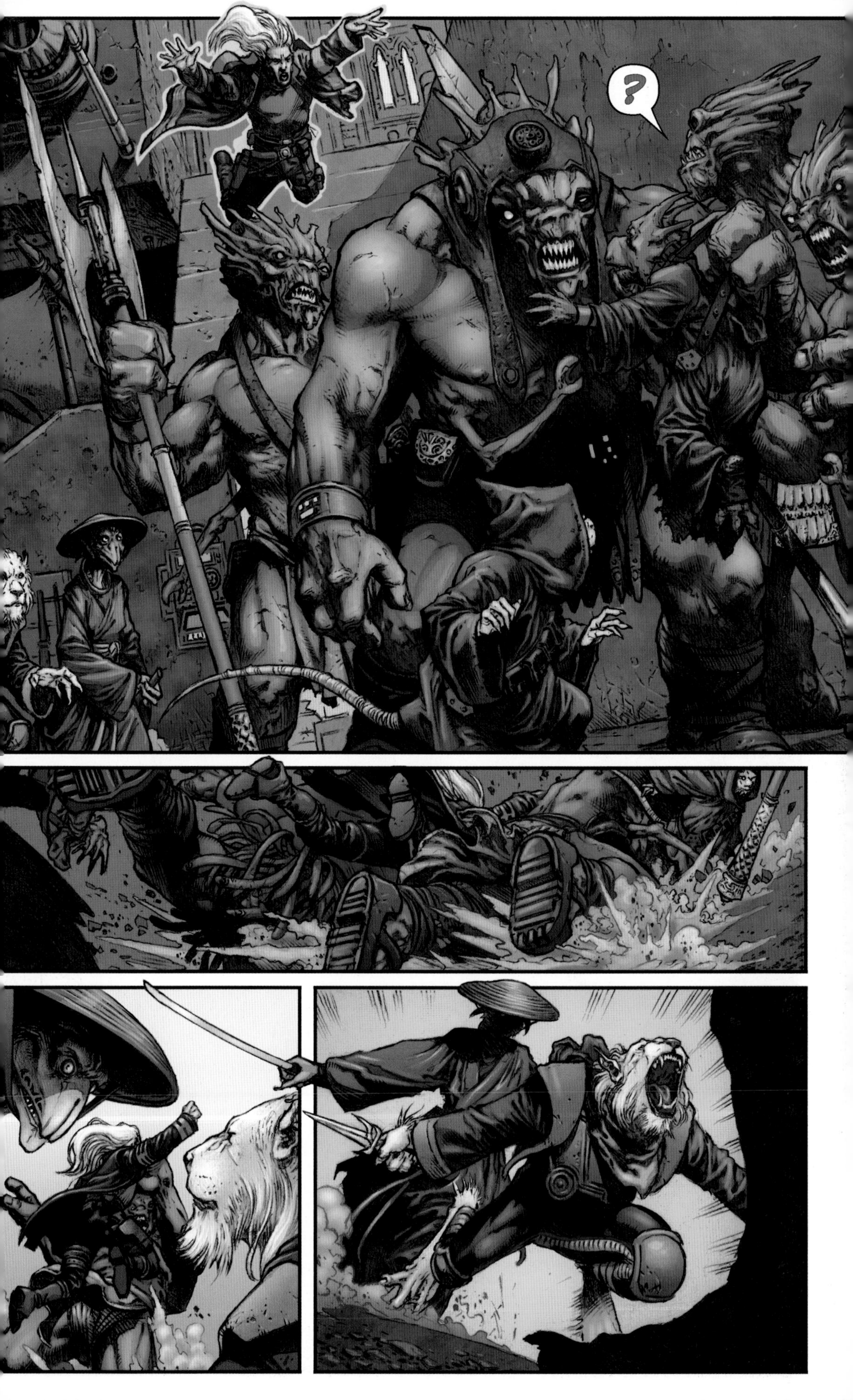
?

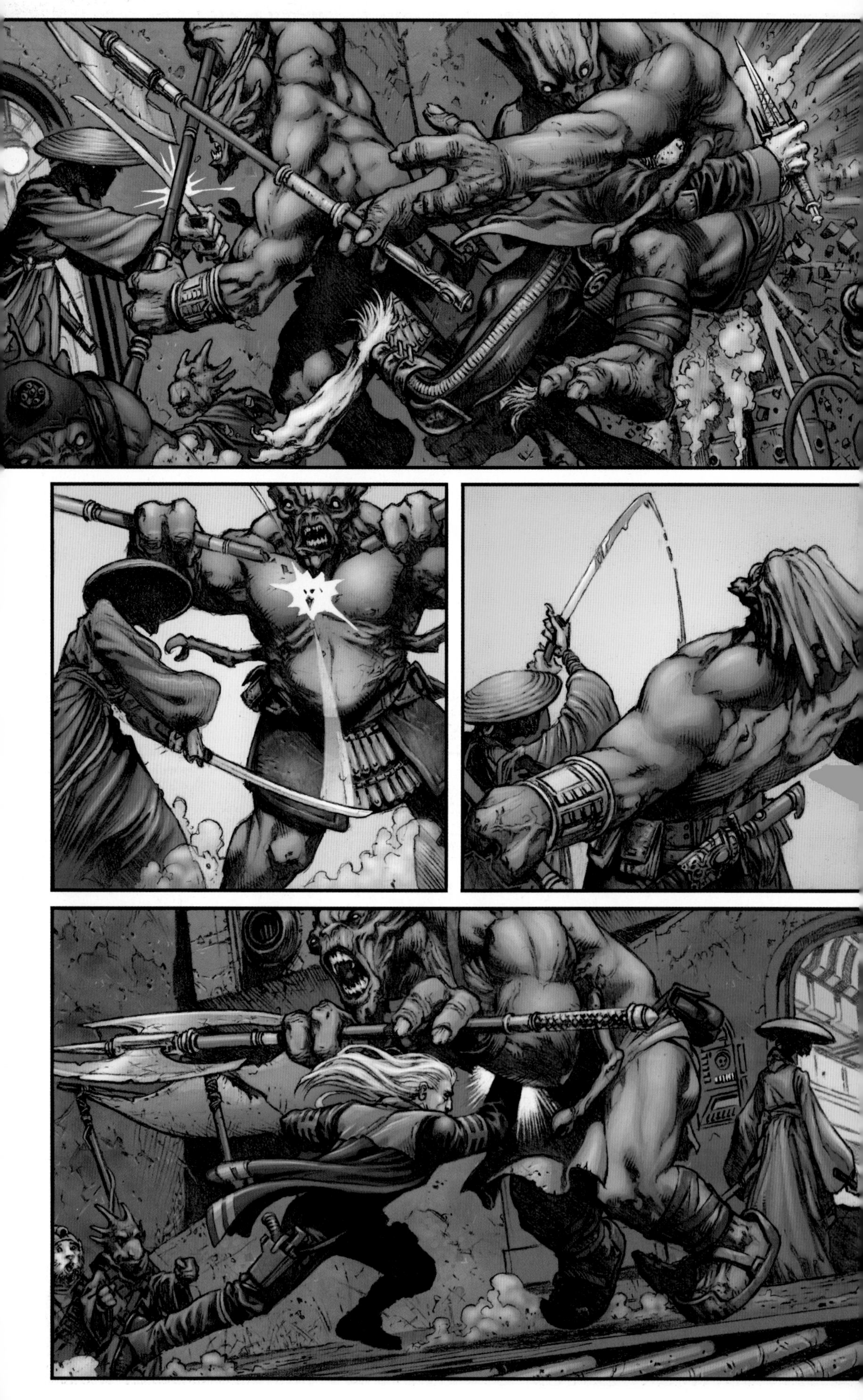

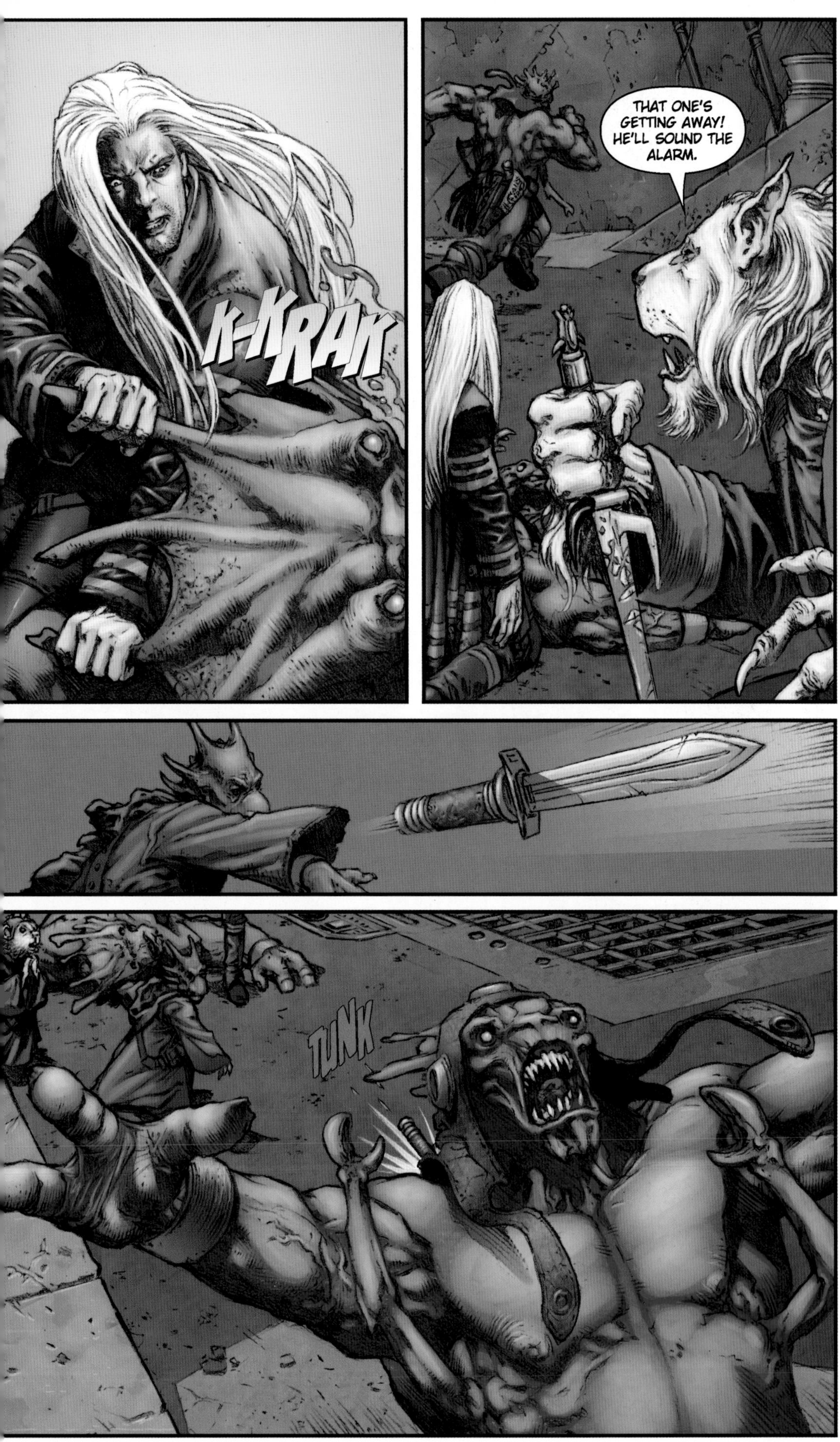
K-KRAK
THAT ONE'S GETTING AWAY! HE'LL SOUND THE ALARM.
TUNK

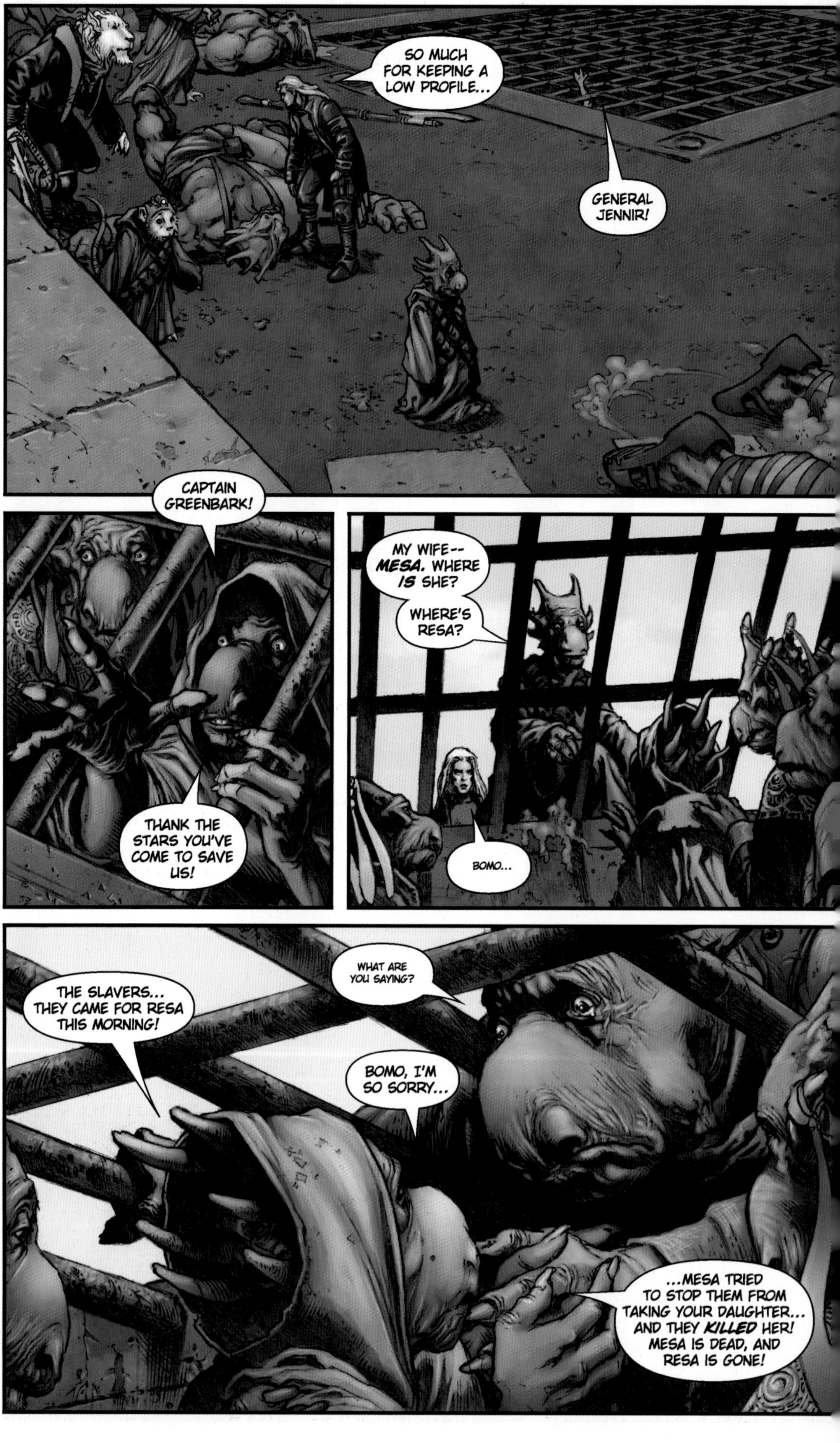
SO MUCH FOR KEEPING A LOW PROFILE...
GENERAL JENNIR!
CAPTAIN GREENBARK!
THANK THE STARS YOU'VE COME TO SAVE US!
MY WIFE-- MESA. WHERE IS SHE?
WHERE'S RESA?
BOMO...
THE SLAVERS... THEY CAME FOR RESA THIS MORNING!
WHAT ARE YOU SAYING?
BOMO, I'M SO SORRY...
...MESA TRIED TO STOP THEM FROM TAKING YOUR DAUGHTER... AND THEY KILLED HER! MESA IS DEAD, AND RESA IS GONE!

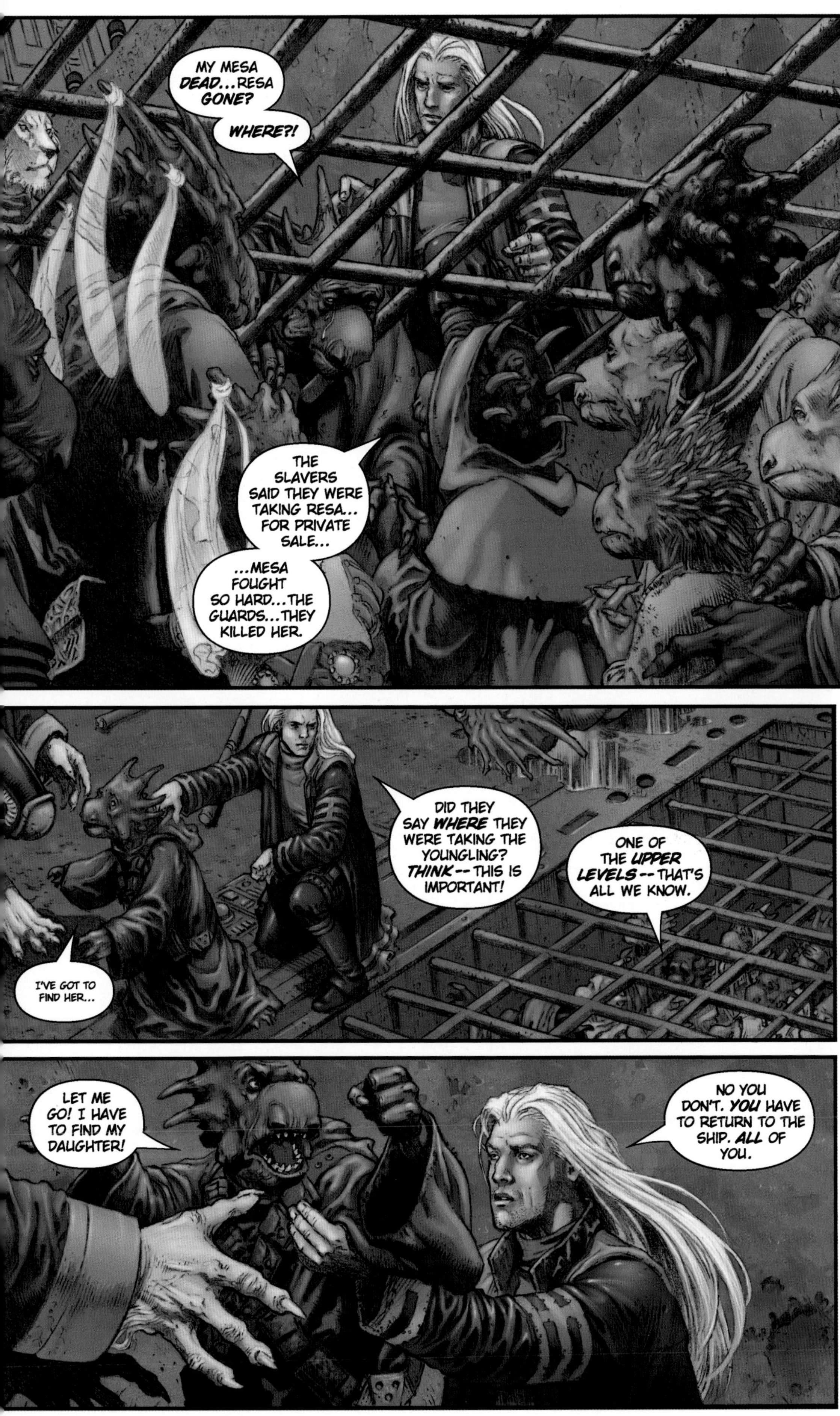

MY MESA *DEAD*...RESA *GONE?*
*WHERE?!*
THE SLAVERS SAID THEY WERE TAKING RESA... FOR PRIVATE SALE...
...MESA FOUGHT SO HARD...THE GUARDS...THEY KILLED HER.
DID THEY SAY *WHERE* THEY WERE TAKING THE YOUNGLING? *THINK* -- THIS IS IMPORTANT!
ONE OF THE *UPPER LEVELS* -- THAT'S ALL WE KNOW.
I'VE GOT TO FIND HER...
LET ME GO! I HAVE TO FIND MY DAUGHTER!
NO YOU DON'T. *YOU* HAVE TO RETURN TO THE SHIP. *ALL* OF YOU.

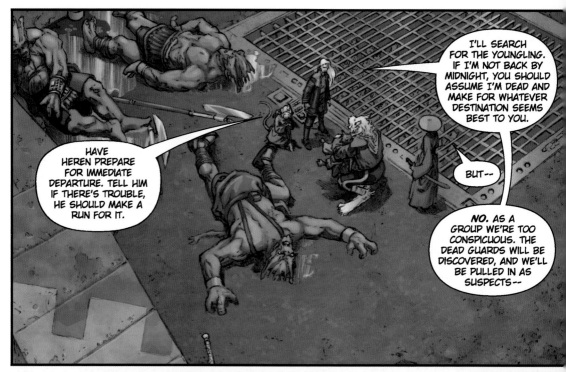

I'LL SEARCH FOR THE YOUNGLING. IF I'M NOT BACK BY MIDNIGHT, YOU SHOULD ASSUME I'M DEAD AND MAKE FOR WHATEVER DESTINATION SEEMS BEST TO YOU.

HAVE HEREN PREPARE FOR IMMEDIATE DEPARTURE. TELL HIM IF THERE'S TROUBLE, HE SHOULD MAKE A RUN FOR IT.

BUT--

*NO.* AS A GROUP WE'RE TOO CONSPICUOUS. THE DEAD GUARDS WILL BE DISCOVERED, AND WE'LL BE PULLED IN AS SUSPECTS--

-- BUT ALONE I MIGHT HAVE A CHANCE.

KEEP A CLOSE WATCH ON BOMO. DON'T LET HIM DO ANYTHING FOOLISH.

*MMMPF!*

WAIT.

*MMMMG!*

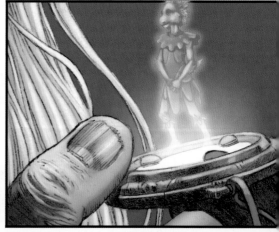

I MAY NEED THIS.

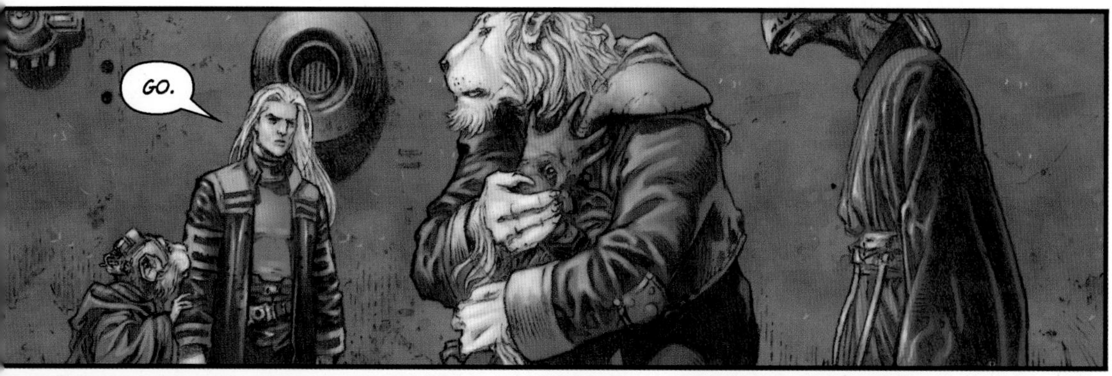
GO.

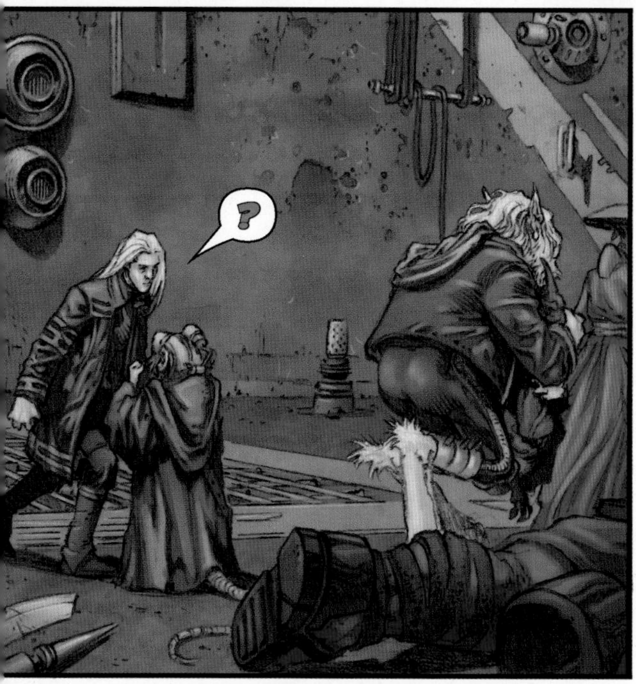
?

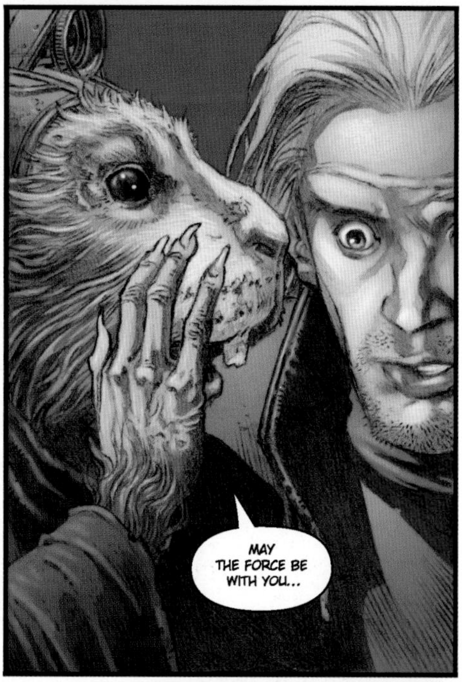
MAY THE FORCE BE WITH YOU...

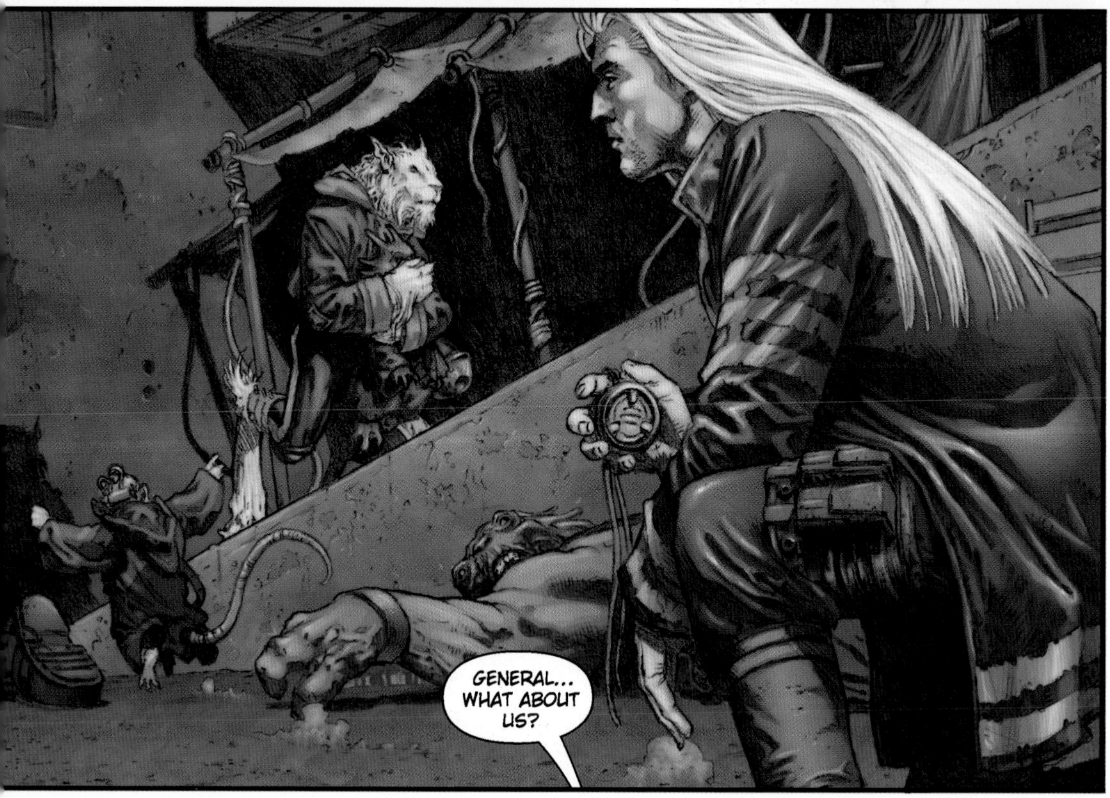
GENERAL... WHAT ABOUT US?

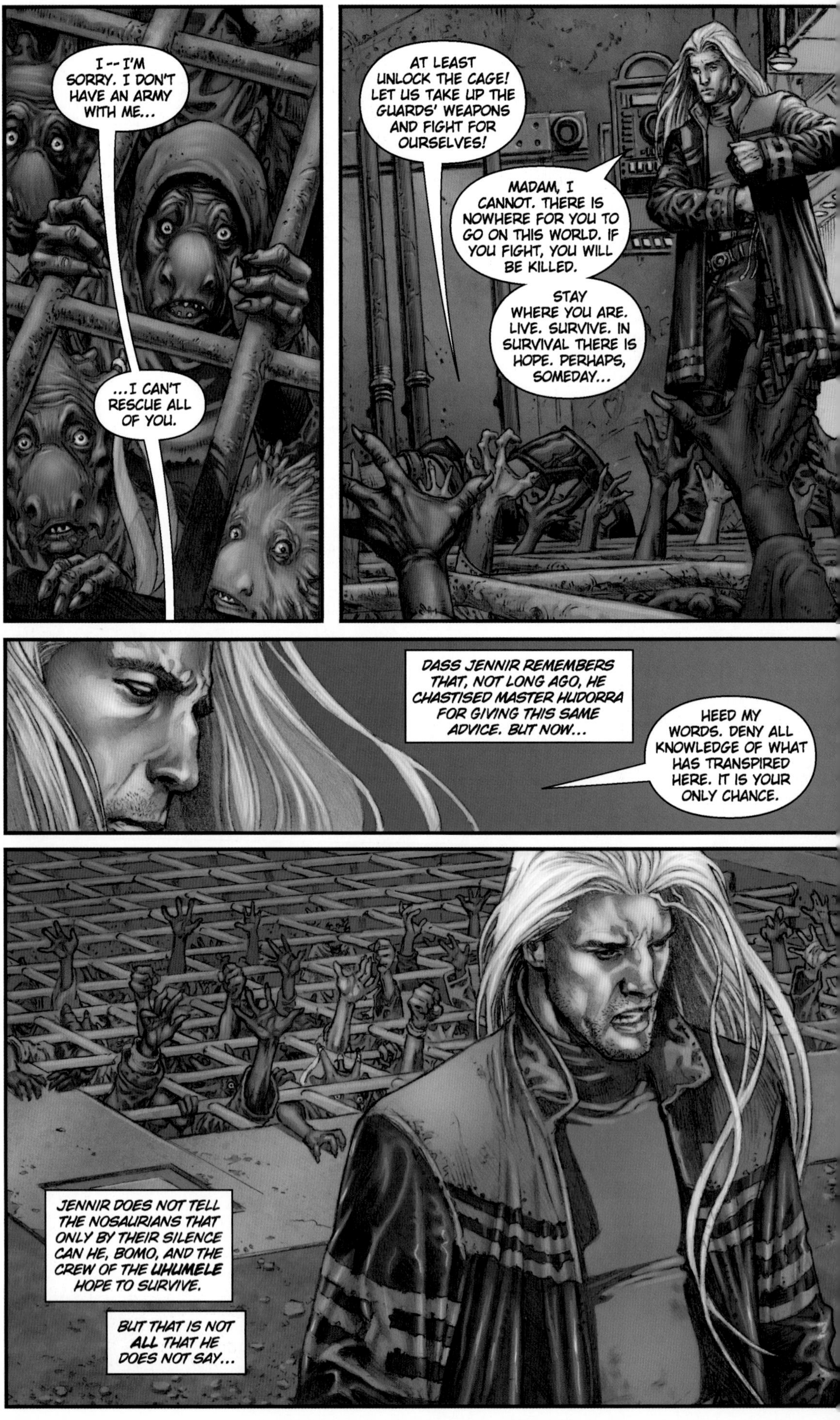
I -- I'M SORRY. I DON'T HAVE AN ARMY WITH ME...
...I CAN'T RESCUE ALL OF YOU.
AT LEAST UNLOCK THE CAGE! LET US TAKE UP THE GUARDS' WEAPONS AND FIGHT FOR OURSELVES!
MADAM, I CANNOT. THERE IS NOWHERE FOR YOU TO GO ON THIS WORLD. IF YOU FIGHT, YOU WILL BE KILLED.
STAY WHERE YOU ARE. LIVE. SURVIVE. IN SURVIVAL THERE IS HOPE. PERHAPS, SOMEDAY...
DASS JENNIR REMEMBERS THAT, NOT LONG AGO, HE CHASTISED MASTER HUDORRA FOR GIVING THIS SAME ADVICE. BUT NOW...
HEED MY WORDS. DENY ALL KNOWLEDGE OF WHAT HAS TRANSPIRED HERE. IT IS YOUR ONLY CHANCE.
JENNIR DOES NOT TELL THE NOSAURIANS THAT ONLY BY THEIR SILENCE CAN HE, BOMO, AND THE CREW OF THE UHUMELE HOPE TO SURVIVE.
BUT THAT IS NOT ALL THAT HE DOES NOT SAY...

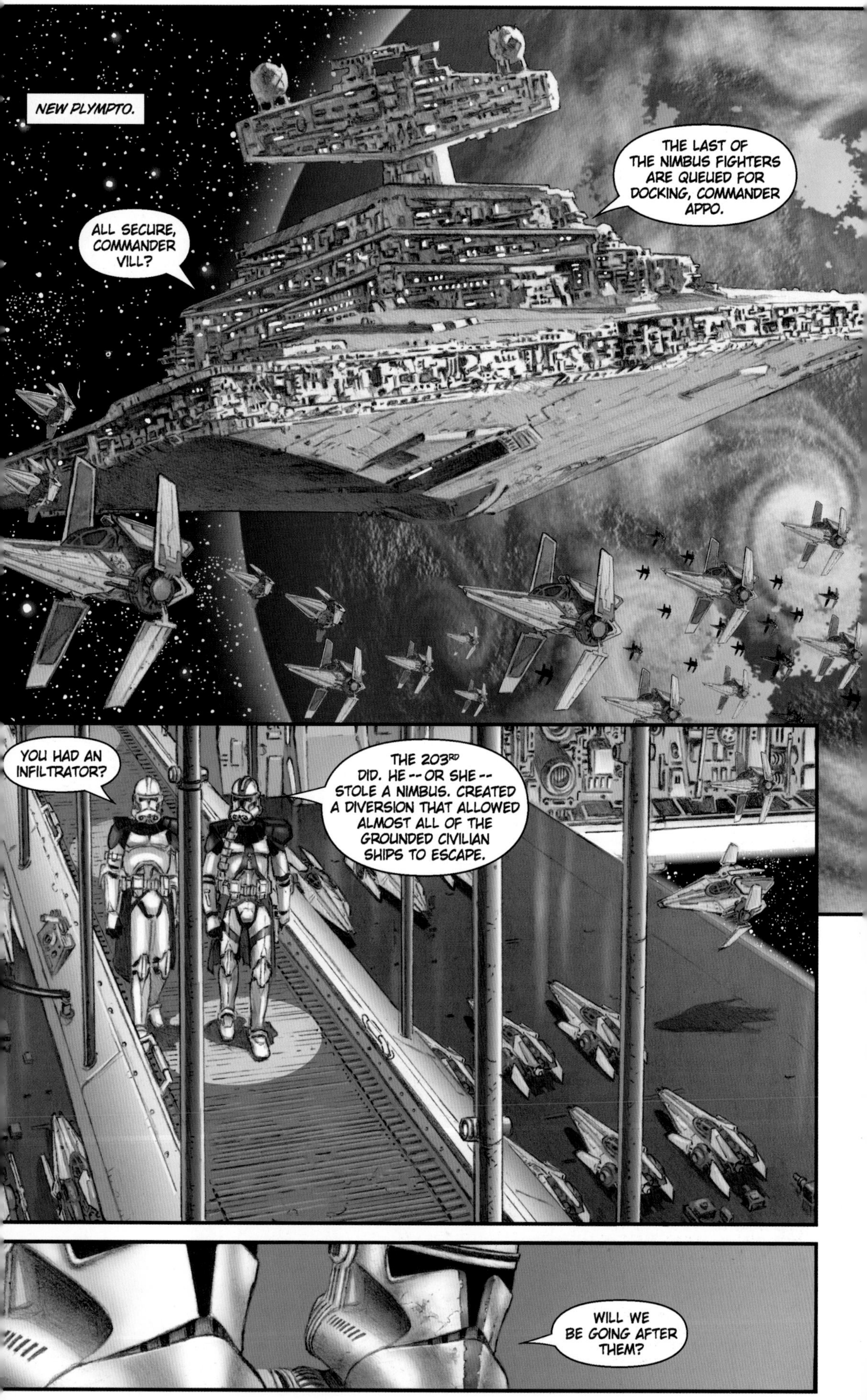
NEW PLYMPTO.
ALL SECURE, COMMANDER VILL?
THE LAST OF THE NIMBUS FIGHTERS ARE QUEUED FOR DOCKING, COMMANDER APPO.
YOU HAD AN INFILTRATOR?
THE 203RD DID. HE -- OR SHE -- STOLE A NIMBUS. CREATED A DIVERSION THAT ALLOWED ALMOST ALL OF THE GROUNDED CIVILIAN SHIPS TO ESCAPE.
WILL WE BE GOING AFTER THEM?

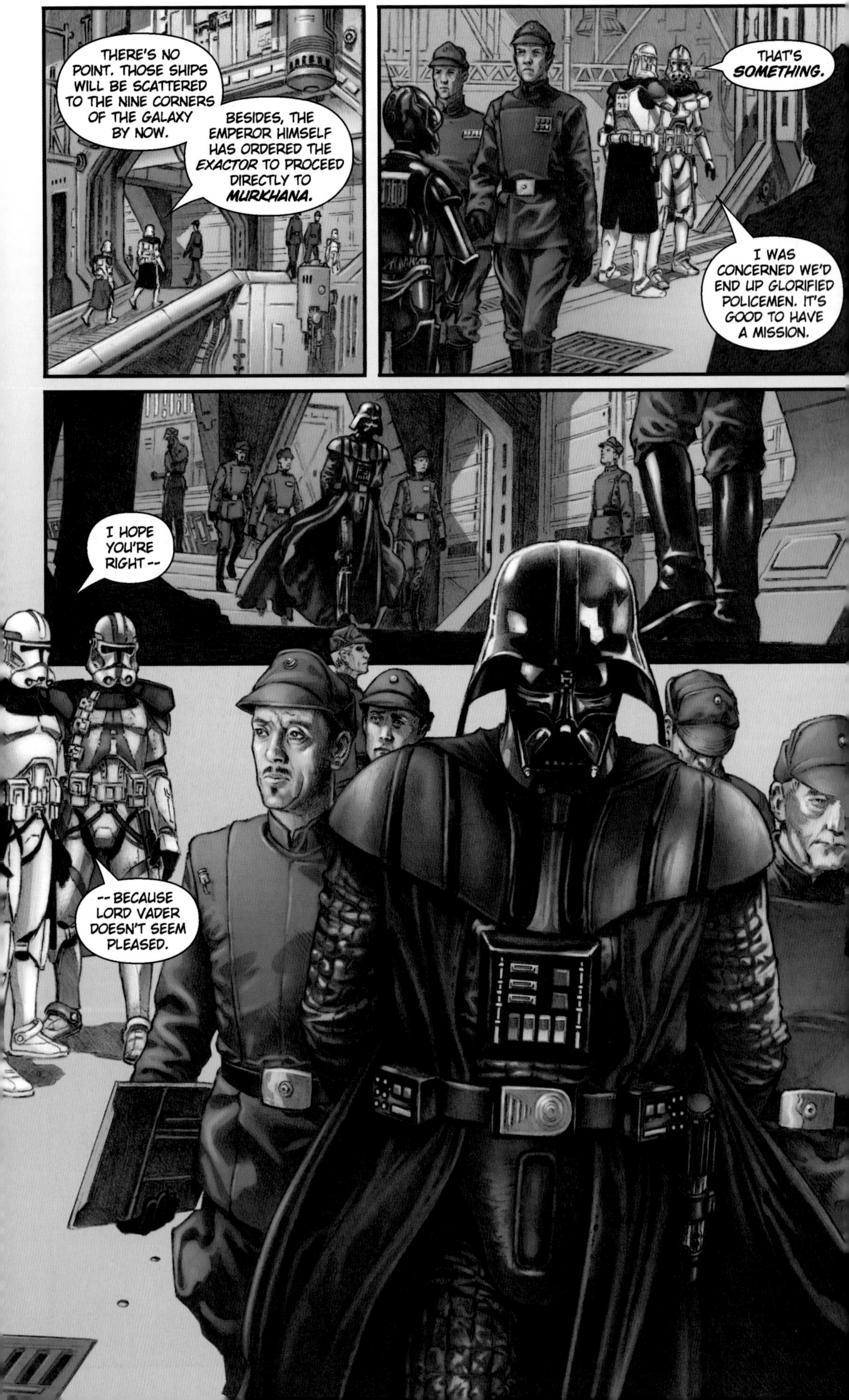
THERE'S NO POINT. THOSE SHIPS WILL BE SCATTERED TO THE NINE CORNERS OF THE GALAXY BY NOW.
BESIDES, THE EMPEROR HIMSELF HAS ORDERED THE *EXACTOR* TO PROCEED DIRECTLY TO ***MURKHANA.***
THAT'S ***SOMETHING.***
I WAS CONCERNED WE'D END UP GLORIFIED POLICEMEN. IT'S GOOD TO HAVE A MISSION.
I HOPE YOU'RE RIGHT --
-- BECAUSE LORD VADER DOESN'T SEEM PLEASED.

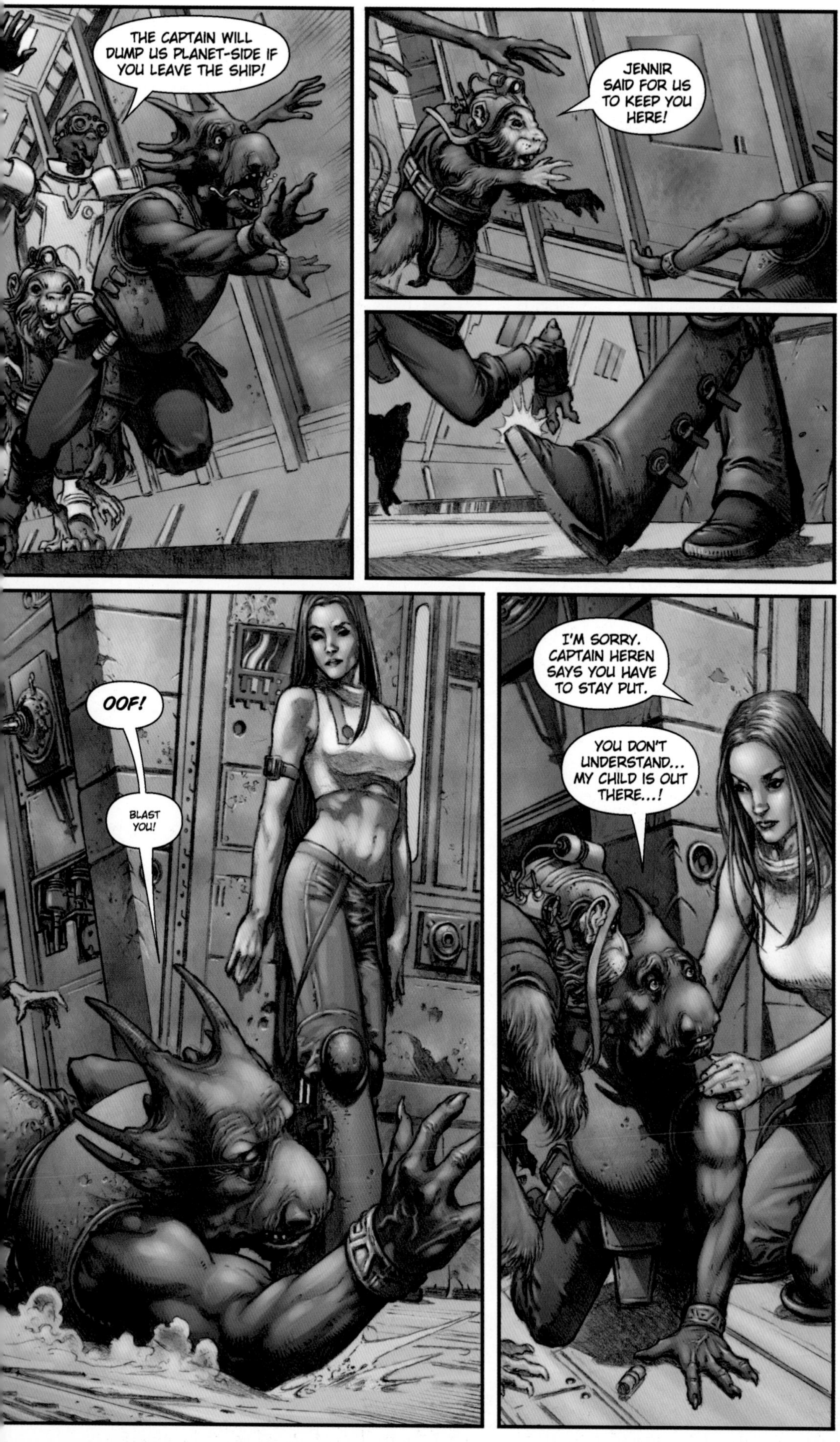
THE CAPTAIN WILL DUMP US PLANET-SIDE IF YOU LEAVE THE SHIP!
JENNIR SAID FOR US TO KEEP YOU HERE!
OOF!
BLAST YOU!
I'M SORRY. CAPTAIN HEREN SAYS YOU HAVE TO STAY PUT.
YOU DON'T UNDERSTAND... MY CHILD IS OUT THERE...!

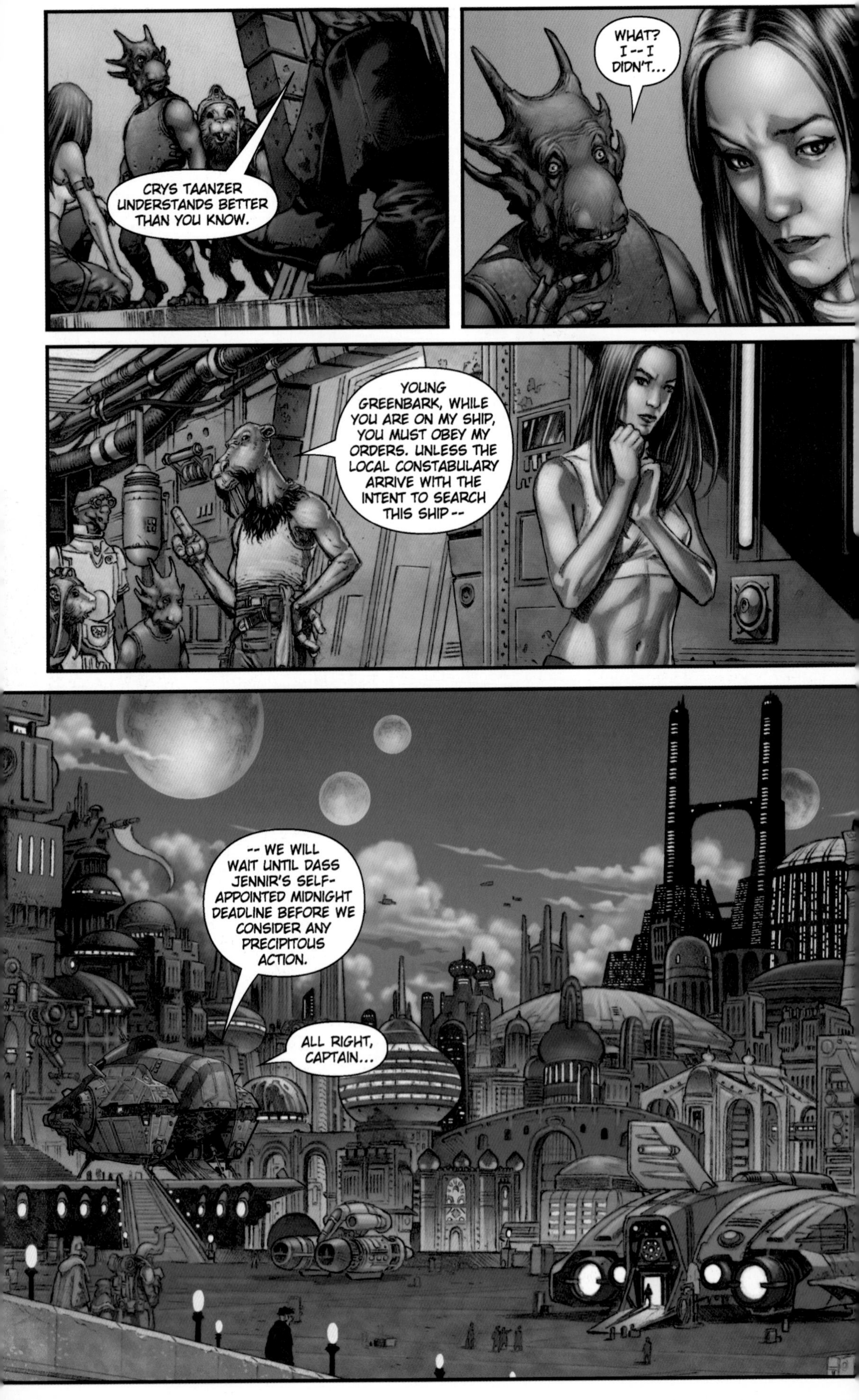
CRYS TAANZER UNDERSTANDS BETTER THAN YOU KNOW.
WHAT? I -- I DIDN'T...
YOUNG GREENBARK, WHILE YOU ARE ON MY SHIP, YOU MUST OBEY MY ORDERS. UNLESS THE LOCAL CONSTABULARY ARRIVE WITH THE INTENT TO SEARCH THIS SHIP --
-- WE WILL WAIT UNTIL DASS JENNIR'S SELF-APPOINTED MIDNIGHT DEADLINE BEFORE WE CONSIDER ANY PRECIPITOUS ACTION.
ALL RIGHT, CAPTAIN...

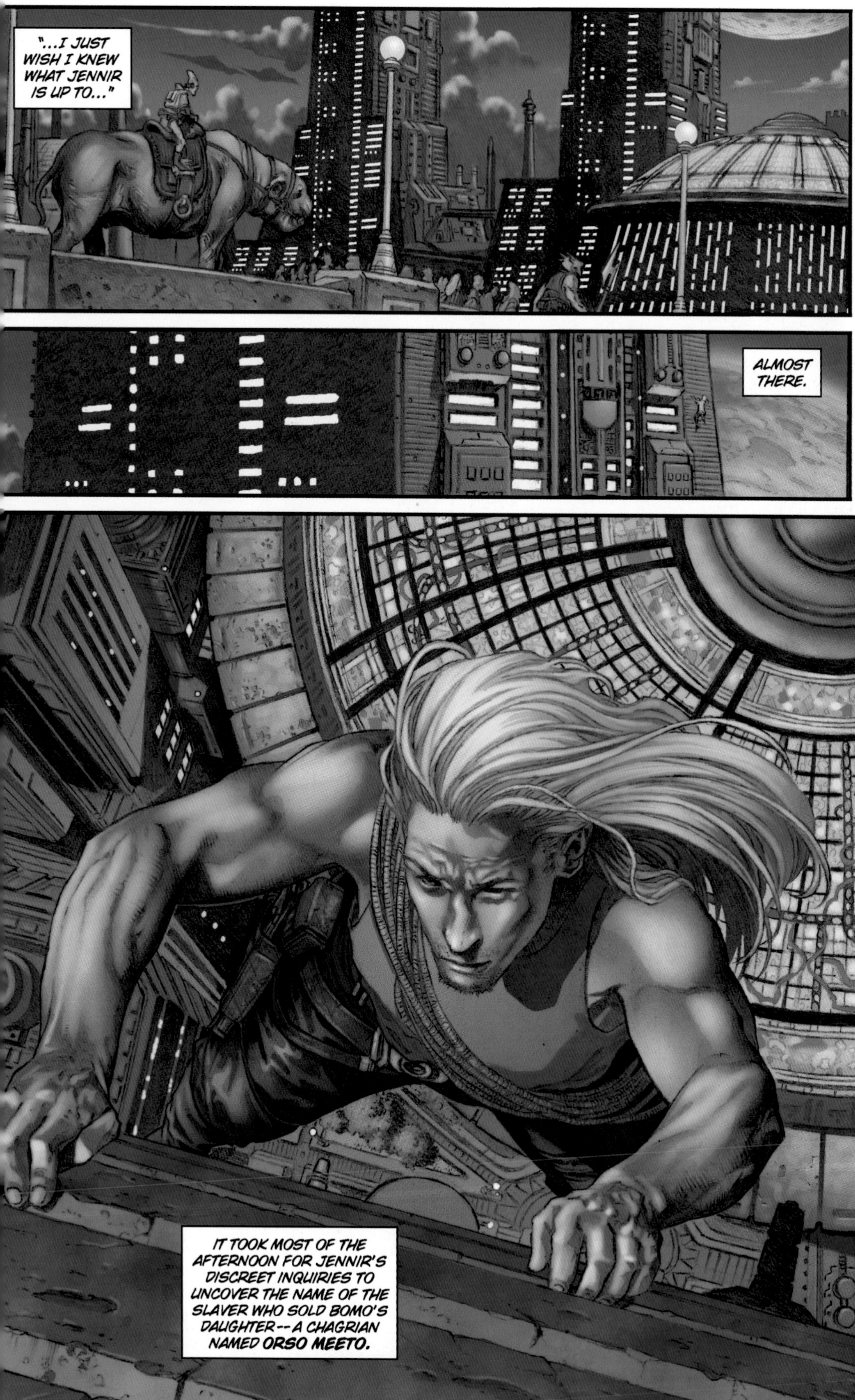
"...I JUST WISH I KNEW WHAT JENNIR IS UP TO..."
ALMOST THERE.
IT TOOK MOST OF THE AFTERNOON FOR JENNIR'S DISCREET INQUIRIES TO UNCOVER THE NAME OF THE SLAVER WHO SOLD BOMO'S DAUGHTER--A CHAGRIAN NAMED ORSO MEETO.

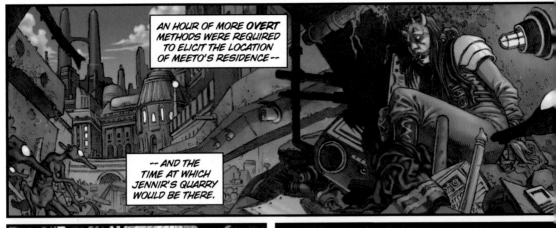

AN HOUR OF MORE *OVERT* METHODS WERE REQUIRED TO ELICIT THE LOCATION OF MEETO'S RESIDENCE --

-- AND THE TIME AT WHICH JENNIR'S QUARRY WOULD BE THERE.

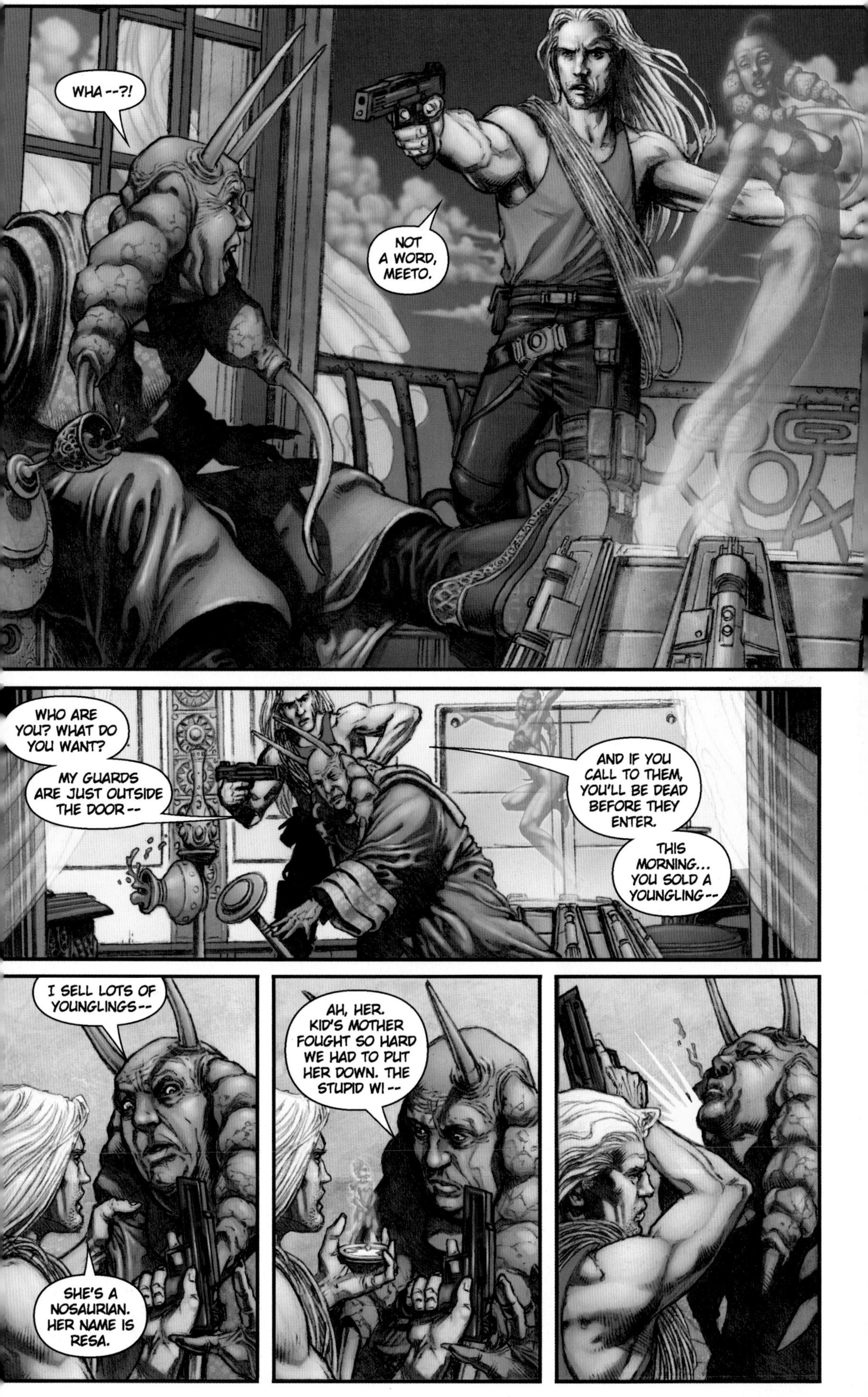
WHA--?!
NOT A WORD, MEETO.
WHO ARE YOU? WHAT DO YOU WANT?
MY GUARDS ARE JUST OUTSIDE THE DOOR--
AND IF YOU CALL TO THEM, YOU'LL BE DEAD BEFORE THEY ENTER.
THIS MORNING... YOU SOLD A YOUNGLING--
I SELL LOTS OF YOUNGLINGS--
SHE'S A NOSAURIAN. HER NAME IS RESA.
AH, HER. KID'S MOTHER FOUGHT SO HARD WE HAD TO PUT HER DOWN. THE STUPID WI--

WHO DID YOU SELL HER TO?

GIVE ME YOUR CLIENT'S NAME AND LOCATION AND I'LL BECOME *HIS* PROBLEM INSTEAD OF YOURS.

GUY'S NAME IS *DEZONO QUA*. HE'S A REGULAR CUSTOMER. FROM *ESSELES*. BUYS A NEW YOUNGLING EVERY TEN ROTATIONS, OR SO...

...HE'S HUMAN -- LIKE *YOU*...

...HEY -- I GAVE YOU WHAT YOU WANTED --

THIS IS THE PART OF THE PLAN JENNIR HADN'T FIGURED OUT.

WHAT'S TO KEEP MEETO FROM ALERTING HIS CLIENT AFTER HE LEAVES?

HEY...!

JUST ONE THING.

NO... DON'T DO IT...

BUT TO DO IT WILL MEAN DEPARTING FROM THE JEDI PATH. POSSIBLY FOREVER.

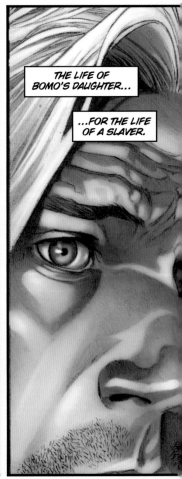

THE LIFE OF BOMO'S DAUGHTER...

...FOR THE LIFE OF A SLAVER.

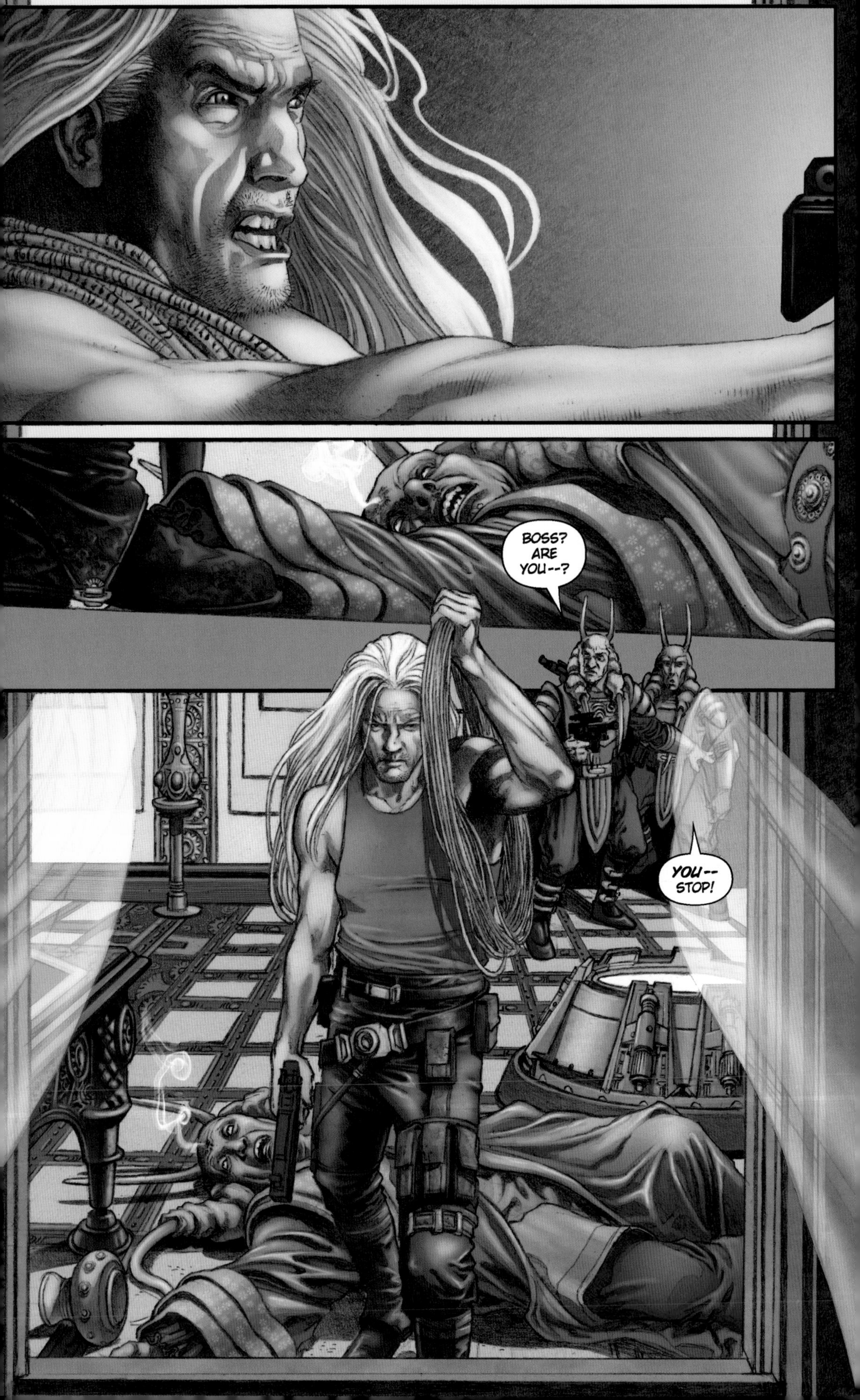
BOSS? ARE YOU--?
YOU-- STOP!

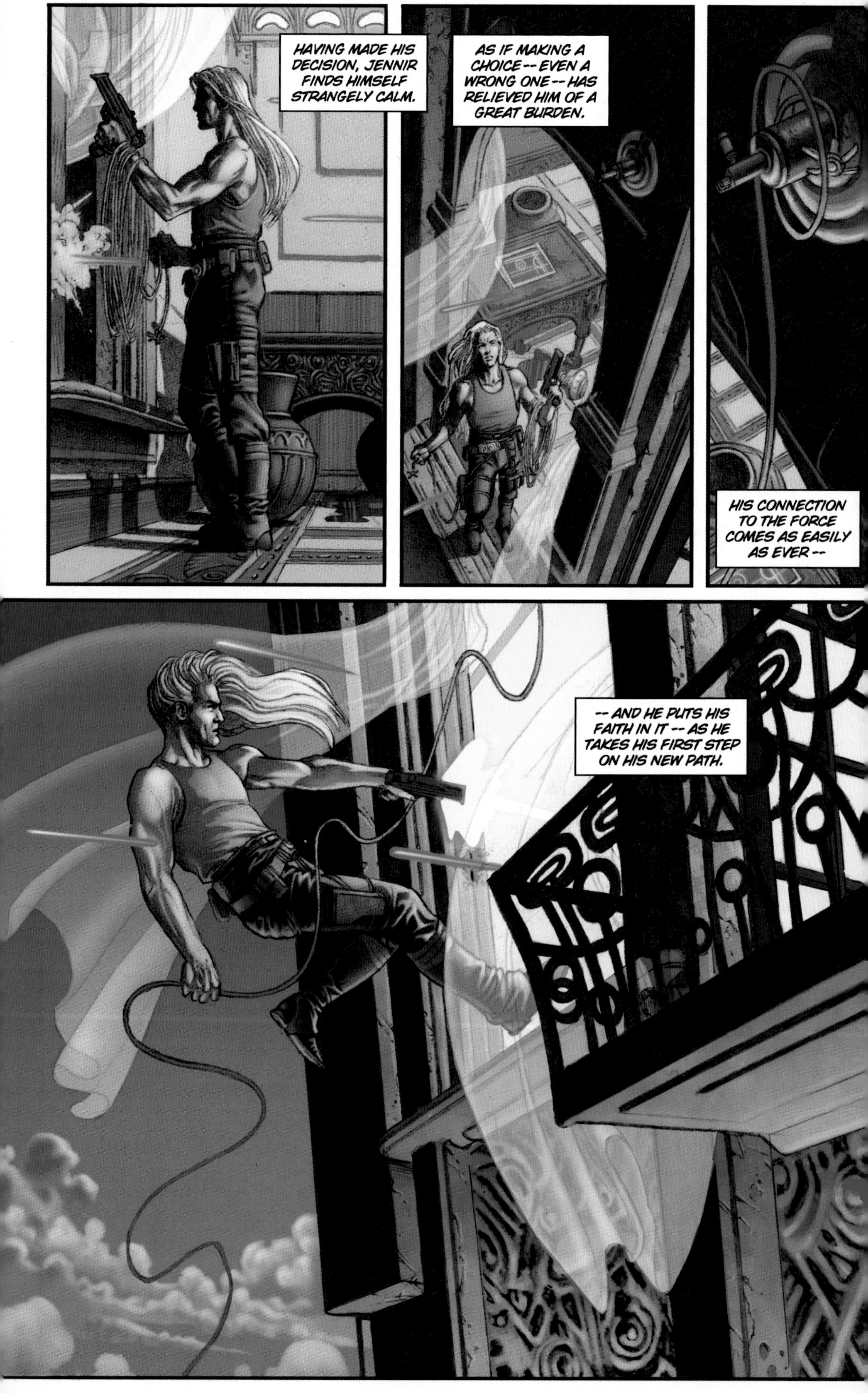
HAVING MADE HIS DECISION, JENNIR FINDS HIMSELF STRANGELY CALM.
AS IF MAKING A CHOICE -- EVEN A WRONG ONE -- HAS RELIEVED HIM OF A GREAT BURDEN.
HIS CONNECTION TO THE FORCE COMES AS EASILY AS EVER --
-- AND HE PUTS HIS FAITH IN IT -- AS HE TAKES HIS FIRST STEP ON HIS NEW PATH.

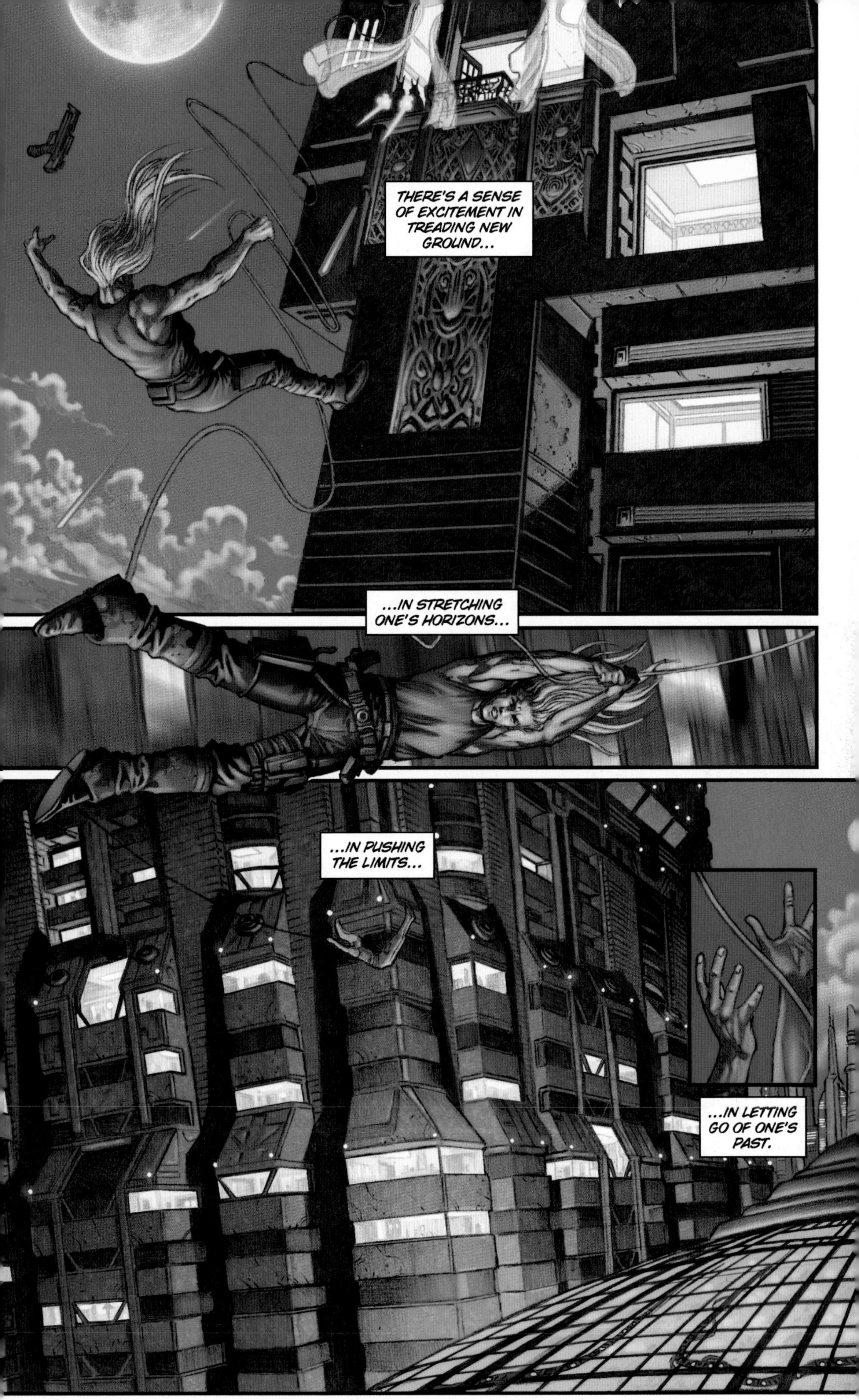
THERE'S A SENSE OF EXCITEMENT IN TREADING NEW GROUND...
...IN STRETCHING ONE'S HORIZONS...
...IN PUSHING THE LIMITS...
...IN LETTING GO OF ONE'S PAST.

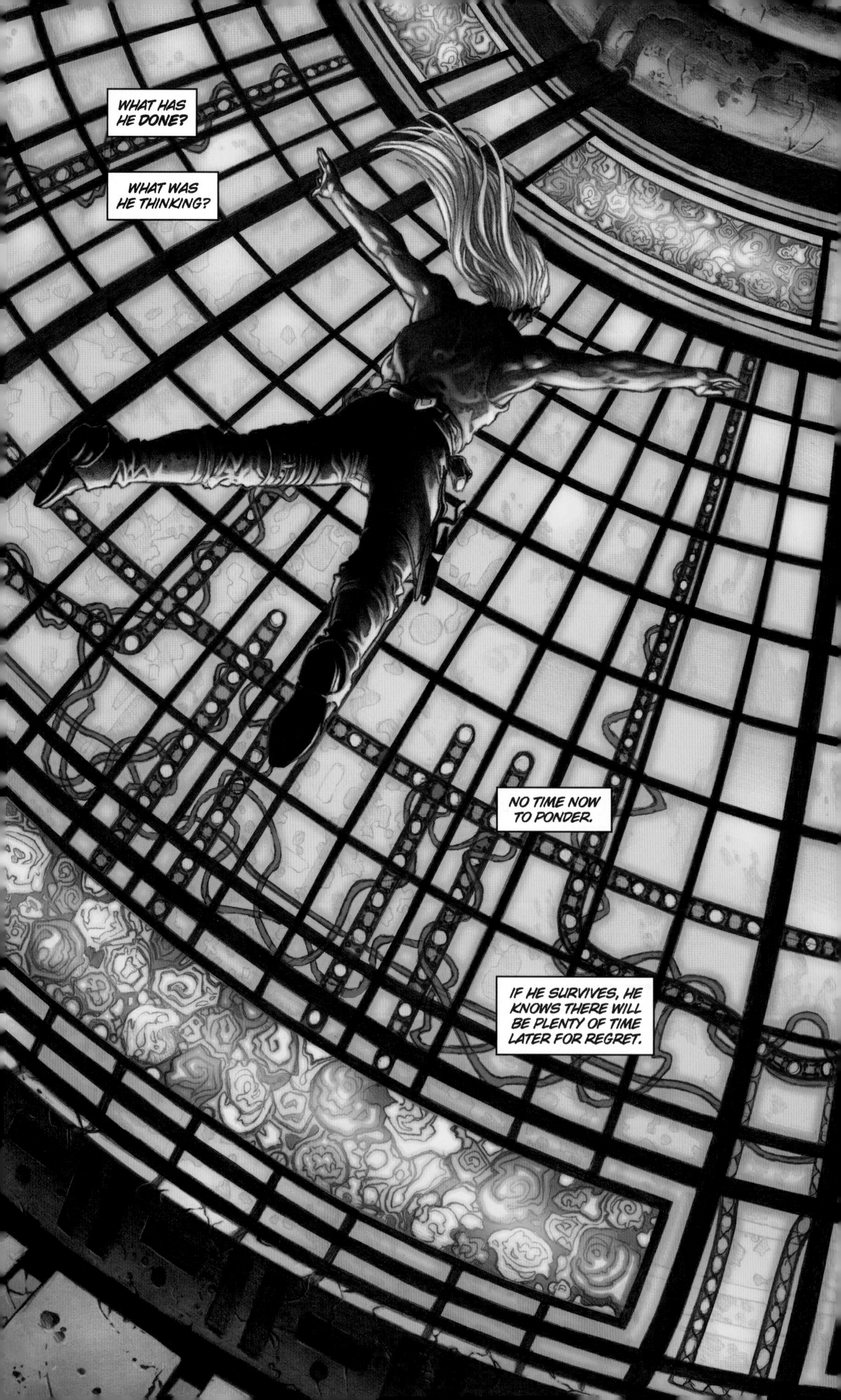
WHAT HAS HE DONE?
WHAT WAS HE THINKING?
NO TIME NOW TO PONDER.
IF HE SURVIVES, HE KNOWS THERE WILL BE PLENTY OF TIME LATER FOR REGRET.

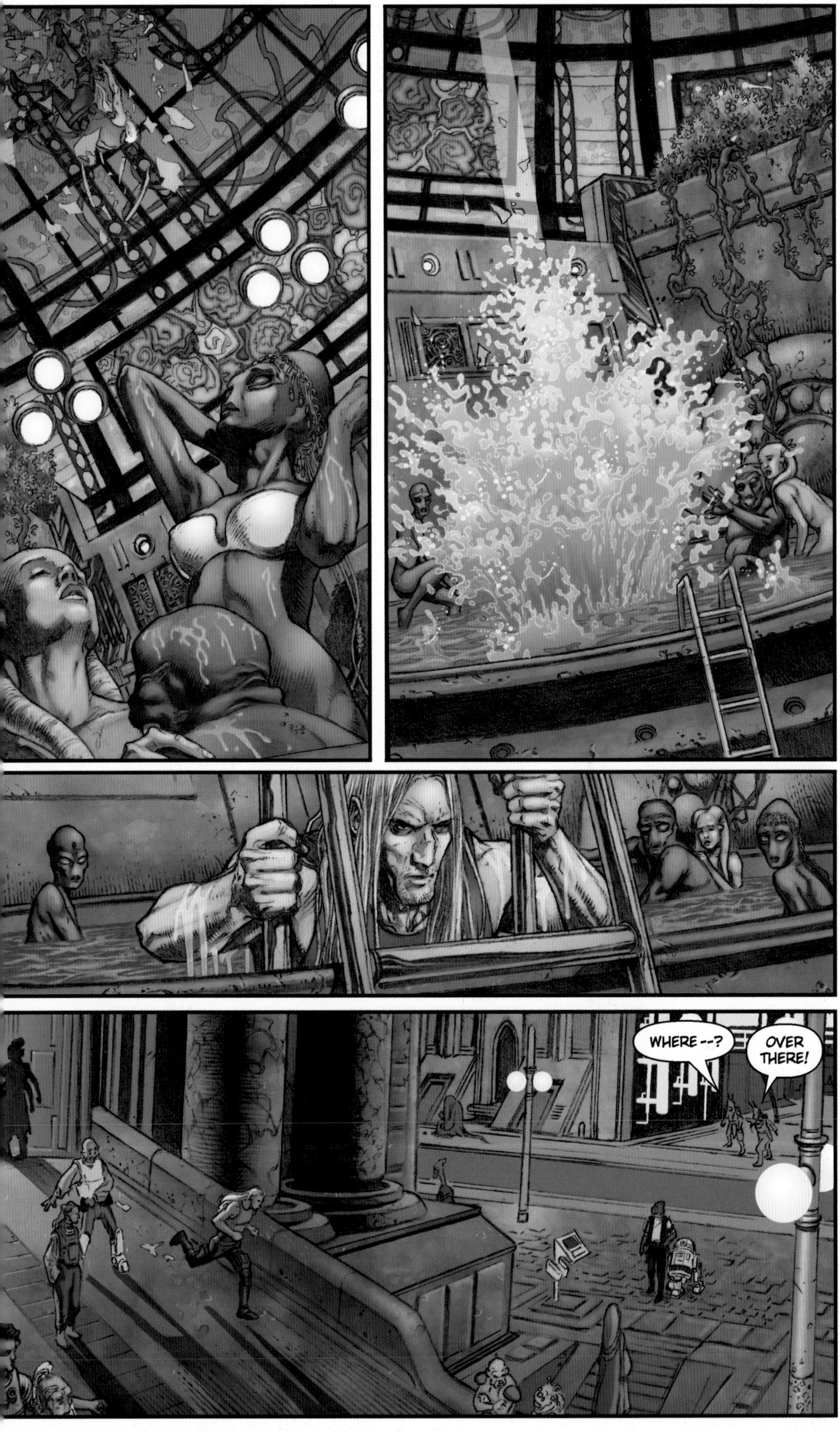
WHERE --?
OVER THERE!

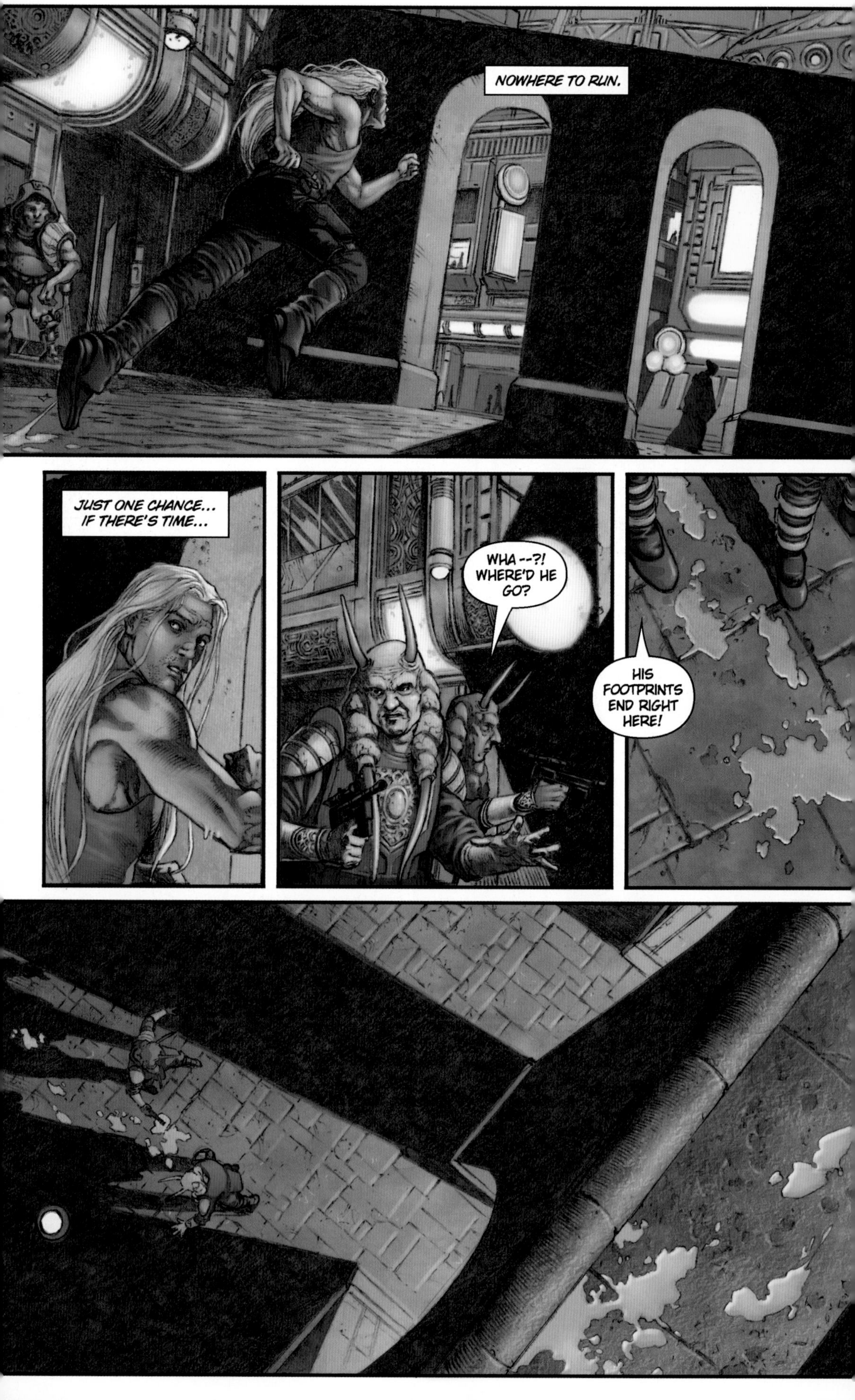
NOWHERE TO RUN.
JUST ONE CHANCE... IF THERE'S TIME...
WHA --?! WHERE'D HE GO?
HIS FOOTPRINTS END RIGHT HERE!

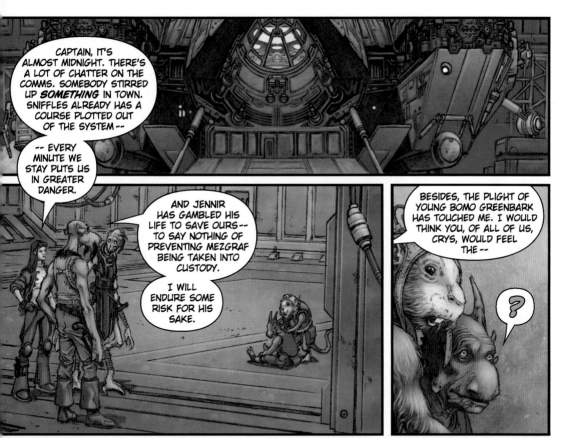

CAPTAIN, IT'S ALMOST MIDNIGHT. THERE'S A LOT OF CHATTER ON THE COMMS. SOMEBODY STIRRED UP *SOMETHING* IN TOWN. SNIFFLES ALREADY HAS A COURSE PLOTTED OUT OF THE SYSTEM --

-- EVERY MINUTE WE STAY PUTS US IN GREATER DANGER.

AND JENNIR HAS GAMBLED HIS LIFE TO SAVE OURS -- TO SAY NOTHING OF PREVENTING MEZGRAF BEING TAKEN INTO CUSTODY.

I WILL ENDURE SOME RISK FOR HIS SAKE.

BESIDES, THE PLIGHT OF YOUNG BOMO GREENBARK HAS TOUCHED ME. I WOULD THINK YOU, OF ALL OF US, CRYS, WOULD FEEL THE --

?

JENNIR!

ARE YOU ALL RIGHT? DID YOU --?

I'LL LIVE. AND YES --

-- I FOUND WHERE RESA HAS BEEN TAKEN.

HERE ARE THE COORDINATES.

SNIFFLES, NEW COURSE. ESSELES. WE'RE LEAVING.

IT'S ABOUT TIME!

IT'S A GOOD THING THAT WE'RE *USED* TO THESE SHORT-NOTICE TAKE-OFFS --

-- BECAUSE IT SEEMS TO BE A REGULAR THING WITH YOU.

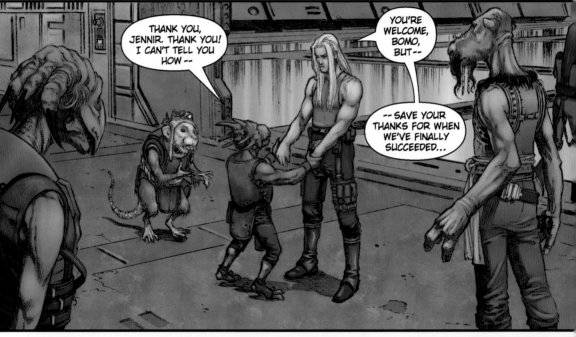

THANK YOU, JENNIR. THANK YOU! I CAN'T TELL YOU HOW --

YOU'RE WELCOME, BOMO, BUT--

-- SAVE YOUR THANKS FOR WHEN WE'VE FINALLY SUCCEEDED...

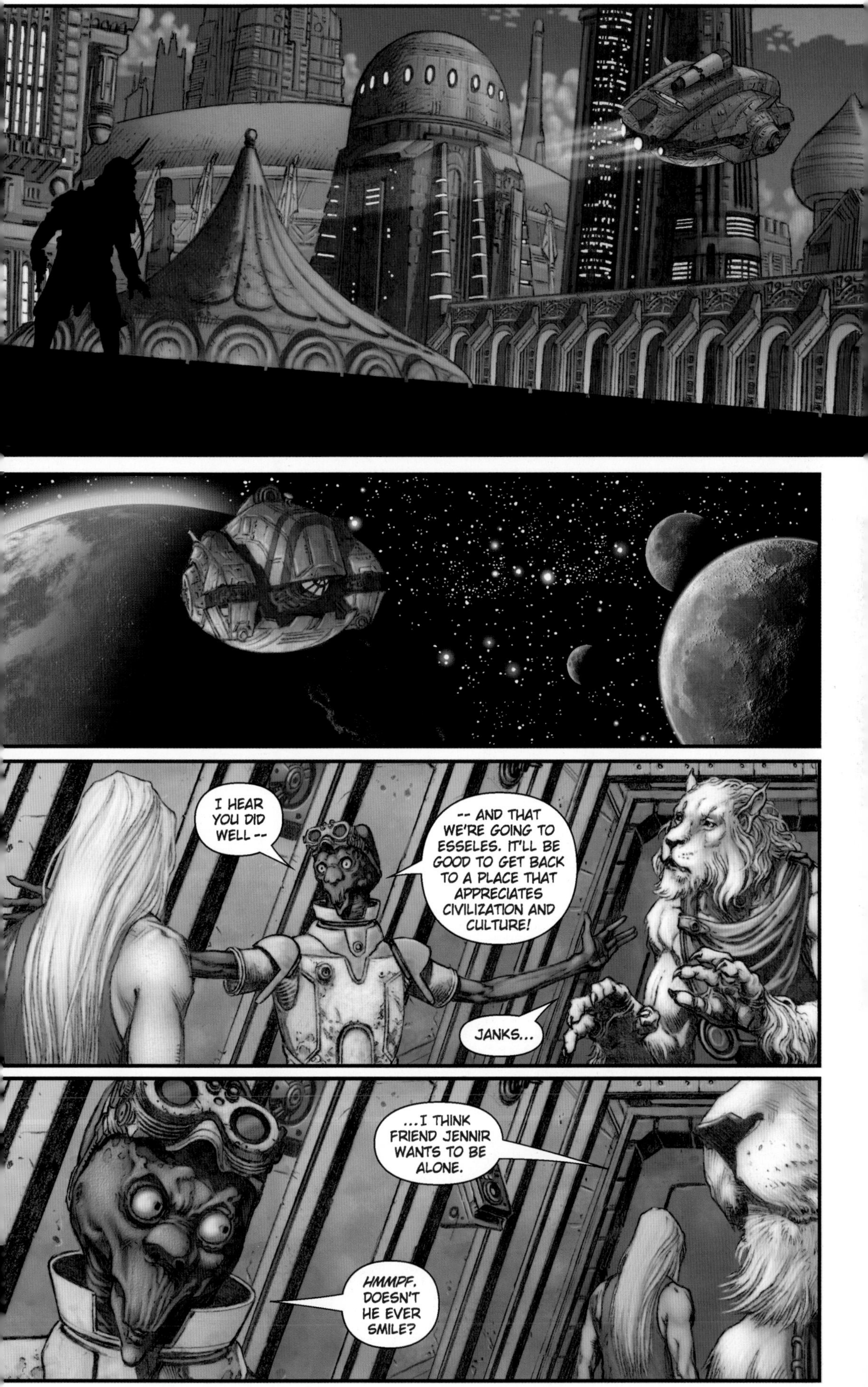
I HEAR YOU DID WELL --
-- AND THAT WE'RE GOING TO ESSELES. IT'LL BE GOOD TO GET BACK TO A PLACE THAT APPRECIATES CIVILIZATION AND CULTURE!
JANKS...
...I THINK FRIEND JENNIR WANTS TO BE ALONE.
HMMPF. DOESN'T HE EVER SMILE?

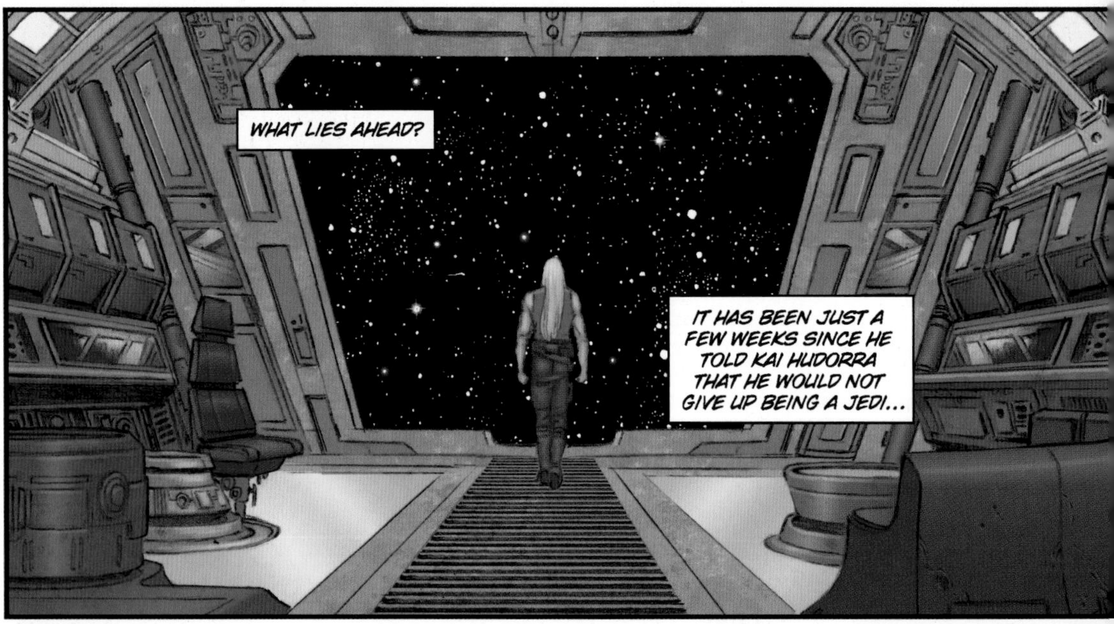
WHAT LIES AHEAD?
IT HAS BEEN JUST A FEW WEEKS SINCE HE TOLD KAI HUDORRA THAT HE WOULD NOT GIVE UP BEING A JEDI...
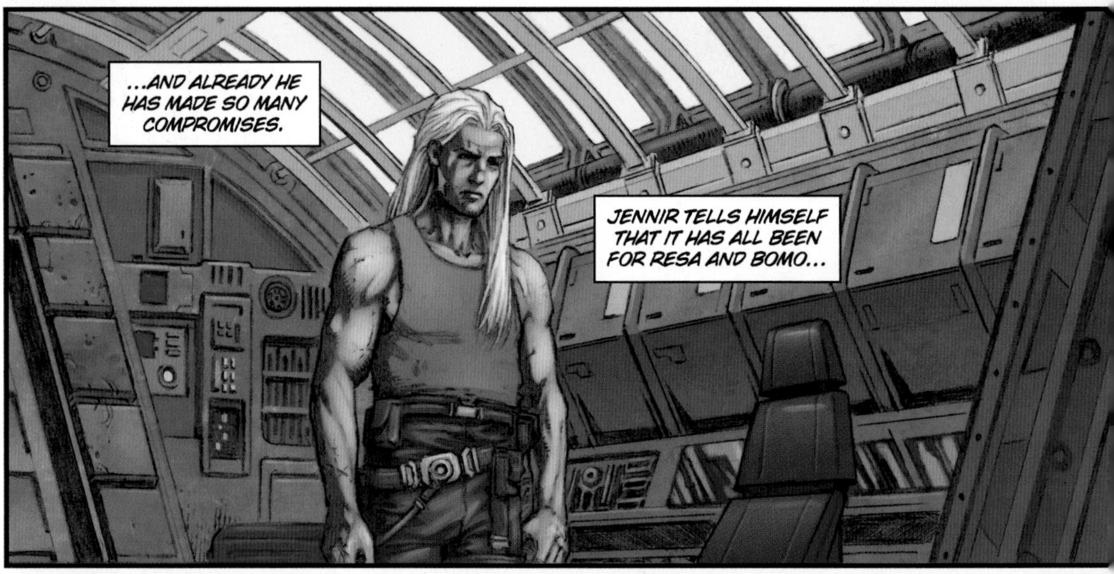
...AND ALREADY HE HAS MADE SO MANY COMPROMISES.
JENNIR TELLS HIMSELF THAT IT HAS ALL BEEN FOR RESA AND BOMO...
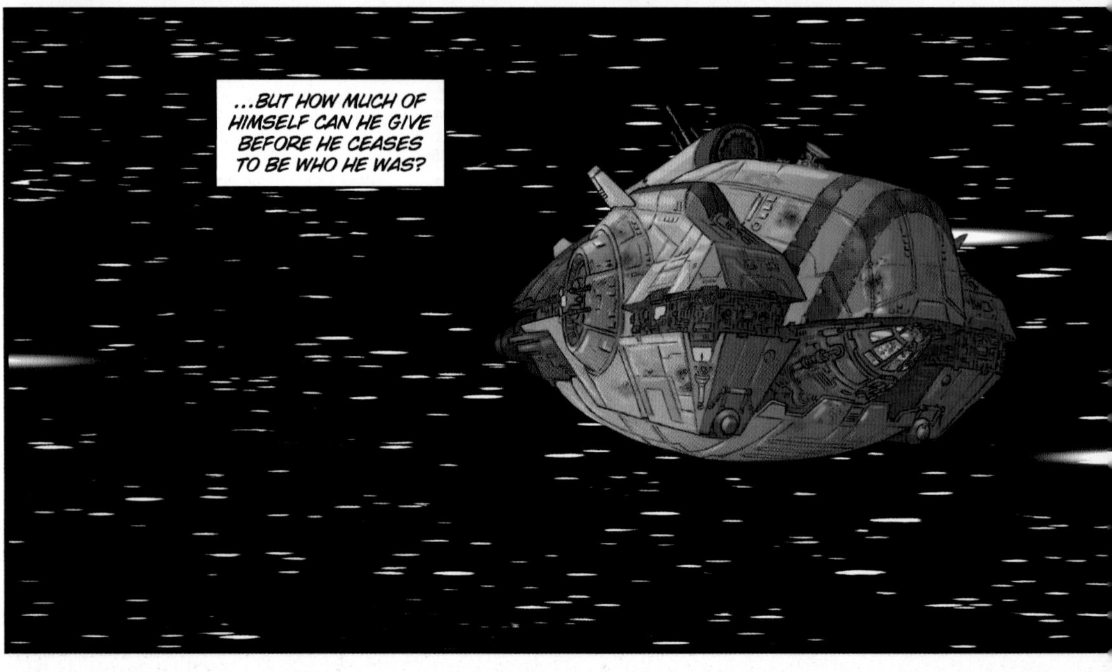
...BUT HOW MUCH OF HIMSELF CAN HE GIVE BEFORE HE CEASES TO BE WHO HE WAS?

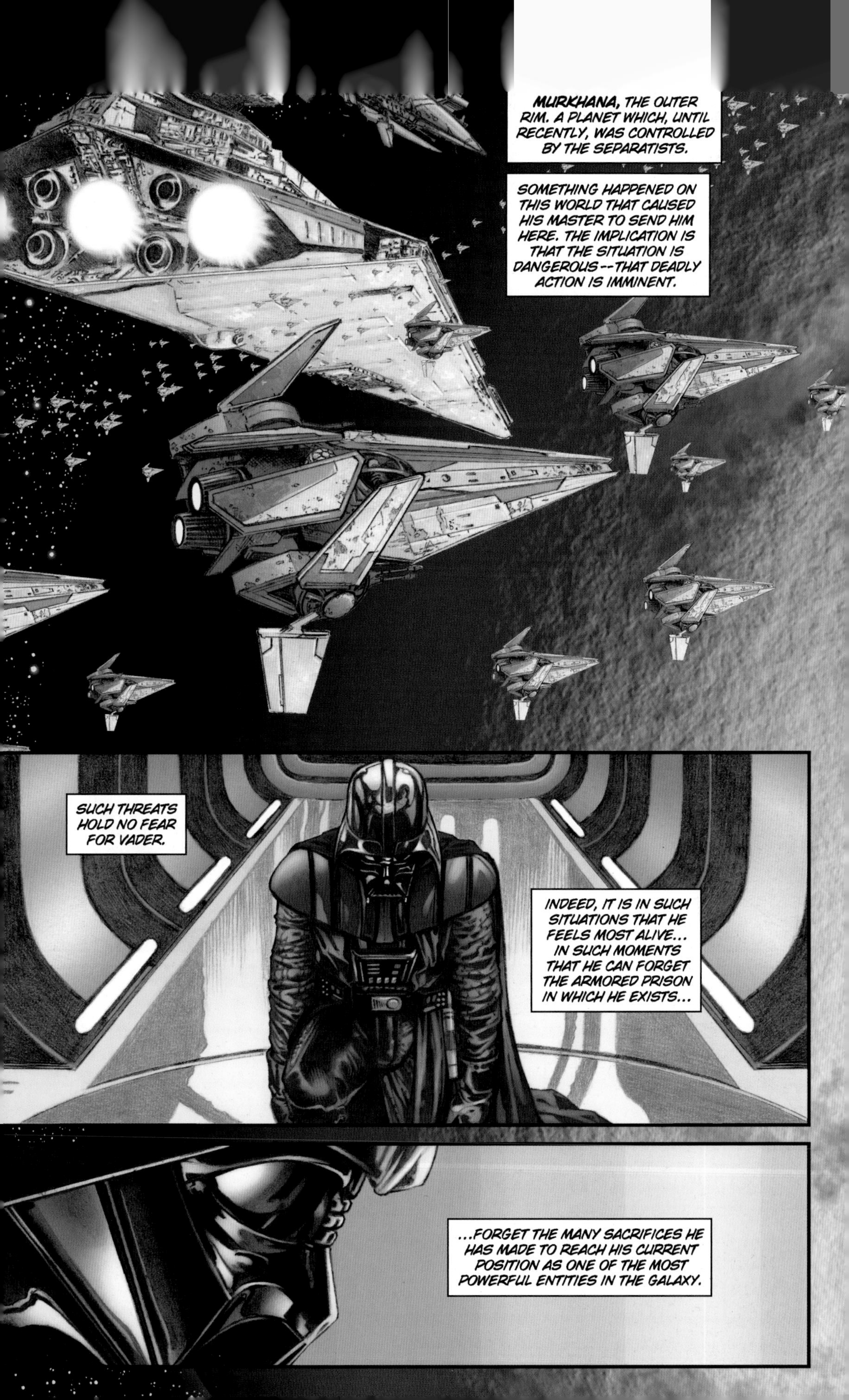
MURKHANA, THE OUTER RIM. A PLANET WHICH, UNTIL RECENTLY, WAS CONTROLLED BY THE SEPARATISTS.
SOMETHING HAPPENED ON THIS WORLD THAT CAUSED HIS MASTER TO SEND HIM HERE. THE IMPLICATION IS THAT THE SITUATION IS DANGEROUS--THAT DEADLY ACTION IS IMMINENT.
SUCH THREATS HOLD NO FEAR FOR VADER.
INDEED, IT IS IN SUCH SITUATIONS THAT HE FEELS MOST ALIVE... IN SUCH MOMENTS THAT HE CAN FORGET THE ARMORED PRISON IN WHICH HE EXISTS...
...FORGET THE MANY SACRIFICES HE HAS MADE TO REACH HIS CURRENT POSITION AS ONE OF THE MOST POWERFUL ENTITIES IN THE GALAXY.

IT IS A FACT VADER WISHES HIS MASTER WAS NOT SO KEENLY AWARE.

...IN DUE TIME, POWER WILL FILL THE VACUUM CREATED BY THE DECISIONS YOU MADE...THE ACTS YOU CARRIED OUT. *MARRIED* TO THE ORDER OF THE SITH --

" --YOU WILL NEED *NO OTHER COMPANION* THAN THE DARK SIDE OF THE FORCE."

WORD HAS REACHED ME THAT A GROUP OF CLONE TROOPERS ON MURKHANA MAY HAVE DELIBERATELY REFUSED TO COMPLY WITH *ORDER SIXTY-SIX...*

I HAD NOT HEARD.

WHAT WAS THE CAUSE OF THE TROOPERS' INSUBORDINATION, MASTER?

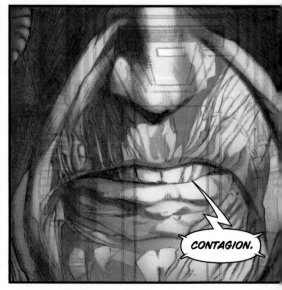

CONTAGION.

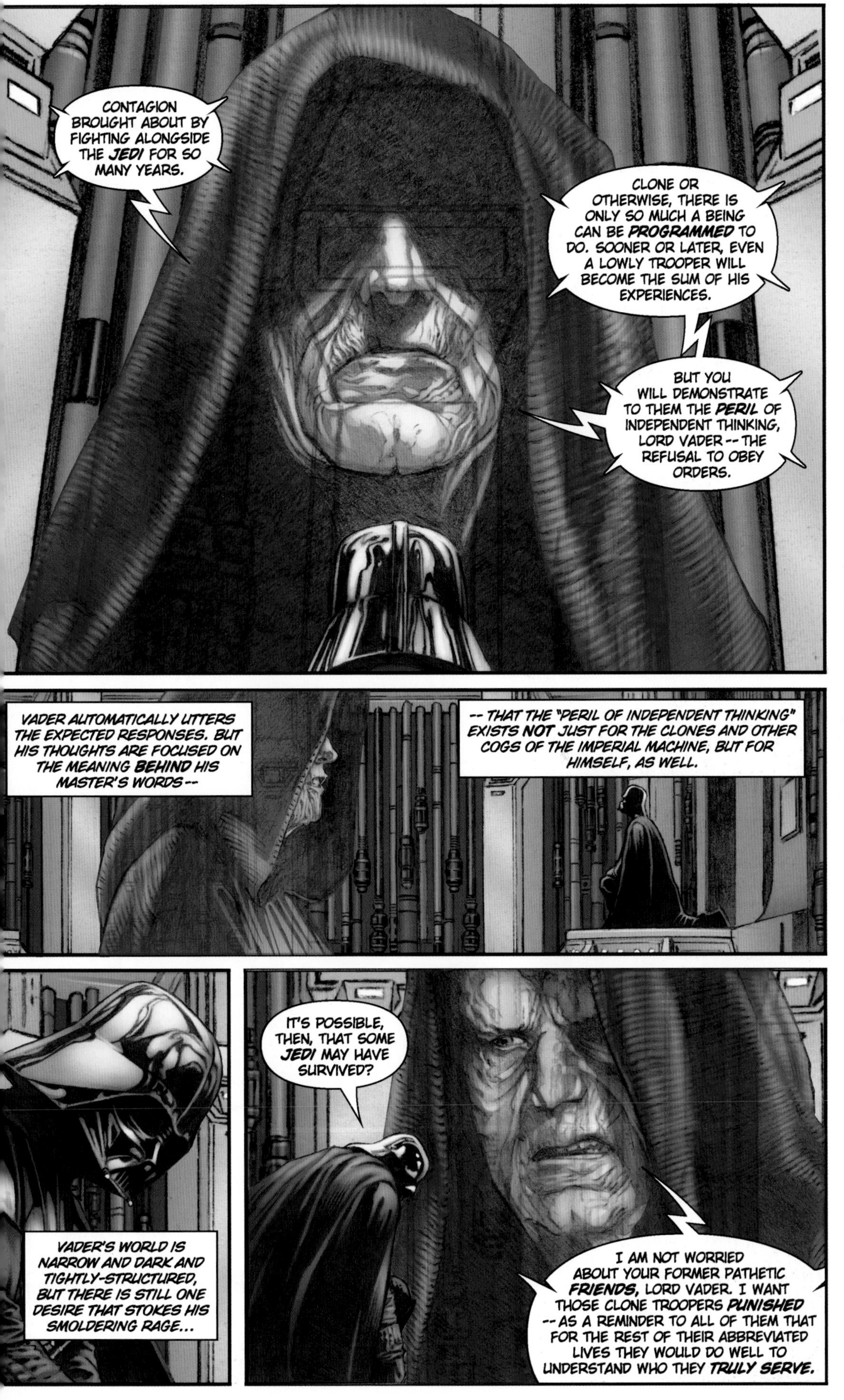
CONTAGION BROUGHT ABOUT BY FIGHTING ALONGSIDE THE JEDI FOR SO MANY YEARS.
CLONE OR OTHERWISE, THERE IS ONLY SO MUCH A BEING CAN BE PROGRAMMED TO DO. SOONER OR LATER, EVEN A LOWLY TROOPER WILL BECOME THE SUM OF HIS EXPERIENCES.
BUT YOU WILL DEMONSTRATE TO THEM THE PERIL OF INDEPENDENT THINKING, LORD VADER -- THE REFUSAL TO OBEY ORDERS.
VADER AUTOMATICALLY UTTERS THE EXPECTED RESPONSES. BUT HIS THOUGHTS ARE FOCUSED ON THE MEANING BEHIND HIS MASTER'S WORDS--
-- THAT THE "PERIL OF INDEPENDENT THINKING" EXISTS NOT JUST FOR THE CLONES AND OTHER COGS OF THE IMPERIAL MACHINE, BUT FOR HIMSELF, AS WELL.
VADER'S WORLD IS NARROW AND DARK AND TIGHTLY-STRUCTURED, BUT THERE IS STILL ONE DESIRE THAT STOKES HIS SMOLDERING RAGE...
IT'S POSSIBLE, THEN, THAT SOME JEDI MAY HAVE SURVIVED?
I AM NOT WORRIED ABOUT YOUR FORMER PATHETIC FRIENDS, LORD VADER. I WANT THOSE CLONE TROOPERS PUNISHED -- AS A REMINDER TO ALL OF THEM THAT FOR THE REST OF THEIR ABBREVIATED LIVES THEY WOULD DO WELL TO UNDERSTAND WHO THEY TRULY SERVE.

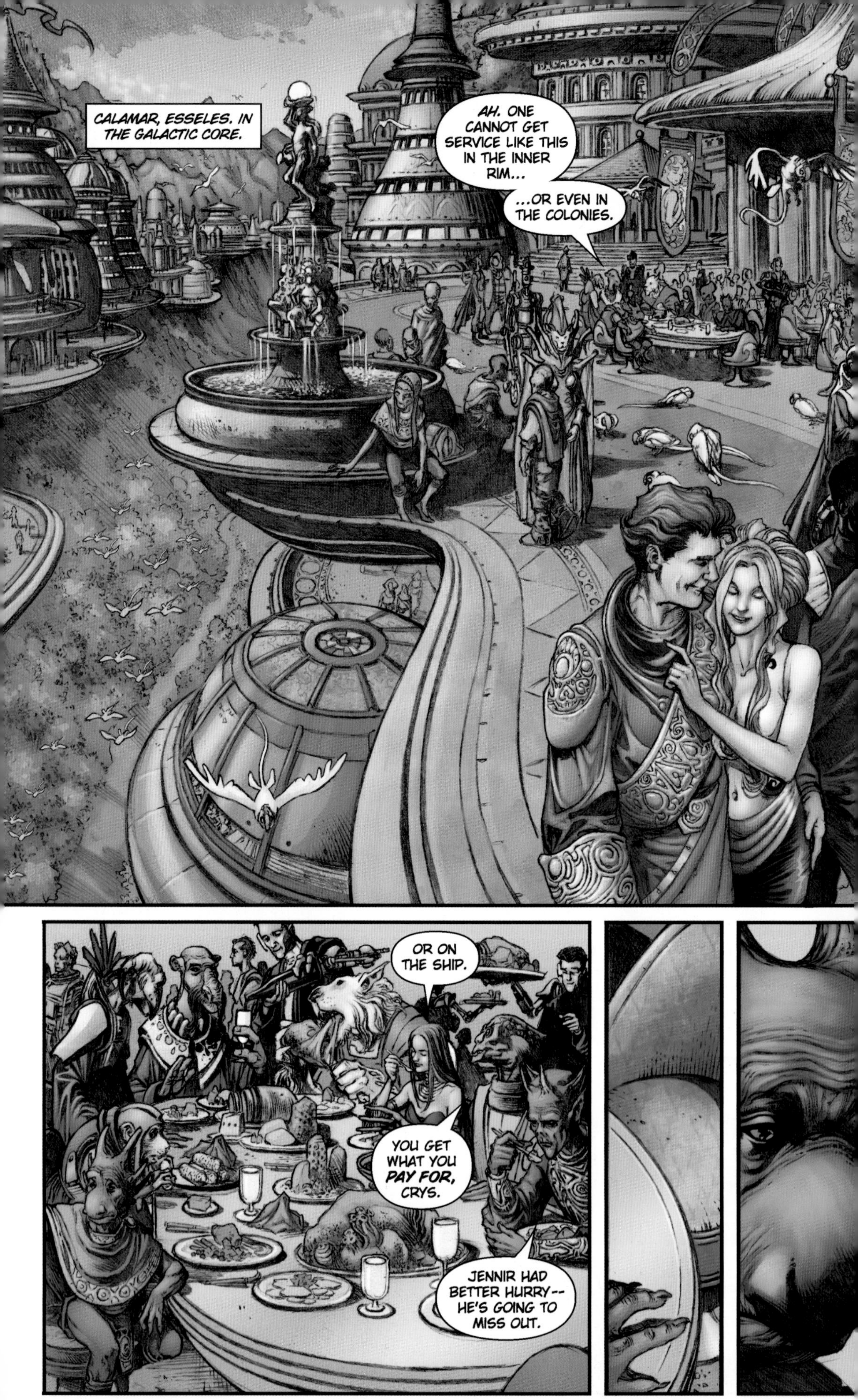
CALAMAR, ESSELES. IN THE GALACTIC CORE.
AH. ONE CANNOT GET SERVICE LIKE THIS IN THE INNER RIM...
...OR EVEN IN THE COLONIES.
OR ON THE SHIP.
YOU GET WHAT YOU PAY FOR, CRYS.
JENNIR HAD BETTER HURRY--HE'S GOING TO MISS OUT.

YES...
I HOPE HE
HASN'T RUN INTO
TROUBLE...

"...LOCAL OFFICIALS CAN
BE SO...OFFICIOUS."

DON'T
WORRY,
BOMO --

" -- I'M SURE JENNIR
CAN TAKE CARE OF
HIMSELF."

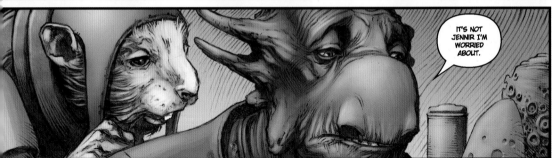

IT'S NOT
JENNIR I'M
WORRIED
ABOUT.

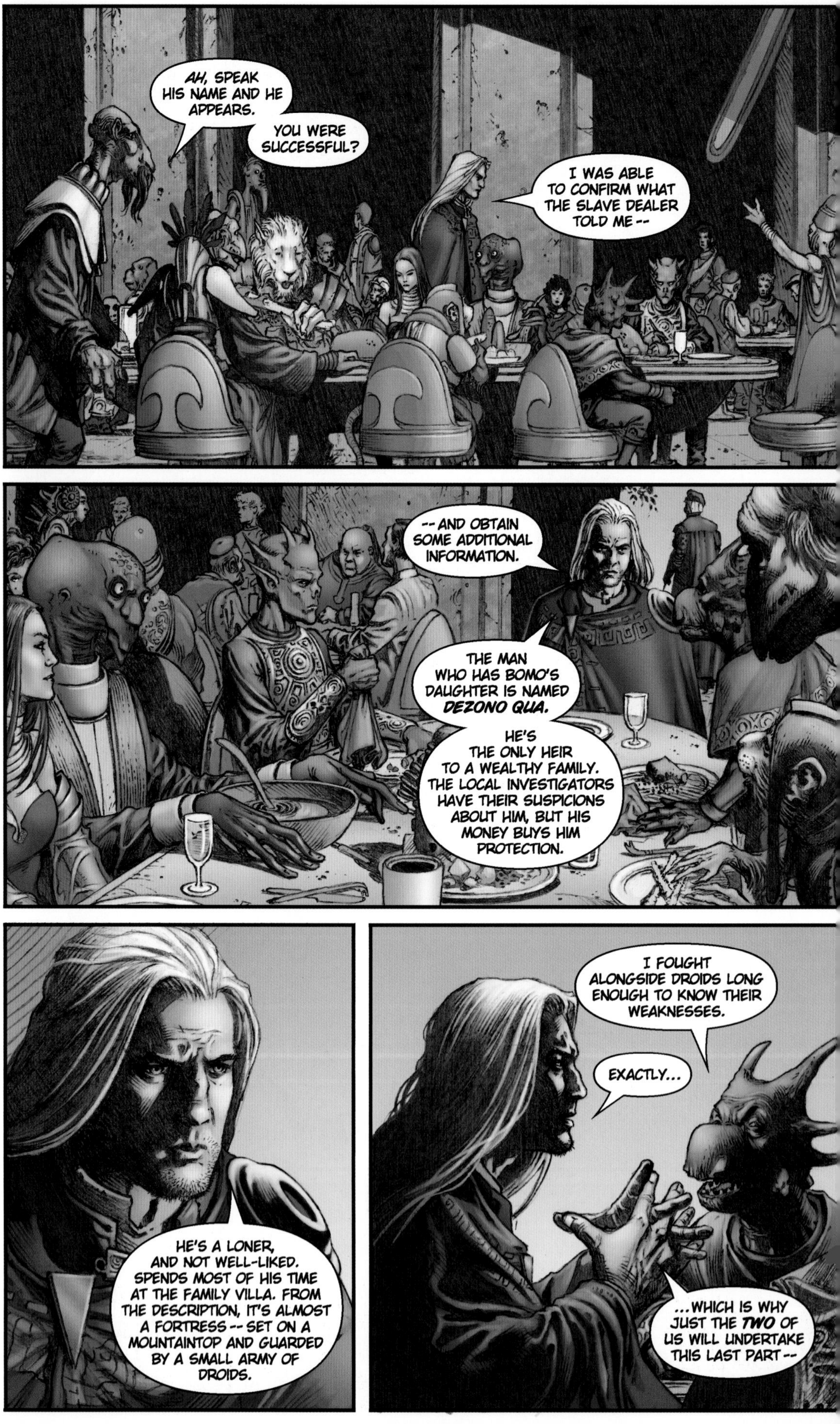
AH, SPEAK HIS NAME AND HE APPEARS.
YOU WERE SUCCESSFUL?
I WAS ABLE TO CONFIRM WHAT THE SLAVE DEALER TOLD ME --
-- AND OBTAIN SOME ADDITIONAL INFORMATION.
THE MAN WHO HAS BOMO'S DAUGHTER IS NAMED DEZONO QUA.
HE'S THE ONLY HEIR TO A WEALTHY FAMILY. THE LOCAL INVESTIGATORS HAVE THEIR SUSPICIONS ABOUT HIM, BUT HIS MONEY BUYS HIM PROTECTION.
HE'S A LONER, AND NOT WELL-LIKED. SPENDS MOST OF HIS TIME AT THE FAMILY VILLA. FROM THE DESCRIPTION, IT'S ALMOST A FORTRESS -- SET ON A MOUNTAINTOP AND GUARDED BY A SMALL ARMY OF DROIDS.
I FOUGHT ALONGSIDE DROIDS LONG ENOUGH TO KNOW THEIR WEAKNESSES.
EXACTLY...
...WHICH IS WHY JUST THE TWO OF US WILL UNDERTAKE THIS LAST PART --

NO! I WON'T HEAR OF IT!

I PLEDGED MY SWORD TO THIS CAUSE, AND THERE IS YET MORE CUTTING TO BE DONE.

I WILL SEE IT THROUGH!

AS WILL I.

SLAVERY DOES NOT SIT WELL WITH ME. THE ENSLAVEMENT OF CHILDREN LEAST OF ALL. I BELIEVE YOU CAN COUNT ON ALL OF US.

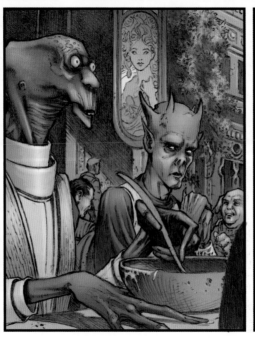

OH, SURE. EVERYBODY STARE AT THE PHINDIAN.

I NEVER SAID I WASN'T IN!

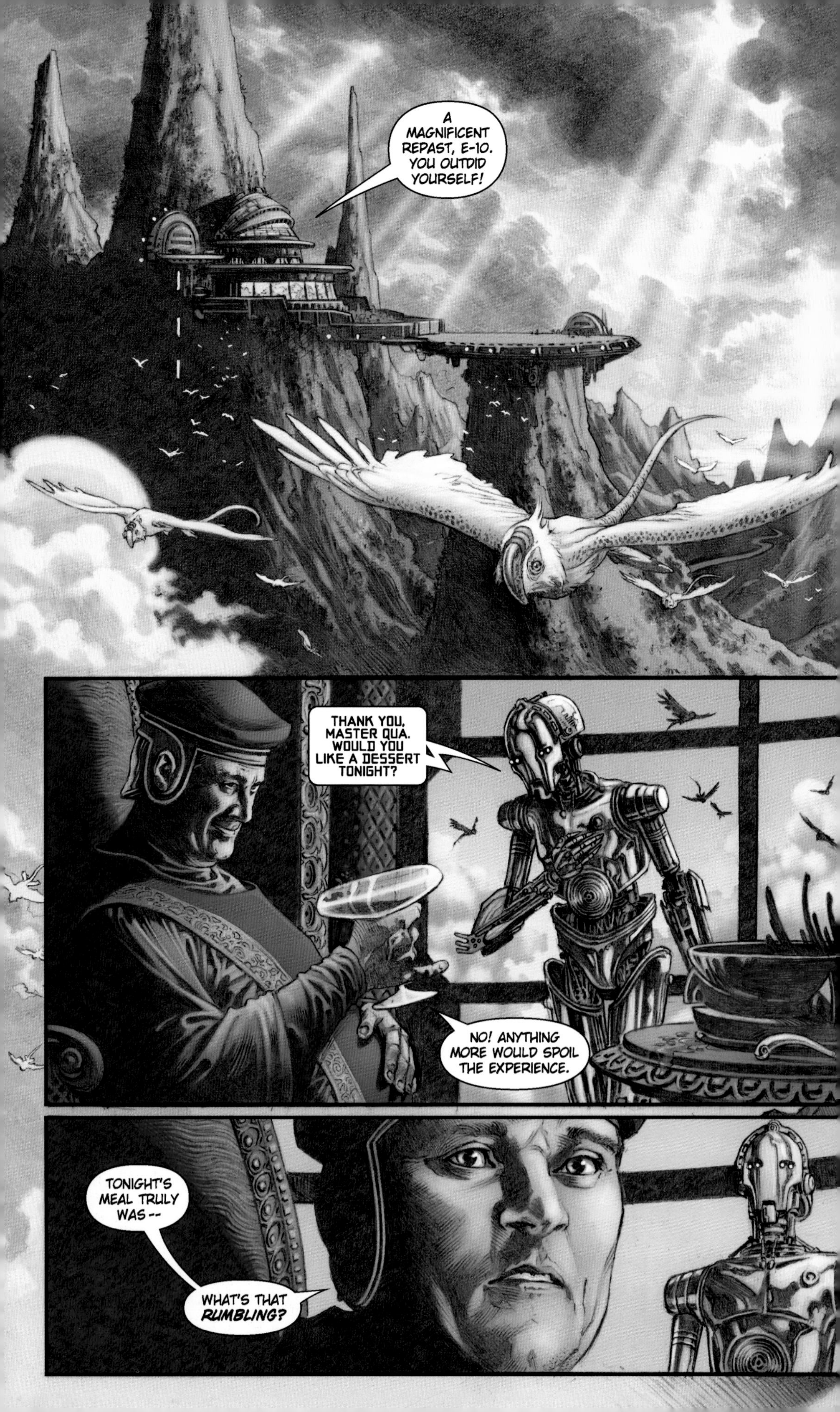
A MAGNIFICENT REPAST, E-10. YOU OUTDID YOURSELF!
THANK YOU, MASTER QUA. WOULD YOU LIKE A DESSERT TONIGHT?
NO! ANYTHING MORE WOULD SPOIL THE EXPERIENCE.
TONIGHT'S MEAL TRULY WAS --
WHAT'S THAT *RUMBLING?*

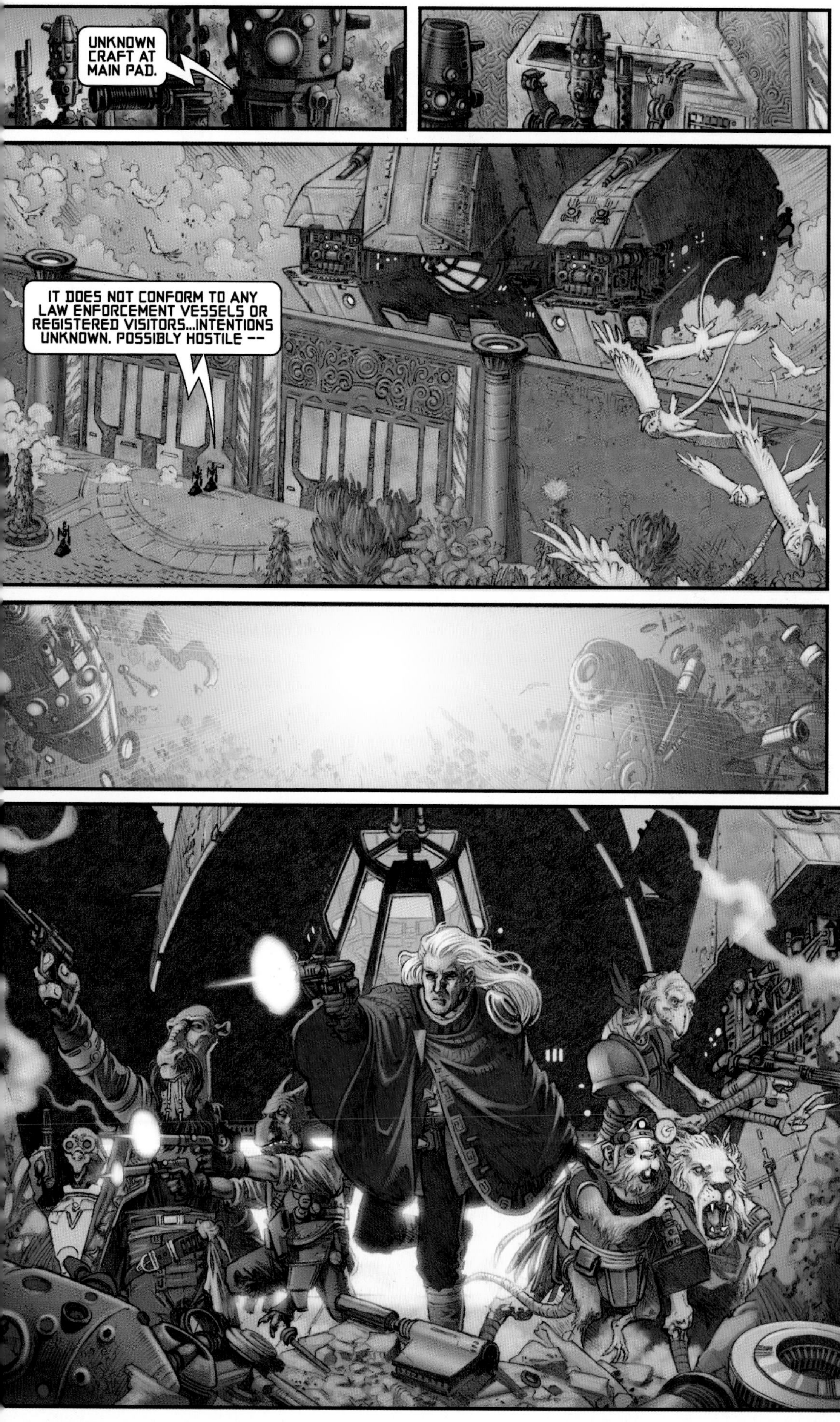
UNKNOWN CRAFT AT MAIN PAD.
IT DOES NOT CONFORM TO ANY LAW ENFORCEMENT VESSELS OR REGISTERED VISITORS...INTENTIONS UNKNOWN. POSSIBLY HOSTILE --

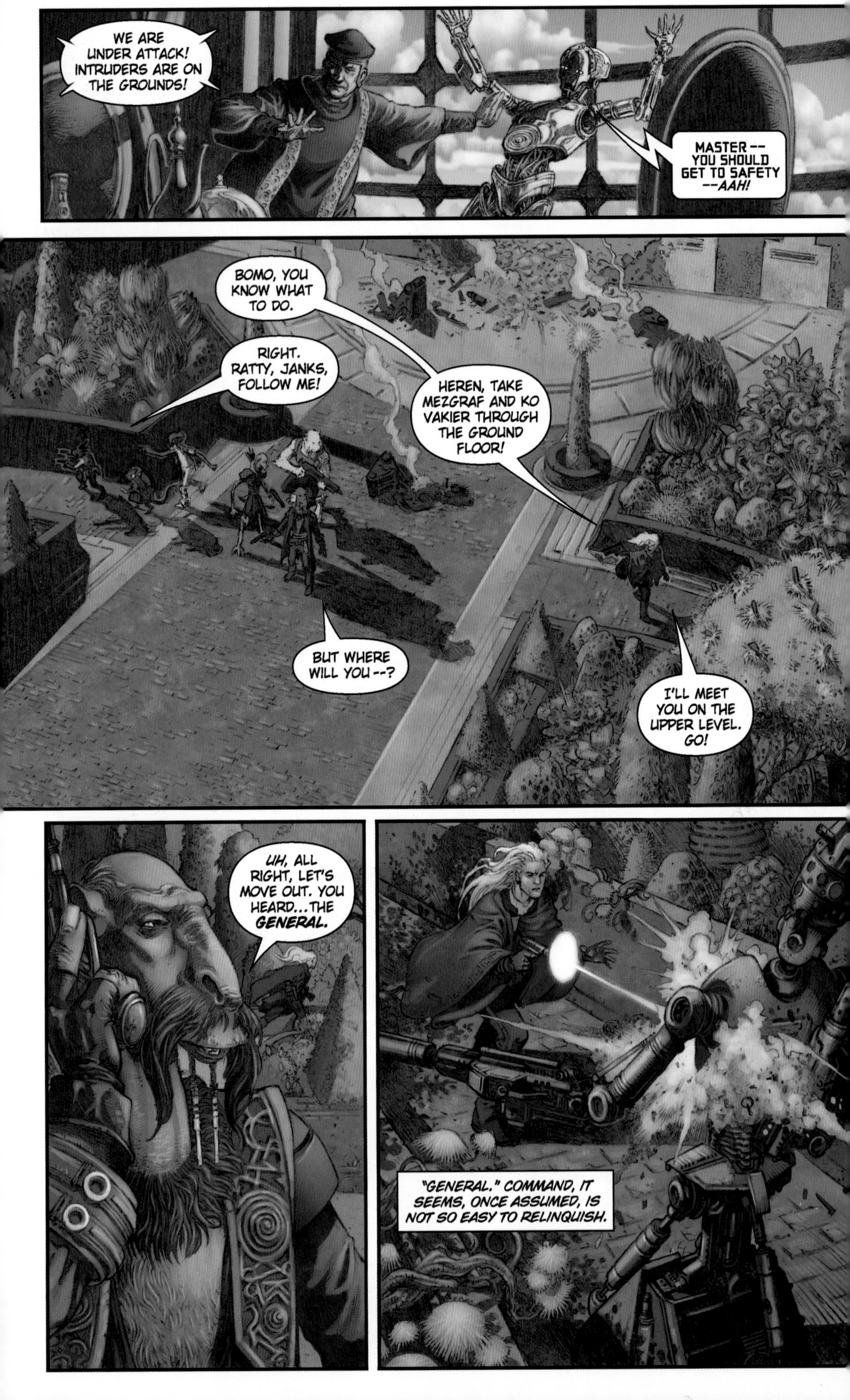
WE ARE UNDER ATTACK! INTRUDERS ARE ON THE GROUNDS!
MASTER -- YOU SHOULD GET TO SAFETY --AAH!
BOMO, YOU KNOW WHAT TO DO.
RIGHT. RATTY, JANKS, FOLLOW ME!
HEREN, TAKE MEZGRAF AND KO VAKIER THROUGH THE GROUND FLOOR!
BUT WHERE WILL YOU --?
I'LL MEET YOU ON THE UPPER LEVEL. GO!
UH, ALL RIGHT, LET'S MOVE OUT. YOU HEARD... THE GENERAL.
"GENERAL." COMMAND, IT SEEMS, ONCE ASSUMED, IS NOT SO EASY TO RELINQUISH.

AT ONE TIME JENNIR WOULD HAVE SAID THE SAME THING OF HIS JEDI TRAINING.

-- AND *THAT* ONLY FOR THE SAKE OF EXPEDIENCY.

BUT HE HAS DISCARDED SO MUCH OF IT IN HIS QUEST TO ARRIVE AT THIS MOMENT.

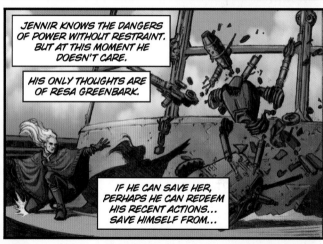

JENNIR KNOWS THE DANGERS OF POWER WITHOUT RESTRAINT. BUT AT THIS MOMENT HE DOESN'T CARE.

HIS ONLY THOUGHTS ARE OF RESA GREENBARK.

HE FEARS THAT ALL HE HAS RETAINED OF IT IS HIS CONNECTION TO THE FORCE --

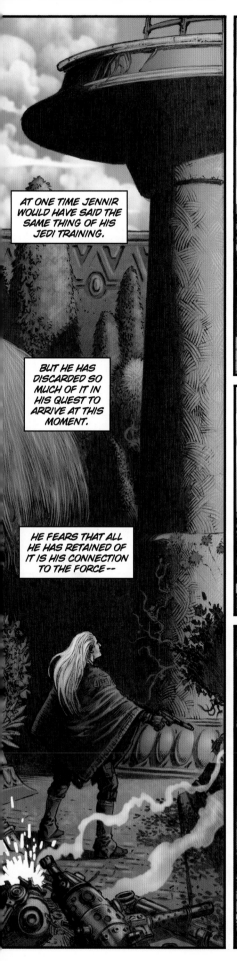

IF HE CAN SAVE HER, PERHAPS HE CAN REDEEM HIS RECENT ACTIONS... SAVE HIMSELF FROM...

...DARKNESS.

THIS IS IT -- THIS CONNECTION TIES DIRECTLY TO THE DROIDS' CONTROL CENTER.

GOOD. HOOK UP THE CHARGE!

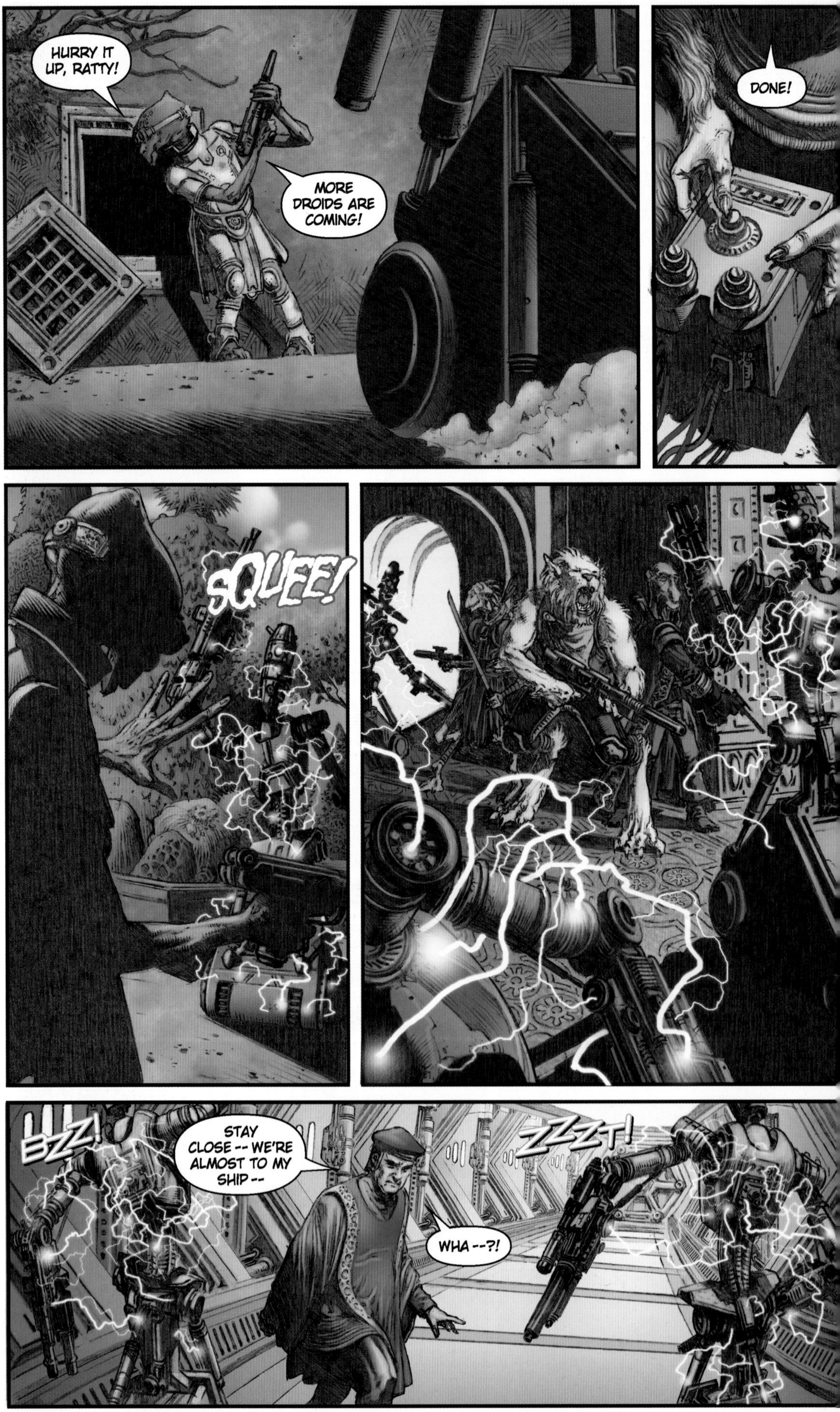
HURRY IT UP, RATTY!
MORE DROIDS ARE COMING!
DONE!
SQUEE!
BZZ!
STAY CLOSE -- WE'RE ALMOST TO MY SHIP --
ZZZT!
WHA --?!

H2! QUICKLY--

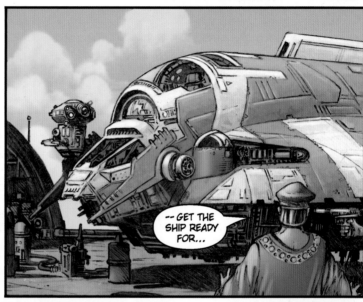

--GET THE SHIP READY FOR...

WHERE'S THE NOSAURIAN YOUNGLING?

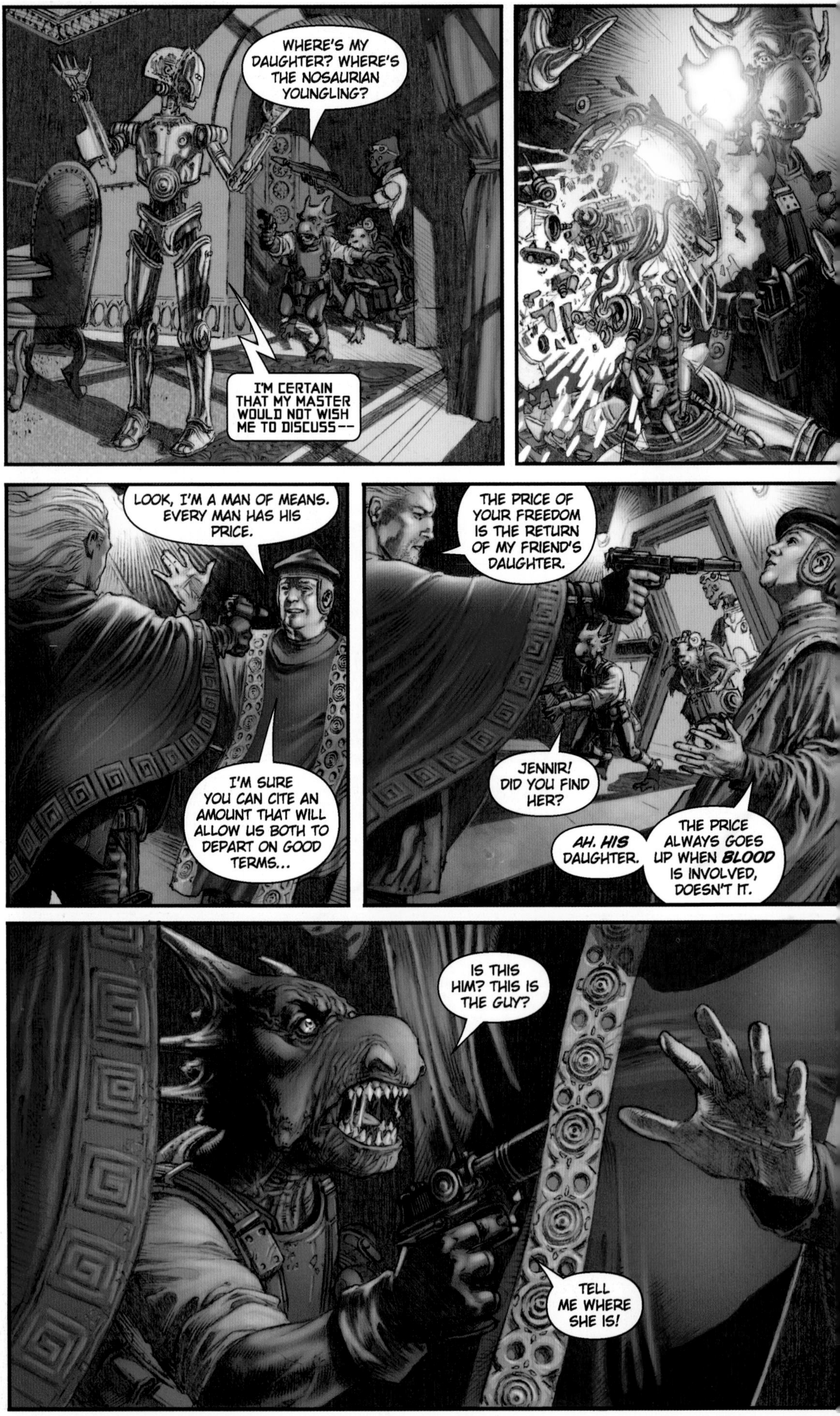
WHERE'S MY DAUGHTER? WHERE'S THE NOSAURIAN YOUNGLING?
I'M CERTAIN THAT MY MASTER WOULD NOT WISH ME TO DISCUSS--
LOOK, I'M A MAN OF MEANS. EVERY MAN HAS HIS PRICE.
I'M SURE YOU CAN CITE AN AMOUNT THAT WILL ALLOW US BOTH TO DEPART ON GOOD TERMS...
THE PRICE OF YOUR FREEDOM IS THE RETURN OF MY FRIEND'S DAUGHTER.
JENNIR! DID YOU FIND HER?
AH. HIS DAUGHTER.
THE PRICE ALWAYS GOES UP WHEN BLOOD IS INVOLVED, DOESN'T IT.
IS THIS HIM? THIS IS THE GUY?
TELL ME WHERE SHE IS!

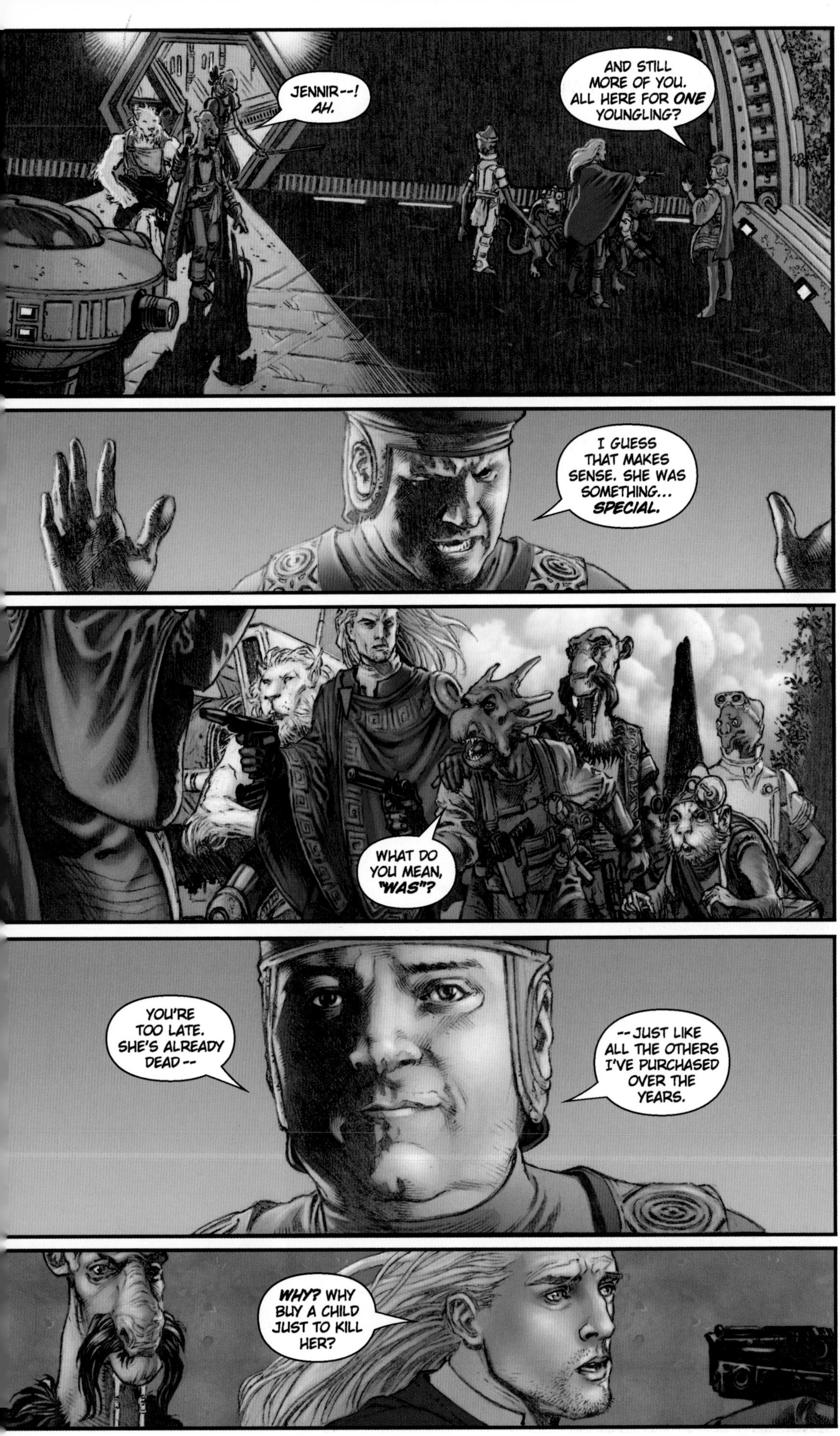
JENNIR--! AH.
AND STILL MORE OF YOU. ALL HERE FOR ONE YOUNGLING?
I GUESS THAT MAKES SENSE. SHE WAS SOMETHING... SPECIAL.
WHAT DO YOU MEAN, "WAS"?
YOU'RE TOO LATE. SHE'S ALREADY DEAD --
-- JUST LIKE ALL THE OTHERS I'VE PURCHASED OVER THE YEARS.
WHY? WHY BUY A CHILD JUST TO KILL HER?

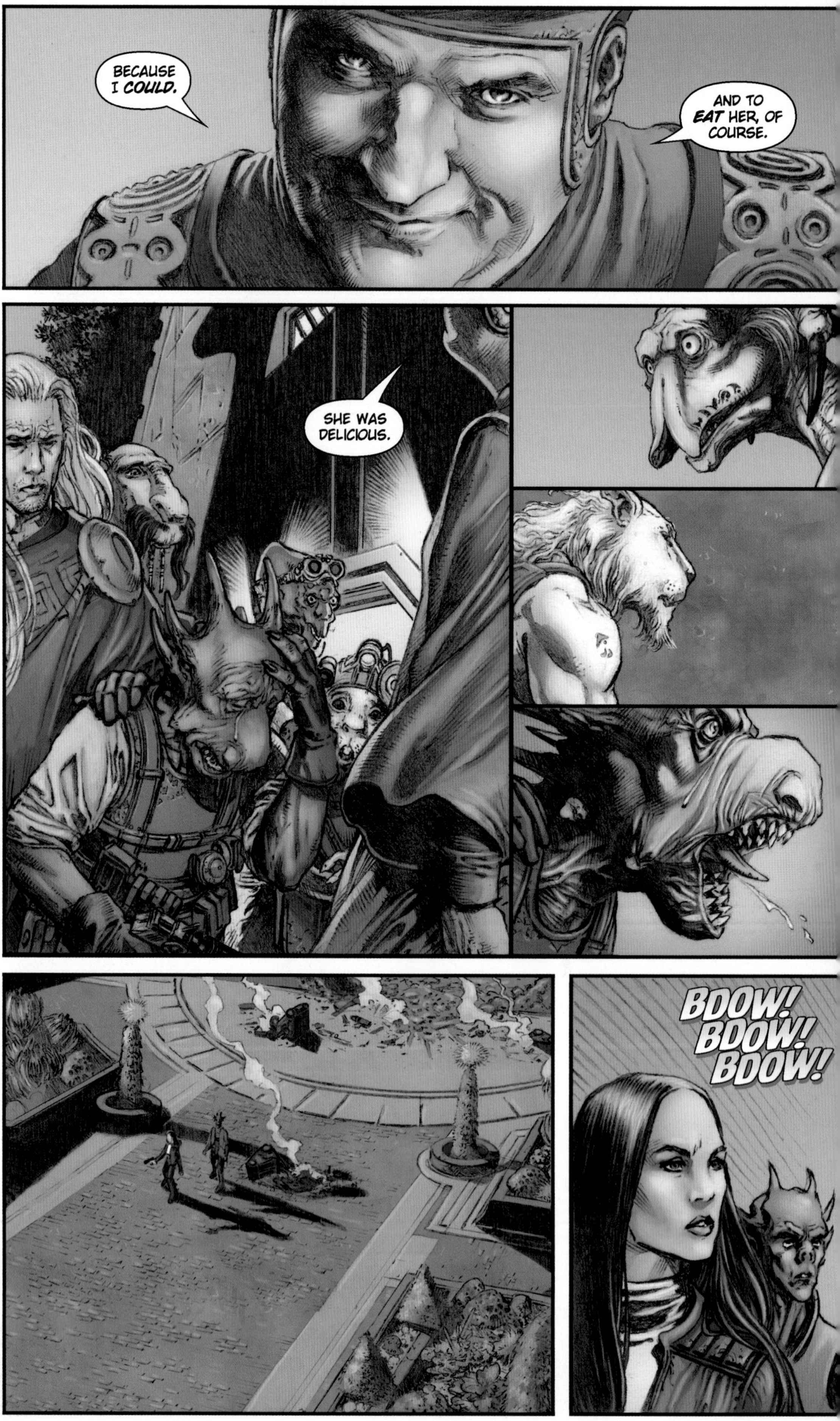
BECAUSE I COULD.
AND TO EAT HER, OF COURSE.
SHE WAS DELICIOUS.
BDOW! BDOW! BDOW!

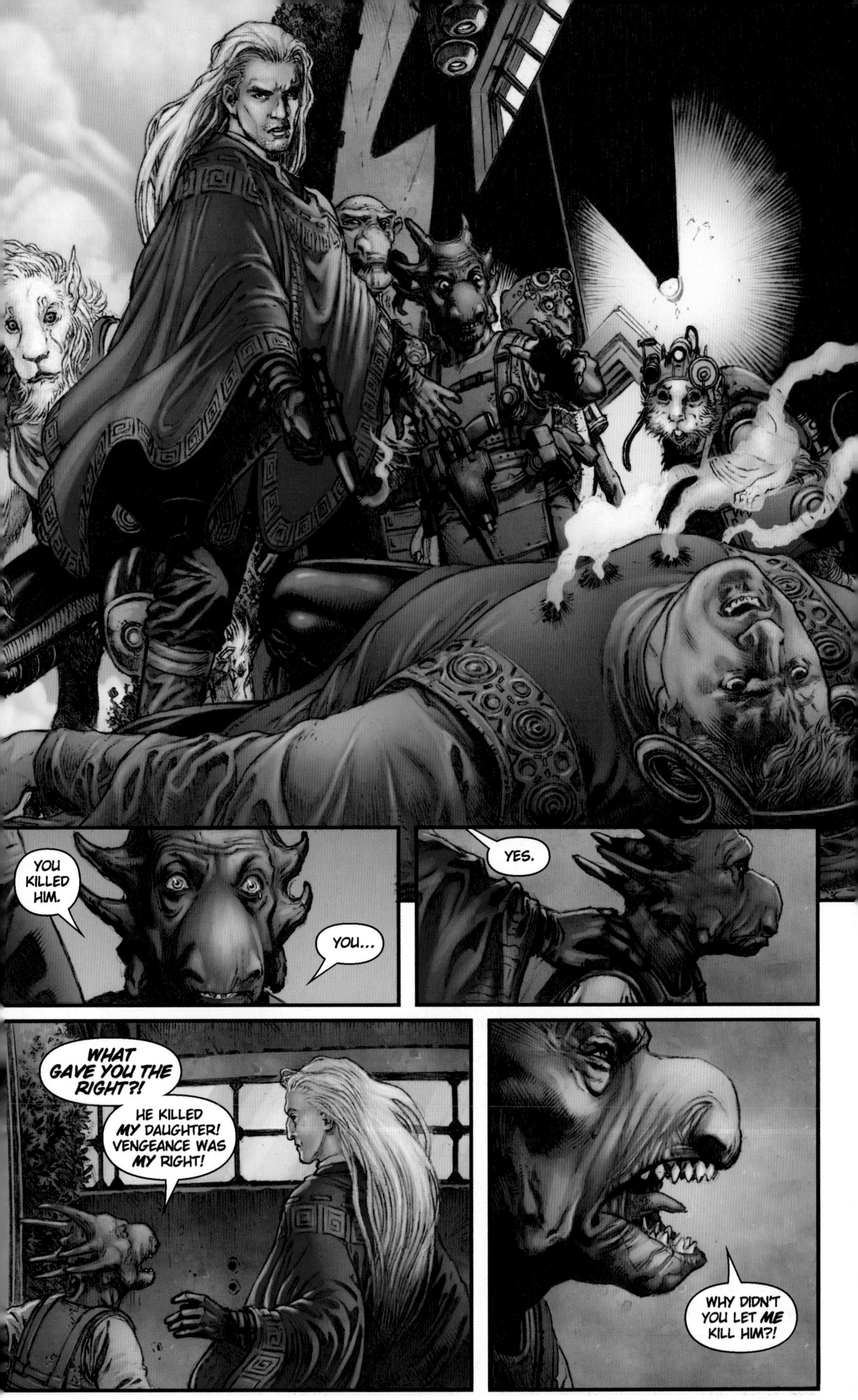
YOU KILLED HIM.
YOU...
YES.
WHAT GAVE YOU THE RIGHT?!
HE KILLED MY DAUGHTER! VENGEANCE WAS MY RIGHT!
WHY DIDN'T YOU LET ME KILL HIM?!

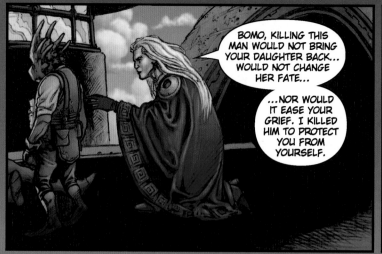

BOMO, KILLING THIS MAN WOULD NOT BRING YOUR DAUGHTER BACK... WOULD NOT CHANGE HER FATE...

...NOR WOULD IT EASE YOUR GRIEF. I KILLED HIM TO PROTECT YOU FROM YOURSELF.

KILLING HIM WOULD HAVE TAKEN SOMETHING FROM YOUR SOUL.

MY SOUL?!

WITHOUT MESA -- WITHOUT RESA -- MY SOUL WAS ALREADY GONE! AND NOW YOU'VE ROBBED ME OF THE ONE THING I HAD LEFT!

DIDN'T YOU LEARN ANYTHING FROM THE WAR?

YOU ALWAYS THINK YOU KNOW WHAT'S BEST FOR EVERYBODY? WELL, BLAST YOU, JEDI!

JEDI --?

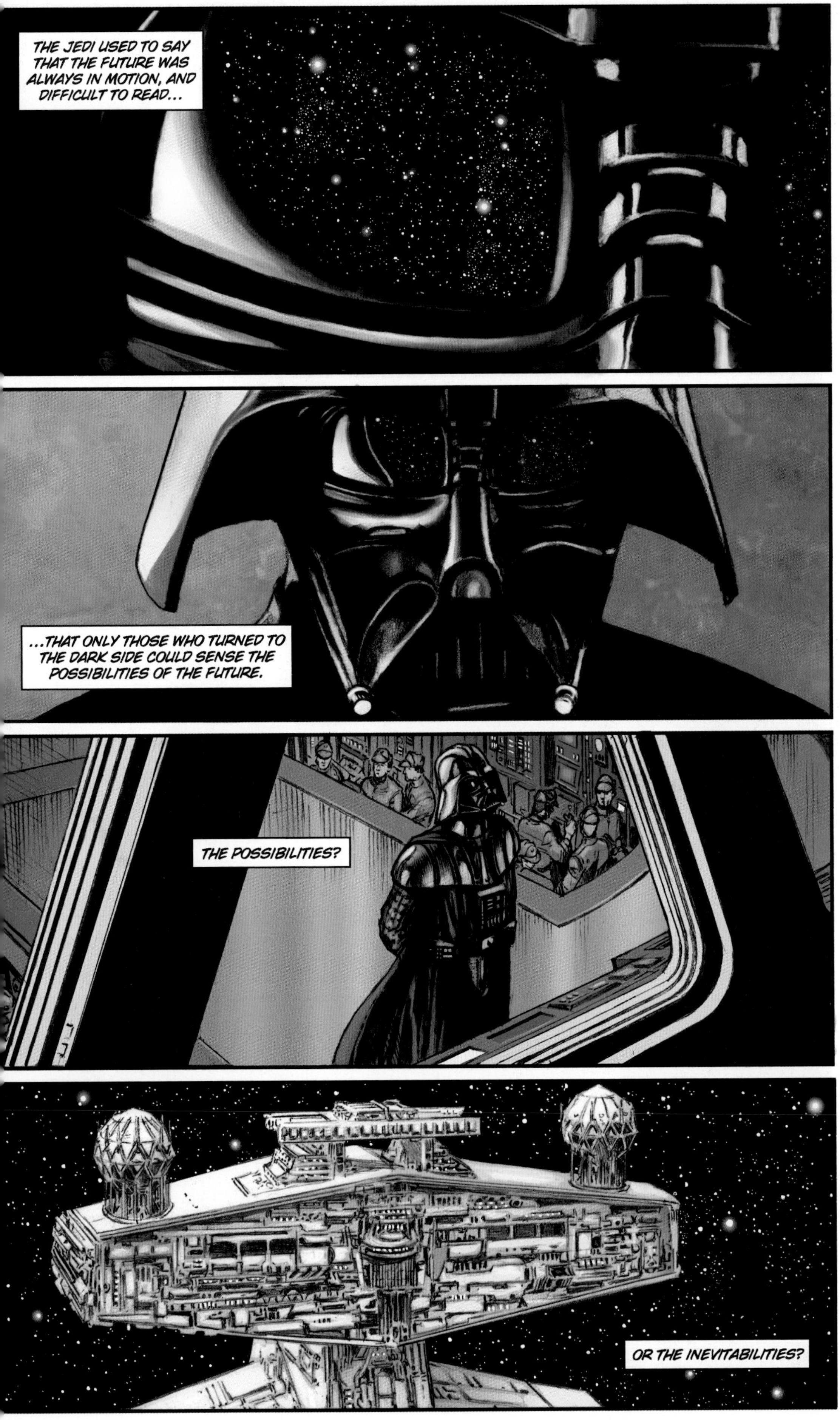
THE JEDI USED TO SAY THAT THE FUTURE WAS ALWAYS IN MOTION, AND DIFFICULT TO READ...
...THAT ONLY THOSE WHO TURNED TO THE DARK SIDE COULD SENSE THE POSSIBILITIES OF THE FUTURE.
THE POSSIBILITIES?
OR THE INEVITABILITIES?

YOU KNOW, IT MIGHT NOT BE A BAD THING TO HAVE A JEDI ON BOARD...

SURE -- AS IF *ONE* BOUNTY ON OUR HEADS WASN'T ENOUGH.

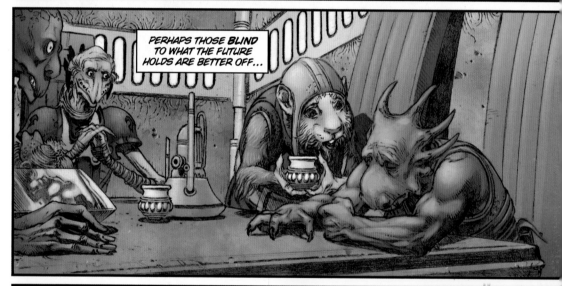

PERHAPS THOSE *BLIND* TO WHAT THE FUTURE HOLDS ARE BETTER OFF...

...THERE ARE CERTAINLY MISERIES ENOUGH FOR THEM IN THE PRESENT.

LET THE FUTURE BE UNKNOWN... A MYSTERY.

BUT DASS JENNIR CANNOT RUN FROM HIS PAST.

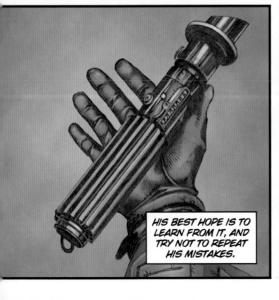

HIS BEST HOPE IS TO LEARN FROM IT, AND TRY NOT TO REPEAT HIS MISTAKES.

ALL HE HAS TO HOLD ONTO IS WHAT HIS TRAINING TELLS HIM TO BE TRUE.

BUT THEN HE THINKS ABOUT THE MANY UN-JEDI-LIKE THINGS HE HAS DONE...

...THE EVILS HE HAS COMMITTED IN THE NAME OF RIGHT...

...AND THE PLACING OF HIS "CERTAINTY" OVER THE NEEDS AND LIVES OF THOSE HE WOULD CALL FRIENDS...

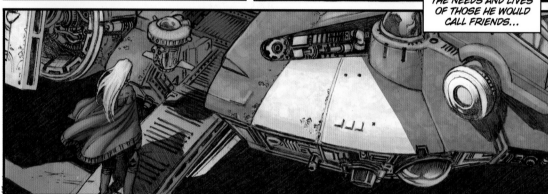

SO WHAT IF THE FUTURE IS A PATH THAT LEADS TO NOWHERE?

ALL HE CAN DO IS WALK THAT PATH ONE STEP AT A TIME...

THE END